W9-BKI-031

PARTIAL PORTRAITS

PARTIAL PORTRAITS

BY

HENRY JAMES

New Introduction by Leon Edel

Ann Arbor Paperbacks
THE UNIVERSITY OF MICHIGAN PRESS

First edition as an Ann Arbor Paperback 1970
Copyright © by The University of Michigan 1970
All rights reserved
SBN 472–06161–5 (paperback)
SBN 472–09161–1 (cloth)
Published in the United States of America by
The University of Michigan Press and simultaneously
in Don Mills, Canada, by Longmans Canada Limited
Originally published in 1888
Manufactured in the United States of America

Introduction
by
LEON EDEL

Partial Portraits was assembled by Henry James in
the autumn of 1887 from the large backlog of his
periodical writings published over more than a dec-
ade. The immediate impulse for the book was eco-
nomic. He had just returned from a long stay in Italy
and his first concern was with his depleted bank account. "I have during the last few years," he told
his publisher, "written certain little articles of a
critical nature which I should like to collect into a
small volume, if for such a volume I can get some
money." Macmillan, who had brought out his earlier
volume of literary essays, *French Poets and Novelists*, readily agreed. The book appeared in May
1888.

Although James spoke of a *small* book he began
by wanting to include eighteen essays—a review of
Zola's *Nana*, papers on Sainte-Beuve, Renan, Arnold,
sketches of Salvini and Coquelin, art essays on Sar-
gent and Abbey. He discarded half of his list, the
papers dealing with critics, actors, artists. What re-

mained was a series on novelists and to these he ultimately added the imaginary conversation on *Daniel Deronda* and his tribute to George du Maurier. As for the title of the volume, he toyed with Essays in Portraiture, Likenesses, Appreciations, Portraits Reduced, Figures Reduced, Half-Length Portraits, and by this process arrived at *Partial Portraits*.

The essays in *Partial Portraits* deal with novels and novelists, but the art which gives the volume its fundamental character can be seen in the list of titles James successively discarded. Portraits, portraiture, figures, likenesses—what are these but words from the lexicon of painting? Everywhere in James we see him functioning as a painter in prose. An earlier volume of travel papers is titled *Portraits of Places;* he is the celebrated author of *The Portrait of a Lady*. In the opening lines of his essay on Robert Louis Stevenson he gives us the key to his conception of "literary portraiture." It is not biographical. He is not concerned with the curriculum vitae of his author. He speaks instead of "the effort to fix a face and a figure, to seize a literary character and transfer it to the canvas of the critic." The face is the author's imagination, the figure is his work. James is thinking of Sainte-Beuve, whose literary portraits he admired when he was young. Sainte-Beuve had built his causeries out of minute details derived from many sources. He had sought to read the poet in his poems, the novelist in his novels. To be sure, his psychology was inclined to be primitive, and in this Henry James ultimately surpassed him, for he could read his fellow craftsmen with a creative imagination Sainte-Beuve did not possess.

In modern terms, James placed himself at the opposite pole from those forms of criticism which insist that the critic must read the poem, not the poet, the novel, not the novelist. For this kind of criticism, for the academic shallows of "explication" and measurement, James had the amused condescension of an artist who knows his own presence in every line that he writes. He reminds us of this in his essay on Maupassant, where he rejects the idea that the Frenchman was so "objective" that he "kept himself out of his books." "They speak of him eloquently," he remarks, "even if it only be to tell us how easy—how easy, given his talent of course—he has found this impersonality." Observation of the artist at work was for James the very essence of the critical act. And in the passage about the art of literary portraiture, he deplores "the mere multiplication of little private judgment-seats," the putting on by critics of judicial wigs and their holding up scales to measure the importance and permanence of this or that reputation. "It has become the fashion," wrote James, "to be effective at the expense of the sitter, to make some little point, or inflict some little dig, with a heated party air, rather than to catch a talent in the fact."

To catch a talent in the fact. This is the essential method of *Partial Portraits,* and James catches his talents with an easy mastery, with brevity, wit, charm, and a generosity he found lacking in the private little judgment seats. The literary portraits are "partial" in the sense that they are neither definitive nor exhaustive: they are "half-length," mostly head and shoulders. But they are "partial" also because they are not impartial: because James liked his subjects, and had had—like a portrait painter— the opportunity of looking at them in life. And yet he avoids, with the greatest care, and with that respect for privacy which the Victorians had, all the pitfalls of "reminiscence." His eulogy of Turgenev, to be sure, is reminiscence, with the delight of an artist in his own memories; but this was his deliberate intention. Otherwise he keeps his eye on the essential task, on the terms of his artistic purpose. His is the quest for "the caught image"—the talent to be captured "in the fact."

By insisting upon literary portraiture as a form of criticism, Henry James revealed himself a great natural psychologist—long before modern psychology. The twentieth century would learn how to discern the motivations of behavior, to read the implications of outward acts. But long before, James had taught himself to notice the smile that accompanies an aggressive remark, the gesture of despair that illustrates a joke, the shrug of denial that is in reality an affirmation. He penetrated human masks and understood, in all he wrote, the way in which we publish the truths of ourselves, even when we believe we are dissimulating them. As early as *The Portrait of a Lady* Madame Merle remarks "one's self—for other people—is one's expression of one's self; and one's house, one's furniture, one's garments . . . these things are all expressive." In his essay on Maupassant he is prompt to challenge that writer's contention that "psychology should be hidden in a book, as it is hidden in reality under the facts of existence." James contends that this is impossible. "From whom is it hidden?" he inquires. Perhaps from people who do not pay attention; but to the alert—to those who are curious and observant —motives, reasons, relations, explanations "are a part of the very surface of the drama." An act, an incident, an attitude may be a sharp, detached, isolated thing in one person, but to another (to someone like James) "it may be hung about with implications, with relations, and conditions as necessary to help you to recognize it as the clothes of your friends are to help you know them in the street." This is crystallized in a memorable passage in "The Art of Fiction."

What is character but the determination of incident?
What is incident but the illustration of character?

What is either a picture or a novel that is *not* of
character? What else do we seek in it and find in it?
It is an incident for a woman to stand up with her
hand resting on a table and look out at you in a certain way; or if it be not an incident I think it will be
hard to say what it is. And at the same time it is an
expression of character.

In these essays James has the advantage of a
double vision. He reads the writers in their works;
but he has also seen them in the flesh; in the portrait
painter's sense they have "sat" for him. He had
known Emerson from early childhood. Robert Louis
Stevenson and Miss Woolson were close friends. He
had met Daudet at Flaubert's in the 1870's; and he
had cultivated the friendship of Turgenev during
his Parisian year of 1875–76. George du Maurier
was, and remained to the end, a walking companion
and deeply loved friend in London. The partial portraits thus possess still another kind of partiality.
Nevertheless, James does not abuse the privileges he
has had. His primary task is not to depict the writers
as he has seen them, but to read them. We can discern the tact and taste of his use of what his eyes
have seen—as distinct from what his eyes have
learned—in the way in which he tells us that he
had visited George Eliot in her home. "People who
had the honour of penetrating into the sequestered
precinct of the Priory—the house in London in which
she lived from 1863 to 1880—remember well a kind

of sanctity in the place, an atmosphere of stillness and concentration, something that suggested a literary temple." The testimony is delicately conveyed. By the same token he mentions in passing how he went with Emerson to the Louvre and the Vatican sculpture gallery. But in this he offers eyewitness testimony to a singular fact—the way in which "I was struck with the anomaly of a man so refined and intelligent being so little spoken to by works of art." At such moments, these portraits contain touches of autobiography. They show us James in his artist's world looking at his fellow artists. Yet he keeps his distance; he does not fall into the error of personal description; he will not invade privacy; and he will not commit the human fault of self-aggrandizement by the company he has kept.

What we get in these pages is a constant illustration of how a man of genius uses his eyes, how he watches, and reads, and keeps all his senses alert. A casual reader might have looked at Du Maurier's cartoons and laughed at their satire. But James notices his "feminine line and surface, curves of shoulder, stretches of arm, turns of head, undulations of step." Or he records out of his boyhood, Leech's drawings in *Punch*—"the expansive back of an old lady getting into an omnibus, the attitude of a little girl bending from her pony in the park, the demureness of a maid-servant opening a street-door in Brompton." He picks up what is characterized prosaically in the psychology texts as "body-posture." In the same fashion he gives us a catalog of the ways in which Maupassant uses physical detail—the latter's "concert of odours" or his close awareness of human depravity; nor is the "brutality" of the French writer lost upon James.

Beyond his ability to describe how his sitters have uniquely used their talents, we have the manner in which James does the describing. That is we have the brilliance of his style. His gift of verbal characterization is everywhere evident; he is pithy, vivid, graceful, good-humored. Everything is transfigured by irony and by wit. When he alludes to Anthony Trollope's "complete appreciation of the usual," wit is turned into a critical dictum. Some of James's sentences are pure aphorism. "In life without art you can find your account; but art without life is a poor affair." "Character in itself is plot, while plot is by no means character." Or we might quote, for the pleasure of it, another of his psychological remarks, "if our emotions in general are interesting, the *form* of those emotions has the merit of being the most definite thing about them." And how well James would have understood our student activists! He speaks in his imaginary conversation on *Daniel Deronda* of that anonymity which is the lot of men (and which youth today finds unbearable in an over-populated world)—"the discovery by each of us that we are at best but a rather ridiculous fifth wheel to the coach, after we have sat cracking our whip and believing that we are at least the coachman in person." Much existential fiction of our time could be wrapped up in that sentence, and the entire student revolt. We have also examples of his subtle humor, as when James explains Turgenev's modesty, "he was absolutely without that eagerness of self-reference which sometimes accompanies great, and even small, reputations." We are face to face everywhere with the critic's perceptions, the power of his intellect, his broad humanity.

The essay on "The Art of Fiction," with which James ended *Partial Portraits,* remains the most significant statement ever made by a working novelist about his art. It began as a rejoinder to Walter Besant, a prolific Victorian writer, who had asked that fiction be given greater recognition. Novelists had received few of the accolades of the Victorian world that today are taken to be their due. Turgenev alone had been given an honorary degree by Oxford, which had overlooked Scott, Dickens, Thackeray, Trollope. On the other hand, the Victorian painters were smothered with adulation and wealth —particularly royal recognition, for Buckingham Palace was essentially visual rather than literary. The Victorian novelists could boast of the admiration of their readers. But the painters received the knighthoods and peerages. This was one of Besant's complaints. He had gone on to speak of novel-writing as a craft and had set down a series of rules for would-be novelists. This prompted James's spontaneous rejoinder and he was little aware at the time that he was writing a veritable manifesto on behalf of his art. He demanded complete freedom; there were no rules save those of the artist and his imagination. James underlined the great areas of life which the novel had yet to annex. With urbanity, humor, good-natured chiding, vivid example, and with depths of knowledge on the question of métier, James issued a supreme summons to novelists to allow themselves to deduce the unseen from the seen, and to cultivate "the atmosphere of the mind." There was no limit to the novelist's "experiments, efforts, discoveries, successes."

> Experience is never limited, and it is never complete; it is an immense sensibility, a kind of huge spiderweb of the finest silken threads suspended in the chamber of consciousness, and catching every air-borne particle in its tissue. It is the very atmosphere of the mind; and when the mind is imaginative—much more when it happens to be that of a man of genius—it takes to itself the faintest hints of life, it converts the very pulses of the air into revelations.

Joyce, Virginia Woolf, Kafka, the whole twentieth-century experimental novel are implicit in this memorable essay.

Each paper in this volume has its own particular brilliance, its own scale of fictional values. But something might be said about the two American writers James included. Emerson, of course, was not a novelist and James placed him at the beginning of the book probably because it was the essay he had most recently written, and also because it represented an act of homage to the memory of a very old and very particular friend of the James family. Emerson is posed for us almost at full-length; and no one in all the annals of American literary criticism has given us as succinct and beautiful a vision of Concord and transcendentalism as James does in these pages. The exquisite qualities of Emerson's mind and its expression in his writings are suggestively traced; and with much finesse James reaches the heart of the Emersonian innocence, his blindness to the existence of evil in this world. "Life never bribed him to look at anything but the soul." There are also a few suggestive words about Thoreau, concerning whom James said very little. However, he discerns, in the poet of Walden, "the violent and limited" application of Emerson's thought, a side of Thoreau—exemplified in his championship of John Brown—few of his admirers have wanted to see.

The second American writer is Constance Fenimore Woolson, a figure now forgotten. One wonders indeed what her claim can be to stand in this book between two such remarkable stylists as Stevenson

and Daudet; for she was a writer of simple sketches
of the reconstruction South and regional pictures of
the lake country in which she grew up. Her claims to
art were modest; and if the other essays in this
book are half-length portraits, the sketch of Miss
Woolson must be called a miniature. But she was an
intimate friend of Henry James's; and James was
not without a Napoleonic propensity to remember
those who were loyal and those to whom he was devoted. In the fullness of time, we must recognize the
success of his gesture. Miss Woolson remains a
footnote in the literary histories; but in touching her
with his prose and style, James conferred a little of
his greatness upon her, gave her a place in literary
memory.

Partial Portraits is a book about an interesting
group of nineteenth-century figures, but it must be
said that no figure in the book is more interesting
than that of Henry James himself. He too, as he said
of Maupassant, has not been able to keep himself out
of his book. And if we apply his own methods, we
are able to get a large portrait of James's critical
mind at its work. What he shows us is that the critic
serves criticism best when he concerns himself gen-
erously and disinterestedly with the creative imagination—defines the talent, the process, the
uniqueness of each artist's experience of the world.
The real lawgiver, James implies, is not the critic,

but the man of imagination, who furnishes the critic with his materials. Proust would say this later on, perhaps more sharply, when he suggested that critics were incomplete men who had to complete themselves with the work of another.

Seen in this way, *Partial Portraits,* which began as a miscellany to refill James's bank account, ends up as an enduring book of American criticism. Its style raises it above the flood of critical writing in recent decades; and then it has a quality that journeyman critics can never possess—that of the great practicing artist, talking out of his workshop, exploring the workshops of his contemporaries, surveying his and their world and—in the very process of earning his bread—achieving a new and durable work of art.

Honolulu, 1969

CONTENTS

I

EMERSON

EMERSON

MR. ELLIOT CABOT has made a very interesting contribution to a class of books of which our literature, more than any other, offers admirable examples : he has given us a biography [1] intelligently and carefully composed. These two volumes are a model of responsible editing—I use that term because they consist largely of letters and extracts from letters : nothing could resemble less the manner in which the mere bookmaker strings together his frequently questionable pearls and shovels the heap into the presence of the public. Mr. Cabot has selected, compared, discriminated, steered an even course between meagreness and redundancy, and managed to be constantly and happily illustrative. And his work, moreover, strikes us as the better done from the fact that it stands for one of the two things that make an absorbing memoir a good deal more than for the other. If these two things be the conscience of the writer and the career of his hero, it is not

[1] *A Memoir of Ralph Waldo Emerson;* by James Elliot Cabot. Two volumes : London, 1887.

difficult to see on which side the biographer of
Emerson has found himself strongest.   Ralph Waldo
Emerson was a man of genius, but he led for nearly
eighty years a life in which the sequence of events
had little of the rapidity, or the complexity, that a
spectator loves.   There is something we miss very
much as we turn these pages—something that has
a kind of accidental, inevitable presence in almost
any personal record—something that may be most
definitely indicated under the name of colour.   We
lay down the book with a singular impression of
paleness—an impression that comes partly from the
tone of the biographer and partly from the moral
complexion of his subject, but mainly from the
vacancy of the page itself.   That of Emerson's personal history is condensed into the single word Concord, and all the condensation in the world will not
make it look rich.   It presents a most continuous
surface.   Mr. Matthew Arnold, in his *Discourses in
America*, contests Emerson's complete right to the
title of a man of letters ; yet letters surely were the
very texture of his history.   Passions, alternations,
affairs, adventures had absolutely no part in it.   It
stretched itself out in enviable quiet—a quiet in
which we hear the jotting of the pencil in the note-
book.   It is the very life for literature (I mean for
one's own, not that of another): fifty years of residence in the home of one's forefathers, pervaded by
reading, by walking in the woods and the daily
addition of sentence to sentence.

If the interest of Mr. Cabot's pencilled portrait is incontestable and yet does not spring from variety, it owes nothing either to a source from which it might have borrowed much and which it is impossible not to regret a little that he has so completely neglected: I mean a greater reference to the social conditions in which Emerson moved, the company he lived in, the moral air he breathed. If his biographer had allowed himself a little more of the ironic touch, had put himself once in a way under the protection of Sainte-Beuve and had attempted something of a general picture, we should have felt that he only went with the occasion. I may overestimate the latent treasures of the field, but it seems to me there was distinctly an opportunity—an opportunity to make up moreover in some degree for the white tint of Emerson's career considered simply in itself. We know a man imperfectly until we know his society, and we but half know a society until we know its manners. This is especially true of a man of letters, for manners lie very close to literature. From those of the New England world in which Emerson's character formed itself Mr. Cabot almost averts his lantern, though we feel sure that there would have been delightful glimpses to be had and that he would have been in a position—that is that he has all the knowledge that would enable him—to help us to them. It is as if he could not trust himself, knowing the subject only too well. This adds to the effect of extreme discretion that we find in his

volumes, but it is the cause of our not finding certain
things, certain figures and scenes, evoked. What is
evoked is Emerson's pure spirit, by a copious, sifted
series of citations and comments. But we must read
as much as possible between the lines, and the picture of the transcendental time (to mention simply
one corner) has yet to be painted—the lines have
yet to be bitten in. Meanwhile we are held and
charmed by the image of Emerson's mind and the
extreme appeal which his physiognomy makes to
our art of discrimination. It is so fair, so uniform
and impersonal, that its features are simply fine
shades, the gradations of tone of a surface whose
proper quality was of the smoothest and on which
nothing was reflected with violence. It is a pleasure of the critical sense to find, with Mr. Cabot's
extremely intelligent help, a notation for such
delicacies.

We seem to see the circumstances of our author's
origin, immediate and remote, in a kind of high, ver-
tical moral light, the brightness of a society at once
very simple and very responsible. The rare single-
ness that was in his nature (so that he was *all* the
warning moral voice, without distraction or counter-
solicitation), was also in the stock he sprang from,
clerical for generations, on both sides, and clerical in
the Puritan sense. His ancestors had lived long (for
nearly two centuries) in the same corner of New
England, and during that period had preached and
studied and prayed and practised. It is impossible

to imagine a spirit better prepared in advance to be exactly what it was—better educated for its office in its far-away unconscious beginnings. There is an inner satisfaction in seeing so straight, although so patient, a connection between the stem and the flower, and such a proof that when life wishes to produce something exquisite in quality she takes her measures many years in advance. A conscience like Emerson's could not have been turned off, as it were, from one generation to another: a succession of attempts, a long process of refining, was required. His perfection, in his own line, comes largely from the non-interruption of the process.

As most of us are made up of ill-assorted pieces, his reader, and Mr. Cabot's, envies him this trans mitted unity, in which there was no mutual hustling or crowding of elements. It must have been a kind of luxury to be—that is to feel—so homogeneous, and it helps to account for his serenity, his power of acceptance, and that absence of personal passion which makes his private correspondence read like a series of beautiful circulars or expanded cards *pour prendre congé.* He had the equanimity of a result ; nature had taken care of him and he had only to speak. He accepted himself as he accepted others, accepted everything ; and his absence of eagerness, or in other words his modesty, was that of a man with whom it is not a question of success, who has nothing invested or at stake. The investment, the stake, was that of the race, of all the past Emersons

and Bulkeleys and Waldos.   There is much that
makes us smile, to-day, in the commotion produced
by his secession from the mild Unitarian pulpit : we
wonder at a condition of opinion in which any utterance of his should appear to be wanting in superior
piety—in the essence of good instruction.   All that
is changed : the great difference has become the infinitely small, and we admire a state of society in
which scandal and schism took on no darker hue ;
but there is even yet a sort of drollery in the spectacle of a body of people among whom the author of
The American Scholar and of the Address of 1838 at
the Harvard Divinity College passed for profane,
and who failed to see that he only gave his plea for
the spiritual life the advantage of a brilliant expression.   They were so provincial as to think that
brilliancy came ill - recommended, and they were
shocked at his ceasing to care for the prayer and the
sermon.   They might have perceived that he *was* the
prayer and the sermon : not in the least a seculariser,
but in his own subtle insinuating way a sanctifier.

Of the three periods into which his life divides
itself, the first was (as in the case of most men)
that of movement, experiment and selection—that
of effort too and painful probation.   Emerson had
his message, but he was a good while looking for
his form—the form which, as he himself would have
said, he never completely found and of which it was
rather characteristic of him that his later years (with
their growing refusal to give him the *word*), wishing

to attack him in his most vulnerable point, where his tenure was least complete, had in some degree the effect of despoiling him. It all sounds rather bare and stern, Mr. Cabot's account of his youth and early manhood, and we get an impression of a terrible paucity of alternatives. If he would be neither a farmer nor a trader he could " teach school "; that was the main resource and a part of the general educative process of the young New Englander who proposed to devote himself to the things of the mind. There was an advantage in the nudity, however, which was that, in Emerson's case at least, the things of the mind did get themselves admirably well considered. If it be his great distinction and his special sign that he had a more vivid conception of the moral life than any one else, it is probably not fanciful to say that he owed it in part to the limited way in which he saw our capacity for living illustrated. The plain, God-fearing, practical society which surrounded him was not fertile in variations : it had great intelligence and energy, but it moved altogether in the straightforward direction. On three occasions later—three journeys to Europe—he was introduced to a more complicated world; but his spirit, his moral taste, as it were, abode always within the undecorated walls of his youth. There he could dwell with that ripe unconsciousness of evil which is one of the most beautiful signs by which we know him. His early writings are full of quaint animadversion upon the vices of the place and time,

but there is something charmingly vague, light and
general in the arraignment.　Almost the worst he
can say is that these vices are negative and that his
fellow-townsmen are not heroic.　We feel that his
first impressions were gathered in a community from
which misery and extravagance, and either extreme,
of any sort, were equally absent.　What the life of
New England fifty years ago offered to the observer
was the common lot, in a kind of achromatic picture,
without particular intensifications.　It was from this
table of the usual, the merely typical joys and sorrows that he proceeded to generalise—a fact that
accounts in some degree for a certain inadequacy
and thinness in his enumerations.　But it helps to
account also for his direct, intimate vision of the soul
itself—not in its emotions, its contortions and perversions, but in its passive, exposed, yet healthy
form.　He knows the nature of man and the long
tradition of its dangers ; but we feel that whereas
he can put his finger on the remedies, lying for the
most part, as they do, in the deep recesses of virtue,
of the spirit, he has only a kind of hearsay, un-
informed acquaintance with the disorders.　It would
require some ingenuity, the reader may say too
much, to trace closely this correspondence between
his genius and the frugal, dutiful, happy but decidedly lean Boston of the past, where there was a
great deal of will but very little fulcrum—like a
ministry without an opposition.

　　The genius itself it seems to me impossible to con-

test—I mean the genius for seeing character as a
real and supreme thing. Other writers have arrived
at a more complete expression : Wordsworth and
Goethe, for instance, give one a sense of having
found their form, whereas with Emerson we never
lose the sense that he is still seeking it. But no
one has had so steady and constant, and above all
so natural, a vision of what we require and what we
are capable of in the way of aspiration and independence. With Emerson it is ever the special
capacity for moral experience—always that and only
that. We have the impression, somehow, that life
had never bribed him to look at anything but the
soul ; and indeed in the world in which he grew up
and lived the bribes and lures, the beguilements and
prizes, were few. He was in an admirable position
for showing, what he constantly endeavoured to
show, that the prize was within. Any one who in
New England at that time could do that was sure of
success, of listeners and sympathy : most of all, of
course, when it was a question of doing it with such
a divine persuasiveness. Moreover, the way in
which Emerson did it added to the charm—by word
of mouth, face to face, with a rare, irresistible voice
and a beautiful mild, modest authority. If Mr.
Arnold is struck with the limited degree in which
he was a man of letters I suppose it is because he is
more struck with his having been, as it were, a man
of lectures. But the lecture surely was never more
purged of its grossness—the quality in it that sug-

gests a strong light and a big brush—than as it issued from Emerson's lips; so far from being a vulgarisation, it was simply the esoteric made audible, and instead of treating the few as the many, after the usual fashion of gentlemen on platforms, he treated the many as the few. There was probably no other society at that time in which he would have got so many persons to understand that; for we think the better of his audience as we read him, and wonder where else people would have had so much moral attention to give. It is to be remembered however that during the winter of 1847-48, on the occasion of his second visit to England, he found many listeners in London and in provincial cities. Mr. Cabot's volumes are full of evidence of the satisfactions he offered, the delights and revelations he may be said to have promised, to a race which had to seek its entertainment, its rewards and consolations, almost exclusively in the moral world. But his own writings are fuller still; we find an instance almost wherever we open them.

" All these great and transcendent properties are ours. . . . Let us find room for this great guest in our small houses. . . . Where the heart is, there the muses, there the gods sojourn, and not in any geography of fame. Massachusetts, Connecticut River, and Boston Bay, you think paltry places, and the ear loves names of foreign and classic topography. But here we are, and if we will tarry a little we may come to learn that here is best. . . . The Jerseys were handsome enough ground for Washington to tread, and London streets for the feet of Milton. . . . That country is fairest which is inhabited by the noblest minds."

We feel, or suspect, that Milton is thrown in as a
hint that the London streets are no such great place,
and it all sounds like a sort of pleading consolation
against bleakness.

The beauty of a hundred passages of this kind in
Emerson's pages is that they are effective, that they
do come home, that they rest upon insight and not
upon ingenuity, and that if they are sometimes obscure it is never with the obscurity of paradox.
We seem to see the people turning out into the
snow after hearing them, glowing with a finer glow
than even the climate could give and fortified for a
struggle with overshoes and the east wind.

"Look to it first and only, that fashion, custom, authority,
pleasure, and money, are nothing to you, are not as bandages
over your eyes, that you cannot see ; but live with the privilege
of the immeasurable mind. Not too anxious to visit periodi-
cally all families and each family in your parish connection,
when you meet one of these men or women be to them a divine
man ; be to them thought and virtue ; let their timid aspirations find in you a friend ; let their trampled instincts be
genially tempted out in your atmosphere ; let their doubts
know that you have doubted, and their wonder feel that you
have wondered."

When we set against an exquisite passage like that,
or like the familiar sentences that open the essay on
History ("He that is admitted to the right of reason
is made freeman of the whole estate. What Plato
has thought, he may think ; what a saint has felt,
he may feel ; what at any time has befallen any
man, he can understand"); when we compare the
letters, cited by Mr. Cabot, to his wife from Spring-

field, Illinois (January 1853) we feel that his spiritual tact needed to be very just, but that if it was
so it must have brought a blessing.

" Here I am in the deep mud of the prairies, misled I fear
into this bog, not by a will-of-the-wisp, such as shine in bogs,
but by a young New Hampshire editor, who over-estimated the
strength of both of us, and fancied I should glitter in the
prairie and draw the prairie birds and waders.   It rains and
thaws incessantly, and if we step off the short street we go up
to the shoulders, perhaps, in mud.   My chamber is a cabin ;
my fellow - boarders are legislators. . . . Two or three governors or ex - governors live in the house. . . . I cannot command daylight and solitude for study or for more than a
scrawl." . . .

And another extract :—

" A cold, raw country this, and plenty of night-travelling
and arriving at four in the morning to take the last and worst
bed in the tavern.   Advancing day brings mercy and favour to
me, but not the sleep. . . . Mercury 15° below zero. . . . I
find well-disposed, kindly people among these sinewy farmers
of the North, but in all that is called cultivation they are only
ten years old."

He says in another letter (in 1860), "I saw
Michigan and its forests and the Wolverines pretty
thoroughly ; " and on another page Mr. Cabot shows
him as speaking of his engagements to lecture in the
West as the obligation to " wade, and freeze, and
ride, and run, and suffer all manner of indignities."
This was not New England, but as regards the country
districts throughout, at that time, it was a question of
degree.   Certainly never was the fine wine of philosophy carried to remoter or queerer corners : never

was a more delicate diet offered to "two or three
governors, or ex-governors," living in a cabin. It
was Mercury, shivering in a mackintosh, bearing
nectar and ambrosia to the gods whom he wished
those who lived in cabins to endeavour to feel that
they might be.

I have hinted that the will, in the old New England society, was a clue without a labyrinth ; but it
had its use, nevertheless, in helping the young talent
to find its mould. There were few or none ready-
made : tradition was certainly not so oppressive as
might have been inferred from the fact that the air
swarmed with reformers and improvers. Of the
patient, philosophic manner in which Emerson groped
and waited, through teaching the young and preaching
to the adult, for his particular vocation, Mr. Cabot's
first volume gives a full and orderly account. His
passage from the Unitarian pulpit to the lecture-desk
was a step which at this distance of time can hardly
help appearing to us short, though he was long in
making it, for even after ceasing to have a parish of
his own he freely confounded the two, or willingly,
at least, treated the pulpit as a platform. "The
young people and the mature hint at odium and
the aversion of faces, to be presently encountered in
society," he writes in his journal in 1838 ; but in
point of fact the quiet drama of his abdication was
not to include the note of suffering. The Boston
world might feel disapproval, but it was far too kindly
to make this sentiment felt as a weight: every element

of martyrdom was there but the important ones of
the cause and the persecutors.   Mr. Cabot marks the
lightness of the penalties of dissent ; if they were
light in somewhat later years for the transcendentalists and fruit-eaters they could press but little on a
man of Emerson's distinction, to whom, all his life,
people went not to carry but to ask the right word.
There was no consideration to give up, he could not
have been one of the dingy if he had tried ; but what
he did renounce in 1838 was a material profession.
He was "settled," and his indisposition to administer
the communion unsettled him.   He calls the whole
business, in writing to Carlyle, "a tempest in our
washbowl" ; but it had the effect of forcing him to
seek a new source of income.   His wants were few
and his view of life severe, and this came to him,
little by little, as he was able to extend the field in
which he read his discourses.   In 1835, upon his
second marriage, he took up his habitation at Concord, and his life fell into the shape it was, in a
general way, to keep for the next half-century.   It
is here that we cannot help regretting that Mr. Cabot
had not found it possible to treat his career a little
more pictorially.   Those fifty years of Concord—at
least the earlier part of them—would have been a
subject bringing into play many odd figures, many
human incongruities : they would have abounded in
illustrations of the primitive New England character,
especially during the time of its queer search for
something to expend itself upon.   Objects and occu-

pations have multiplied since then, and now there is no lack; but fifty years ago the expanse was wide and free, and we get the impression of a conscience gasping in the void, panting for sensations, with something of the movement of the gills of a landed fish. It would take a very fine point to sketch Emerson's benignant, patient, inscrutable countenance during the various phases of this democratic communion; but the picture, when complete, would be one of the portraits, half a revelation and half an enigma, that suggest and fascinate. Such a striking personage as old Miss Mary Emerson, our author's aunt, whose high intelligence and temper were much of an influence in his earlier years, has a kind of tormenting representative value: we want to see her from head to foot, with her frame and her background; having (for we happen to have it), an impression that she was a very remarkable specimen of the transatlantic Puritan stock, a spirit that would have dared the devil. We miss a more liberal handling, are tempted to add touches of our own, and end by convincing ourselves that Miss Mary Moody Emerson, grim intellectual virgin and daughter of a hundred ministers, with her local traditions and her combined love of empire and of speculation, would have been an inspiration for a novelist. Hardly less so the charming Mrs. Ripley, Emerson's life-long friend and neighbour, most delicate and accomplished of women, devoted to Greek and to her house, studious, simple and dainty —an admirable example of the old-fashioned New

England lady. It was a freak of Miss Emerson's
somewhat sardonic humour to give her once a broom-
stick to carry across Boston Common (under the
pretext of a " moving "), a task accepted with docility
but making of the victim the most benignant witch
ever equipped with that utensil.

These ladies, however, were very private persons
and not in the least of the reforming tribe : there are
others who would have peopled Mr. Cabot's page to
whom he gives no more than a mention. We must
add that it is open to him to say that their features
have become faint and indistinguishable to-day without more research than the question is apt to be
worth : they are embalmed—in a collective way—
the apprehensible part of them, in Mr. Frothingham's
clever *History of Transcendentalism in New England.*
This must be admitted to be true of even so lively a
"factor," as we say nowadays, as the imaginative,
talkative, intelligent and finally Italianised and shipwrecked Margaret Fuller : she is now one of the
dim, one of Carlyle's "then-celebrated" at most. It
seemed indeed as if Mr. Cabot rather grudged her a
due place in the record of the company that Emerson
kept, until we came across the delightful letter he
quotes toward the end of his first volume—a letter interesting both as a specimen of inimitable, imperceptible
edging away, and as an illustration of the curiously
generalised way, as if with an implicit protest against
personalities, in which his intercourse, epistolary and
other, with his friends was conducted. There is an

extract from a letter to his aunt on the occasion
of the death of a deeply - loved brother (his own)
which reads like a passage from some fine old chas-
tened essay on the vanity of earthly hopes : strangely
unfamiliar, considering the circumstances. Courteous
and humane to the furthest possible point, to the
point of an almost profligate surrender of his attention, there was no familiarity in him, no personal
avidity. Even his letters to his wife are courtesies,
they are not familiarities. He had only one style,
one manner, and he had it for everything—even for
himself, in his notes, in his journals. But he had it
in perfection for Miss Fuller; he retreats, smiling
and flattering, on tiptoe, as if he were advancing.
" She ever seems to crave," he says in his journal,
"something which I have not, or have not for her."
What he had was doubtless not what she craved, but
the letter in question should be read to see how the
modicum was administered. It is only between the
lines of such a production that we read that a part of
her effect upon him was to bore him; for his system
was to practise a kind of universal passive hospitality
—he aimed at nothing less. It was only because he
was so deferential that he could be so detached; he
had polished his aloofness till it reflected the image
of his solicitor. And this was not because he was an
"uncommunicating egotist," though he amuses himself
with saying so to Miss Fuller: egotism is the strongest
of passions, and he was altogether passionless. It
was because he had no personal, just as he had almost

no physical wants. "Yet I plead not guilty to the malice prepense. 'Tis imbecility, not contumacy, though perhaps somewhat more odious. It seems very just, the irony with which you ask whether you may not be trusted and promise such docility. Alas, we will all promise, but the prophet loiters." He would not say even to himself that she bored him ; he had denied himself the luxury of such easy and obvious short cuts. There is a passage in the lecture (1844) called "Man the Reformer," in which he hovers round and round the idea that the practice of trade, in certain conditions likely to beget an underhand competition, does not draw forth the nobler parts of character, till the reader is tempted to interrupt him with, "Say at once that it is impossible for a gentleman ! "

So he remained always, reading his lectures in the winter, writing them in the summer, and at all seasons taking wood-walks and looking for hints in old books.

"Delicious summer stroll through the pastures. . . . On the steep park of Conantum I have the old regret—is all this beauty to perish ? Shall none re-make this sun and wind ; the sky-blue river ; the river-blue sky ; the yellow meadow, spotted with sacks and sheets of cranberry-gatherers ; the red bushes ; the iron-gray house, just the colour of the granite rocks ; the wild orchard ? "

His observation of Nature was exquisite—always the direct, irresistible impression.

" The hawking of the wild geese flying by night ; the thin note of the companionable titmouse in the winter day ; the fall of swarms of flies in autumn, from combats high in the air, pattering down on the leaves like rain ; the angry hiss of the wood-birds ; the pine throwing out its pollen for the benefit of the next century." . . . (*Literary Ethics.*)

I have said there was no familiarity in him, but he was familiar with woodland creatures and sounds. Certainly, too, he was on terms of free association with his books, which were numerous and dear to him ; though Mr. Cabot says, doubtless with justice, that his dependence on them was slight and that he was not "intimate" with his authors. They did not feed him but they stimulated ; they were not his meat but his wine—he took them in sips. But he needed them and liked them ; he had volumes of notes from his reading, and he could not have produced his lectures without them. He liked literature as a thing to refer to, liked the very names of which it is full, and used them, especially in his later writings, for purposes of ornament, to dress the dish, sometimes with an unmeasured profusion. I open *The Conduct of Life* and find a dozen on the page. He mentions more authorities than is the fashion to-day. He can easily say, of course, that he follows a better one—that of his well-loved and irrepressibly allusive Montaigne. In his own bookishness there is a certain contradiction, just as there is a latent incompleteness in his whole literary side. Independence, the return to nature, the finding out and doing for one's self, was ever what he most highly recommended ; and yet he is constantly reminding his

readers of the conventional signs and consecrations
—of what other men have done. This was partly
because the independence that he had in his eye was
an independence without ill-nature, without rudeness
(though he likes that word), and full of gentle
amiabilities, curiosities and tolerances ; and partly
it is a simple matter of form, a literary expedient,
confessing its character—on the part of one who had
never really mastered the art of composition—of
continuous expression. Charming to many a reader,
charming yet ever slightly droll, will remain Emerson's
frequent invocation of the "scholar": there is such
a friendly vagueness and convenience in it. It is of
the scholar that he expects all the heroic and uncomfortable things, the concentrations and relinquish-
ments, that make up the noble life. We fancy this
personage looking up from his book and arm-chair a
little ruefully and saying, "Ah, but why *me* always
and only ? Why so much of me, and is there no one
else to share the responsibility ?" "Neither years
nor books have yet availed to extirpate a prejudice
then rooted in me [when as a boy he first saw the
graduates of his college assembled at their anniver-
sary], that a scholar is the favourite of heaven and
earth, the excellency of his country, the happiest of
men."

In truth, by this term he means simply the cultivated man, the man who has had a liberal education,
and there is a voluntary plainness in his use of it—
speaking of such people as the rustic, or the

vulgar, speak of those who have a tincture of
books. This is characteristic of his humility—that
humility which was nine-tenths a plain fact (for it is
easy for persons who have at bottom a great fund of
indifference to be humble), and the remaining tenth
a literary habit. Moreover an American reader may
be excused for finding in it a pleasant sign of that
prestige, often so quaintly and indeed so extravagantly
acknowledged, which a connection with literature
carries with it among the people of the United
States. There is no country in which it is more
freely admitted to be a distinction—*the* distinction ;
or in which so many persons have become eminent
for showing it even in a slight degree. Gentlemen
and ladies are celebrated there on this ground who
would not on the same ground, though they might
on another, be celebrated anywhere else. Emerson's
own tone is an echo of that, when he speaks of the
scholar—not of the banker, the great merchant, the
legislator, the artist—as the most distinguished figure
in the society about him. It is because he has most
to give up that he is appealed to for efforts and
sacrifices. "Meantime I know that a very different
estimate of the scholar's profession prevails in this
country," he goes on to say in the address from which
I last quoted (the *Literary Ethics*), "and the importunity with which society presses its claim upon
young men tends to pervert the views of the youth
in respect to the culture of the intellect." The
manner in which that is said represents, surely, a

serious mistake : with the estimate of the scholar's profession which then prevailed in New England Emerson could have had no quarrel ; the ground of his lamentation was another side of the matter. It was not a question of estimate, but of accidental practice. In 1838 there were still so many things of prime material necessity to be done that reading was driven to the wall ; but the reader was still thought the cleverest, for he found time as well as intelligence. Emerson's own situation sufficiently indicates it. In what other country, on sleety winter nights, would provincial and bucolic populations have gone forth in hundreds for the cold comfort of a literary discourse ? The distillation anywhere else would certainly have appeared too thin, the appeal too special. But for many years the American people of the middle regions, outside of a few cities, had in the most rigorous seasons no other recreation. A gentleman, grave or gay, in a bare room, with a manuscript, before a desk, offered the reward of toil, the refreshment of pleasure, to the young, the middle-aged and the old of both sexes. The hour was brightest, doubtless, when the gentleman was gay, like Doctor Oliver Wendell Holmes. But Emerson's gravity never sapped his career, any more than it chilled the regard in which he was held among those who were particularly his own people. It was impossible to be more honoured and cherished, far and near, than he was during his long residence in Concord, or more looked upon as the principal gentleman in the place.

This was conspicuous to the writer of these remarks
on the occasion of the curious, sociable, cheerful
public funeral made for him in 1883 by all the
countryside, arriving, as for the last honours to the
first citizen, in trains in waggons, on foot, in multi-
tudes. It was a popular manifestation, the most
striking I have ever seen provoked by the death of a
man of letters.

If a picture of that singular and very illustrative
institution the old American lecture-system would
have constituted a part of the filling-in of the ideal
memoir of Emerson, I may further say, returning to
the matter for a moment, that such a memoir would
also have had a chapter for some of those Concord-
haunting figures which are not so much interesting
in themselves as interesting because for a season
Emerson thought them so. And the pleasure of
that would be partly that it would push us to inquire
how interesting he did really think them. That is,
it would bring up the question of his inner reserves
and scepticisms, his secret ennuis and ironies, the
way he sympathised for courtesy and then, with his
delicacy and generosity, in a world after all given
much to the literal, let his courtesy pass for adhesion
—a question particularly attractive to those for whom
he has, in general, a fascination. Many entertaining
problems of that sort present themselves for such
readers : there is something indefinable for them in
the mixture of which he was made—his fidelity as
an interpreter of the so-called transcendental spirit

and his freedom from all wish for any personal share
in the effect of his ideas.   He drops them, sheds
them, diffuses them, and we feel as if there would be
a grossness in holding him to anything so temporal
as a responsibility.   He had the advantage, for many
years, of having the question of application assumed for
him by Thoreau, who took upon himself to be, in the
concrete, the sort of person that Emerson's "scholar"
was in the abstract, and who paid for it by having a
shorter life than that fine adumbration.   The application, with Thoreau, was violent and limited (it
became a matter of prosaic detail, the non-payment
of taxes, the non-wearing of a necktie, the preparation of one's food one's self, the practice of a rude
sincerity—all things not of the essence), so that,
though he wrote some beautiful pages, which read
like a translation of Emerson into the sounds of the
field and forest and which no one who has ever loved
nature in New England, or indeed anywhere, can
fail to love, he suffers something of the *amoindrisse-*
ment of eccentricity.   His master escapes that reduc-
tion altogether.   I call it an advantage to have had
such a pupil as Thoreau; because for a mind so
much made up of reflection as Emerson's everything
comes under that head which prolongs and reani-
mates the process—produces the return, again and
yet again, on one's impressions.   Thoreau must have
had this moderating and even chastening effect.   It
did not rest, moreover, with him alone; the advantage of which I speak was not confined to Thoreau's

case In 1837 Emerson (in his journal) pronounced Mr. Bronson Alcott the most extraordinary man and the highest genius of his time : the sequence of which was that for more than forty years after that he had the gentleman living but half a mile away. The opportunity for the return, as I have called it, was not wanting.

His detachment is shown in his whole attitude toward the transcendental movement—that remarkable outburst of Romanticism on Puritan ground, as Mr. Cabot very well names it. Nothing can be more ingenious, more sympathetic and charming, than Emerson's account and definition of the matter in his lecture (of 1842) called "The Transcendentalist"; and yet nothing is more apparent from his letters and journals than that he regarded any such label or banner as a mere tiresome flutter. He liked to taste but not to drink—least of all to become intoxicated. He liked to explain the transcendentalists but did not care at all to be explained by them : a doctrine "whereof you know I am wholly guiltless," he says to his wife in 1842, "and which is spoken of as a known and fixed element, like salt or meal. So that I have to begin with endless disclaimers and explanations : 'I am not the man you take me for.'" He was never the man any one took him for, for the simple reason that no one could possibly take him for the elusive, irreducible, merely gustatory spirit for which he took himself.

"It is a sort of maxim with me never to harp on the omnipotence of limitations. Least of all do we need any suggestion

of checks and measures ; as if New England were anything else.
. . . Of so many fine people it is true that being so much
they ought to be a little more, and missing that are naught.
It is a sort of King Renè period ; there is no doing, but rare
thrilling prophecy from bands of competing minstrels."

That is his private expression about a large part of
a ferment in regard to which his public judgment
was that

"That indeed constitutes a new feature in their portrait.
that they are the most exacting and extortionate critics. . . .
These exacting children advertise us of our wants.   There is no
compliment, no smooth speech with them ; they pay you only
this one compliment of insatiable expectation ; they aspire, they
severely exact, and if they only stand fast in this watch-tower,
and stand fast unto the end, and without end, then they are
terrible friends, whereof poet and priest cannot but stand in
awe ; and what if they eat clouds and drink wind, they have
not been without service to the race of man."

That was saying the best for them, as he always
said it for everything; but it was the sense of their
being "bands of competing minstrels" and their
camp being only a "measure and check," in a society
too sparse for a synthesis, that kept him from wishing
to don their uniform.   This was after all but a mis-
fitting imitation of his natural wear, and what he
would have liked was to put that off—he did not
wish to button it tighter.   He said the best for his
friends of the Dial, of Fruitlands and Brook Farm, in
saying that they were fastidious and critical; but he
was conscious in the next breath that what there was
around them to be criticised was mainly a negative.
Nothing is more perceptible to-day than that their

criticism produced no fruit—that it was little else than a very decent and innocent recreation—a kind of Puritan carnival. The New England world was for much the most part very busy, but the Dial and Fruitlands and Brook Farm were the amusement of the leisure-class. Extremes meet, and as in older societies that class is known principally by its connection with castles and carriages, so at Concord it came, with Thoreau and Mr. W. H. Channing, out of the cabin and the wood-lot.

Emerson was not moved to believe in their fastidiousness as a productive principle even when they directed it upon abuses which he abundantly recognised. Mr. Cabot shows that he was by no means one of the professional abolitionists or philanthropists—never an enrolled "humanitarian."

"We talk frigidly of Reform until the walls mock us. It is that of which a man should never speak, but if he have cherished it in his bosom he should steal to it in darkness, as an Indian to his bride. . . . Does he not do more to abolish slavery who works all day steadily in his own garden, than he who goes to the abolition meeting and makes a speech ? He who does his own work frees a slave."

I must add that even while I transcribe these words there comes to me the recollection of the great meeting in the Boston Music Hall, on the first day of 1863, to celebrate the signing by Mr. Lincoln of the proclamation freeing the Southern slaves—of the momentousness of the occasion, the vast excited multitude, the crowded platform and the tall, spare figure of Emerson, in the midst, reading out the stanzas that were published under the name of the Boston Hymn. They are not the happiest he produced for an occasion—they do not compare with the verses on the "embattled farmers," read at Concord in 1857, and there is a certain awkwardness in some of them. But I well remember the immense effect with which his beautiful voice pronounced the lines—

> "Pay ransom to the owner
> And fill the bag to the brim.
> Who is the owner? The slave is owner,
> And ever was. Pay *him!*"

And Mr. Cabot chronicles the fact that the *gran' rifiuto*—the great backsliding of Mr. Webster when he cast his vote in Congress for the Fugitive Slave Law of 1850—was the one thing that ever moved him to heated denunciation. He felt Webster's apostasy as strongly as he had admired his genius. "Who has not helped to praise him? Simply he was the one American of our time whom we could produce as a finished work of nature." There is a passage in his journal (not a rough jotting, but, like most of the entries in it, a finished piece of writing), which is admirably descriptive of the wonderful orator and is moreover one of the very few portraits, or even personal sketches, yielded by Mr. Cabot's selections. It shows that he could observe the human figure and "render" it to good purpose.

"His splendid wrath, when his eyes become fire, is good to see, so intellectual it is—the wrath of the fact and the cause he espouses, and not at all personal to himself. . . . These village

parties must be dish-water to him, yet he shows himself just
good-natured, just nonchalant enough ; and he has his own
way, without offending any one or losing any ground. . . . His
expensiveness seems necessary to him ; were he too prudent a
Yankee it would be a sad deduction from his magnificence.   I
only wish he would not truckle [to the slave-holders].   I do
not care how much he spends."

I doubtless appear to have said more than enough,
yet I have passed by many of the passages I had
marked for transcription from Mr. Cabot's volumes.
There is one, in the first, that makes us stare as we
come upon it, to the effect that Emerson "could see
nothing in Shelley, Aristophanes, Don Quixote, Miss
Austen, Dickens." Mr. Cabot adds that he rarely
read a novel, even the famous ones (he has a point
of contact here as well as, strangely enough, on two
or three other sides with that distinguished moralist
M. Ernest Renan, who, like Emerson, was originally
a dissident priest and cannot imagine why people
should write works of fiction) ; and thought Dante "a
man to put into a museum, but not into your house ;
another Zerah Colburn ; a prodigy of imaginative
function, executive rather than contemplative or
wise." The confession of an insensibility ranging
from Shelley to Dickens and from Dante to Miss
Austen and taking Don Quixote and Aristophanes
on the way, is a large allowance to have to make for
a man of letters, and may appear to confirm but
slightly any claim of intellectual hospitality and
general curiosity put forth for him. The truth was
that, sparely constructed as he was and formed not

wastefully, not with material left over, as it were, for a special function, there were certain chords in Emerson that did not vibrate at all. I well remember my impression of this on walking with him in the autumn of 1872 through the galleries of the Louvre and, later that winter, through those of the Vatican : his perception of the objects contained in these collections was of the most general order. I was struck with the anomaly of a man so refined and intelligent being so little spoken to by works of art. It would be more exact to say that certain chords were wholly absent ; the tune was played, the tune of life and literature, altogether on those that remained. They had every wish to be equal to their office, but one feels that the number was short—that some notes could not be given. Mr. Cabot makes use of a singular phrase when he says, in speaking of Hawthorne, for several years our author's neighbour at Concord and a little—a very little we gather —his companion, that Emerson was unable to read his novels—he thought them "not worthy of him." This is a judgment odd almost to fascination—we circle round it and turn it over and over ; it contains so elusive an ambiguity. How highly he must have esteemed the man of whose genius *The House of the Seven Gables* and *The Scarlet Letter* gave imperfectly the measure, and how strange that he should not have been eager to read almost anything that such a gifted being might have let fall ! It was a rare accident that made them live almost side by side so long in

the same small New England town, each a fruit of a
long Puritan stem, yet with such a difference of
taste. Hawthorne's vision was all for the evil and
sin of the world ; a side of life as to which Emerson's
eyes were thickly bandaged. There were points as
to which the latter's conception of right could be
violated, but he had no great sense of wrong—a
strangely limited one, indeed, for a moralist—no
sense of the dark, the foul, the base. There were
certain complications in life which he never suspected. One asks one's self whether that is why he
did not care for Dante and Shelley and Aristophanes
and Dickens, their works containing a considerable
reflection of human perversity. But that still leaves
the indifference to Cervantes and Miss Austen un-
accounted for.

It has not, however, been the ambition of these
remarks to account for everything, and I have arrived
at the end without even pointing to the grounds on
which Emerson justifies the honours of biography,
discussion and illustration. I have assumed his
importance and continuance, and shall probably not
be gainsaid by those who read him. Those who do
not will hardly rub him out. Such a book as Mr.
Cabot's subjects a reputation to a test—leads people
to look it over and hold it up to the light, to see
whether it is worth keeping in use or even putting
away in a cabinet. Such a revision of Emerson has
no relegating consequences. The result of it is once
more the impression that he serves and will not wear

out, and that indeed we cannot afford to drop him
His instrument makes him precious.   He did something better than any one else ; he had a particular
faculty, which has not been surpassed, for speaking
to the soul in a voice of direction and authority.
There have been many spiritual voices appealing,
consoling, reassuring, exhorting, or even denouncing
and terrifying, but none has had just that firmness
and just that purity.   It penetrates further, it seems
to go back to the roots of our feelings, to where conduct and manhood begin ; and moreover, to us to-day,
there is something in it that says that it is connected
somehow with the virtue of the world, has wrought
and achieved, lived in thousands of minds, produced
a mass of character and life.   And there is this
further sign of Emerson's singular power, that he is
a striking exception to the general rule that writings
live in the last resort by their form ; that they owe
a large part of their fortune to the art with which
they have been composed.   It is hardly too much, or
too little, to say of Emerson's writings in general
that they were not composed at all.   Many and many
things are beautifully said ; he had felicities, inspira-
tions, unforgettable phrases ; he had frequently an
exquisite eloquence.

" O my friends, there are resources in us on which we have
not yet drawn.   There are men who rise refreshed on hearing a
threat ; men to whom a crisis which intimidates and paralyses
the majority—demanding not the faculties of prudence and
thrift, but comprehension, immovableness, the readiness of
sacrifice, come graceful and beloved as a bride. . . .   But these

are heights that we can scarce look up to and remember without contrition and shame. Let us thank God that such things exist."

None the less we have the impression that that search for a fashion and a manner on which he was always engaged never really came to a conclusion; it draws itself out through his later writings—it drew itself out through his later lectures, like a sort of renunciation of success. It is not on these, however, but on their predecessors, that his reputation will rest. Of course the way he spoke was the way that was on the whole most convenient to him; but he differs from most men of letters of the same degree of credit in failing to strike us as having achieved a style. This achievement is, as I say, usually the bribe or toll-money on the journey to posterity; and if Emerson goes his way, as he clearly appears to be doing, on the strength of his message alone, the case will be rare, the exception striking, and the honour great.

1887.

II

THE LIFE OF GEORGE ELIOT

THE LIFE OF GEORGE ELIOT

THE writer of these pages has observed that the first question usually asked in relation to Mr. Cross's long-expected biography is whether the reader has not been disappointed in it. The inquirer is apt to be disappointed if the question be answered in the negative. It may as well be said, therefore, at the threshold of the following remarks, that such is not the feeling with which this particular reader laid down the book. The general feeling about it will depend very much on what has been looked for ; there was probably, in advance, a considerable belief that we were to be treated to "revelations." I know not exactly why it should have been, but certain it is that the announcement of a biography of George Eliot has been construed more or less as a promise that we were to be admitted behind the scenes, as it were, of her life. No such result has taken place. We look at the drama from the point of view usually allotted to the public, and the curtain is lowered whenever it suits the biographer. The most "intimate" pages in the book are those in which

the great novelist notes her derangements of health
and depression of spirits.　This history, to my sense,
is quite as interesting as it might have been ; that is,
it is of the deepest interest, and one misses nothing
that is characteristic or essential except perhaps a
few more examples of the *vis comica* which made
half the fortune of *Adam Bede* and *Silas Marner*.
There is little that is absent that it would have been
in Mr. Cross's power to give us.　George Eliot's
letters and journals are only a partial expression of
her spirit, but they are evidently as full an expression as it was capable of giving itself when she was
not wound up to the epic pitch.　They do not
explain her novels ; they reflect in a singularly
limited degree the process of growth of these great
works ; but it must be added that even a superficial
acquaintance with the author was sufficient to assure
one that her rich and complicated mind did not
overflow in idle confidences.　It was benignant and
receptive in the highest degree, and nothing could
have been more gracious than the manner of its
intercourse ; but it was deeply reserved and very
far from egotistical, and nothing could have been
less easy or agreeable to it, I surmise, than to attempt to tell people how, for instance, the plot of
Romola got itself constructed or the character of
Grandcourt got itself observed.　There are critics
who refuse to the delineator of this gentleman the
title of a genius ; who say that she had only a great
talent overloaded with a great store of knowledge.

The label, the epithet, matters little, but it is certain
that George Eliot had this characteristic of the mind
possessed : that the creations which brought her
renown were of the incalculable kind, shaped themselves in mystery, in some intellectual back-shop or
secret crucible, and were as little as possible implied
in the aspect of her life.   There is nothing more
singular or striking in Mr. Cross's volumes than the
absence of any indication, up to the time the *Scenes
from Clerical Life* were published, that Miss Evans
was a likely person to have written them ; unless it
be the absence of any indication, after they were
published, that the deeply-studious, concentrated,
home-keeping Mrs. Lewes was a likely person to
have produced their successors.   I know very well
that there is no such thing in general as the air of
the novelist, which it behoves those who practise
this art to put on so that they may be recognised in
public places ; but there is such a thing as the air of
the sage, the scholar, the philosopher, the votary of
abstractions and of the lore of the ages, and in this
pale but rich *Life* that is the face that is presented.

The plan on which it is composed is, so far as I
know, without precedent, but it is a plan that could
have occurred only to an " outsider " in literature, if
I may venture to apply this term to one who has
executed a literary task with such tact and success.
The regular *littérateur*, hampered by tradition, would,
I think, have lacked the boldness, the artless artful-
ness, of conjoining in the same text selected morsels

of letters and journals, so as to form a continuous and multifarious *talk*, on the writer's part, punctuated only by marginal names and dates and divisions into chapters. There is something a little violent in the system, in spite of our feeling that it has been applied with a supple hand; but it was probably the best that Mr. Cross could have adopted, and it served especially well his purpose of appearing only as an arranger, or rather of not appearing at all. The modesty, the good taste, the self-effacement of the editorial element in the book are, in a word, complete, and the clearness and care of arrangement, the accuracy of reference, leave nothing to be desired. The form Mr. Cross has chosen, or invented, becomes, in the application, highly agreeable, and his rule of omission (for we have, almost always, only parts and passages of letters) has not prevented his volumes from being as copious as we could wish. George Eliot was not a great letter-writer, either in quantity or quality; she had neither the spirit, the leisure, nor the lightness of mind to conjure with the epistolary pen, and after her union with George Henry Lewes her disposition to play with it was further damped by his quick activity in her service. Letter-writing was part of the trouble he saved her; in this as in other ways he interposed between the world and his sensitive companion. The difference is striking between her habits in this respect and those of Madame George Sand, whose correspondence has lately been collected into six closely-printed volumes which testify afresh to her extraordinary energy and facility. Madame Sand, however, indefatigable producer as she was, was not a woman of study ; she lived from day to day, from hand to mouth (intellectually), as it were, and had no general plan of life and culture. Her English compeer took the problem of production more seriously ; she distilled her very substance into the things she gave the world. There was therefore so much the less of it left for casual utterance.

It was not till Marian Evans was past thirty, indeed, that she became an author by profession, and it may accordingly be supposed that her early letters are those which take us most into her confidence. This is true of those written when she was on tho threshold of womanhood, which form a very full expression of her feelings at the time. The drawback here is that the feelings themselves are rather wanting in interest—one may almost say in amiability. At the age of twenty Marian Evans was a deeply religious young woman, whose faith took the form of a narrow evangelicism. Religious, in a manner, she remained to the end of her life, in spite of her adoption of a scientific explanation of things ; but in the year 1839 she thought it ungodly to go to concerts and to read novels. She writes to her former governess that she can " only sigh " when she hears of the " marrying and giving in marriage that is constantly transacted ; " expresses enjoyment of Hannah More's letters ("the contemplation of so

blessed a character as hers is very salutary ");
wishes that she "might be more useful in her own
obscure and lowly station" ("I feel myself to be a
mere cumberer of the ground"), that she "might
seek to be sanctified wholly." These first fragments
of her correspondence, first glimpses of her mind,
are very curious; they have nothing in common
with the later ones but the deep seriousness of the
tone. Serious, of course, George Eliot continued to
be to the end; the sense of moral responsibility, of
the sadness and difficulty of life, was the most inveterate part of her nature. But the provincial
strain in the letters from which I have quoted is
very marked: they reflect a meagreness and grayness of outward circumstance; have a tinge as of
Dissent in a small English town, where there are
brick chapels in back streets. This was only a
moment in her development; but there is something touching in the contrast between such a state
of mind and that of the woman before whom, at
middle age, all the culture of the world unrolled
itself, and towards whom fame and fortune, and an
activity which at the earlier period she would have
thought very profane, pressed with rapidity. In
1839, as I have said, she thought very meanly of
the art in which she was to attain such distinction.
"I venture to believe that the same causes which
exist in my own breast to render novels and romances
pernicious have their counterpart in every fellow-
creature. . . . The weapons of Christian warfare

were never sharpened at the forge of romance."
The style of these pietistic utterances is singularly
strenuous and hard; the light and familiar are
absent from them, and I think it is not too much
to say that they show scarcely a single premonitory
ray of the genius which had *Silas Marner* in reserve.
This dryness was only a phase, indeed; it was
speedily dispelled by more abundant showers of
emotion—by the overflow of perception. Premonitory rays are still absent, however, after her first
asceticism passes away—a change apparently co-
incident with her removal from the country to the
pleasant old town of Coventry, where all American
pilgrims to midland shrines go and murmur Tenny-
son on the bridge. After the evangelical note began
to fade it was still the desire for faith (a faith which
could reconcile human affection with some of the un-
amiable truths of science), still the religious idea
that coloured her thought; not the love of human
life as a spectacle, nor the desire to spread the wings
of the artist. It must be remembered, though, that
during these years, if she was not stimulating prophecy in any definite form she was inhaling those
impressions which were to make her first books so
full of the delightful midland quality, the air of old-
fashioned provincialism. The first piece of literary
work she attempted (and she brought it to the best
conclusion), was a translation of Strauss's *Life of
Jesus*, which she began in 1844, when she was not
yet twenty-five years of age; a task which indicates

not only the persistence of her religious preoccupations, as well as the higher form they took, but the fact that with the limited facilities afforded by her life at that time she had mastered one of the most difficult of foreign languages and the vocabulary of a German exegetist.   In 1841 she thought it wrong to encourage novels, but in 1847 she confesses to reading George Sand with great delight.   There is no exhibition in Mr. Cross's pages of the steps by which she passed over to a position of tolerant scepticism ; but the details of the process are after all of minor importance : the essential fact is that the change was predetermined by the nature of her mind.

The great event of her life was of course her acquaintance with George Henry Lewes.   I say " of course," because this relation had an importance even more controlling than the publication and success of her first attempt at fiction, inasmuch as it was in consequence of Mr. Lewes's friendly urgency that she wrote the *Scenes of Clerical Life*.   She met him for the first time in London, in the autumn of 1851; but it was not till the summer of 1854 that the connection with him began (it was marked to the world by their going to spend together several months in Germany, where he was bent on researches for his *Life of Goethe*), which was to become so much closer than many formal marriages and to last till his death in 1878.   The episode of Miss Evans's life in London during these three years was already tolerably well known. She had become by this time a professional literary woman, and had regular work as assistant editor of the *Westminster Review*, to which she gave her most conscientious attention. Her accomplishments now were wide. She was a linguist, a copious reader, an earnest student of history and philosophy. She wrote much for her magazine as well as solicited articles from others, and several of her contributions are contained in the volume of essays published after her death— essays of which it is fair to say that they give but a faint intimation of her latent powers. George Henry Lewes was a versatile, hard-working journalist, with a tendency, apparently, of the drifting sort ; and after having been made acquainted with each other by Mr. Herbert Spencer, the pair commingled their sympathies and their efforts. Her letters, at this season, contain constant mention of Lewes (one allusion to the effect that he " has quite won my regard, after having had a good deal of my vituperation ") ; she takes an interest in his health and corrects his proofs for him when he is absent. It was impossible for Mr. Lewes to marry, as he had a wife living, from whom he was separated. He had also three children, of whom the care did not devolve upon their mother. The union Miss Evans formed with him was a deliberate step, of which she accepted all the consequences. These consequences were excellent, so far as the world is at liberty to judge, save in an important particular. This particular is the fact that her false position, as we may call it, produced upon George Eliot's life a certain effect of sequestration which was not favourable to social freedom, or to freedom of observation, and which excited on the part of her companion a protecting, sheltering, fostering, precautionary attitude — the assumption that they lived in special, in abnormal conditions. It would be too much to say that George Eliot had not the courage of the situation she had embraced, but she had, at least, not the levity, the indifference; she was unable, in the premises, to be sufficiently superficial. Her deep, strenuous, much-considering mind, of which the leading mark is the capacity for a sort of luminous brooding, fed upon the idea of her irregularity with an intensity which doubtless only her magnificent intellectual activity and Lewes's brilliancy and ingenuity kept from being morbid. The fault of most of her work is the absence of spontaneity, the excess of reflection; and by her action in 1854 (which seemed superficially to be of the sort usually termed reckless), she committed herself to being nothing if not reflective, to cultivating a kind of compensatory earnestness. Her earnestness, her educated conscience, her exalted sense of responsibility, were coloured by her peculiar position; they committed her to a plan of life, of study, in which the accidental, the unexpected, were too little allowed for, and this is what I mean by speaking of her sequestration. If her relations with the world had been easier, in a word, her books would have been less difficult. Mr. Cross, very justly, merely touches upon this question of her forming a tie which was deprived of the sanction of the law ; but he gives a portion of a letter written to Mrs. Bray more than a year after it had begun, which sufficiently indicates the serenity of her resolution. Repentance, of course, she never had—the success of her experiment was too rare and complete for that ; and I do not mean that her attitude was ever for a moment apologetic. On the contrary, it was only too superabundantly confirmatory. Her effort was to pitch her life ever in the key of the superior wisdom that made her say to Mrs. Bray, in the letter of September 1855, " That any unworldly, unsuperstitious person who is sufficiently acquainted with the realities of life can pronounce my relation to Mr. Lewes immoral, I can only understand when I remember how subtle and complex are the influences that mould opinion." I need not attempt to project the light of criticism on this particular case of conscience ; there remains ever, in the mutual relations of intelligent men and women, an element which is for themselves alone to consider. One reflection, however, forces itself upon the mind : if the connection had not taken place we should have lost the spectacle and influence of one of the most successful partnerships presented to us in the history of human affection. There has been much talk about George Eliot's " example," which is not to be deprecated so long as it is remembered that in speak-

ing of the example of a woman of this value we can
only mean example for good. Exemplary indeed in
her long connection with George Henry Lewes were
the qualities on which beneficent intimacy rests.

She was thirty-seven years old when the *Scenes
from Clerical Life* were published, but this work
opened wide for her the door of success, and fame
and fortune came to her rapidly. Her union with
Lewes had been a union of poverty : there is a
sentence in her journal, of the year 1856, which
speaks of their ascending certain cliffs called the
Tors, at Ilfracombe, " only twice ; for a tax of 3d.
per head was demanded for this luxury, and we
could not afford a sixpenny walk very frequently."
The incentive to writing *Amos Barton* seems to have
been mainly pecuniary. There was an urgent need
to make money, and it appears to have been agreed
between the pair that there was at least no harm in
the lady's trying her hand at a story. Lewes professed a belief that she would really do something in
this line, while she, more sceptical, reserved her
judgment till after the test. The *Scenes from Clerical
Life* were therefore pre-eminently an empirical work
of fiction. With the sending of the first episode to
the late Mr. John Blackwood for approval, there
opened a relation between publisher and author
which lasted to the end, and which was probably
more genial and unclouded than any in the annals
of literature, as well as almost unprecedentedly
lucrative to both parties. This first book of George

Eliot's has little of the usual air of a first book, none of the crudity of an early attempt; it was not the work of a youthful person, and one sees that the material had been long in her mind. The ripeness, the pathos, a sort of considered quality, are as striking to-day as when *Amos Barton* and *Janet's Repentance* were published, and enable us to understand that people should have asked themselves with surprise, at that time, who it was, in the midst of them, that had been taking notes so long and so wisely without giving a sign. *Adam Bede*, written rapidly, appeared in 1859, and George Eliot found herself a consummate novelist without having suspected it. The book was an immense, a brilliant success, and from this moment the author's life took its definite and final direction. She accepted the great obligations which to her mind belonged to a person who had the ear of the public, and her whole effort thenceforth was highly to respond to them — to respond to them by teaching, by vivid moral illustration and even by direct exhortation. It is striking that from the first her conception of the novelist's task is never in the least as the game of art. The most interesting passage in Mr. Cross's volumes is to my sense a simple sentence in a short entry in her journal in the year 1859, just after she had finished the first volume of *The Mill on the Floss* (the original title of which, by the way, had been *Sister Maggie*): "We have just finished reading aloud Père Goriot, a hateful book." That Balzac's masterpiece

should have elicited from her only this remark, at a
time, too, when her mind might have been opened
to it by her own activity of composition, is significant
of so many things that the few words are, in the
whole *Life*, those I should have been most sorry to
lose.   Of course they are not all George Eliot would
have had to say about Balzac, if some other occasion
than a simple jotting in a diary had presented itself.
Still, what even a jotting may *not* have said after a
first perusal of *Le Père Goriot* is eloquent ; it illumin-
ates the author's general attitude with regard to the
novel, which, for her, was not primarily a picture of
life, capable of deriving a high value from its form,
but a moralised fable, the last word of a philosophy
endeavouring to teach by example.

This is a very noble and defensible view, and one
must speak respectfully of any theory of work which
would produce such fruit as *Romola* and *Middlemarch*.
But it testifies to that side of George Eliot's nature
which was weakest—the absence of free æsthetic
life (I venture this remark in the face of a passage
quoted from one of her letters in Mr. Cross's third
volume) ; it gives the hand, as it were, to several
other instances that may be found in the same
pages.   " My function is that of the *æsthetic*, not
the doctrinal teacher ; the rousing of the nobler
emotions, which make mankind desire the social right,
not the prescribing of special measures, concerning which the artistic mind, however strongly
moved by social sympathy, is often not the best

judge." That is the passage referred to in my par-
enthetic allusion, and it is a good general description
of the manner in which George Eliot may be said to
have acted on her generation; but the "artistic
mind," the possession of which it implies, existed in
her with limitations remarkable in a writer whose
imagination was so rich. We feel in her, always,
that she proceeds from the abstract to the concrete;
that her figures and situations are evolved, as the
phrase is, from her moral consciousness, and are only
indirectly the products of observation. They are
deeply studied and massively supported, but they are
not *seen*, in the irresponsible plastic way. The world
was, first and foremost, for George Eliot, the moral,
the intellectual world; the personal spectacle came
after; and lovingly humanly as she regarded it we
constantly feel that she cares for the things she finds
in it only so far as they are types. The philosophic
door is always open, on her stage, and we are aware
that the somewhat cooling draught of ethical purpose
draws across it. This constitutes half the beauty of
her work; the constant reference to ideas may be
an excellent source of one kind of reality—for, after
all, the secret of seeing a thing well is not necessarily
that you see nothing else. Her preoccupation with
the universe helped to make her characters strike
you as also belonging to it; it raised the roof, widened
the area, of her æsthetic structure. Nothing is finer,
in her genius, than the combination of her love of
general truth and love of the special case; without

this, indeed, we should not have heard of her as a
novelist, for the passion of the special case is surely
the basis of the story-teller's art.   All the same, that
little sign of all that Balzac failed to suggest to her
showed at what perils the special case got itself considered.   Such dangers increased as her activity proceeded, and many judges perhaps hold that in her
ultimate work, in *Middlemarch* and *Daniel Deronda*
(especially the latter), it ceased to be considered at
all.   Such critics assure us that Gwendolen and
Grandcourt, Deronda and Myra, are not concrete
images, but disembodied types, pale abstractions, signs
and symbols of a "great lesson."   I give up Deronda
and Myra to the objector, but Grandcourt and Gwendolen seem to me to have a kind of superior reality ;
to be, in a high degree, what one demands of a
figure in a novel, planted on their legs and complete.

The truth is, perception and reflection, at the outset, divided George Eliot's great talent between
them ; but as time went on circumstances led the
latter to develop itself at the expense of the former
—one of these circumstances being apparently the
influence of George Henry Lewes.   Lewes was interested in science, in cosmic problems ; and though his
companion, thanks to the original bent of her versatile, powerful mind, needed no impulse from without
to turn herself to speculation, yet the contagion of
his studies pushed her further than she would otherwise have gone in the direction of scientific observation, which is but another form of what I have called

reflection. Her early novels are full of natural as
distinguished from systematic observation, though
even in them it is less the dominant note, I think,
than the love of the "moral," the reaction of thought
in the face of the human comedy. They had observation sufficient, at any rate, to make their fortune,
and it may well be said that that is enough for any
novel. In *Silas Marner*, in *Adam Bede*, the quality
seems gilded by a sort of autumn haze, an afternoon
light, of meditation, which mitigates the sharpness of
portraiture. I doubt very much whether the author
herself had a clear vision, for instance, of the marriage of Dinah Morris to Adam, or of the rescue of
Hetty from the scaffold at the eleventh hour. The
reason of this may be, indeed, that her perception was
a perception of nature much more than of art, and
that these particular incidents do not belong to nature
(to my sense at least) ; by which I do not mean that
they belong to a very happy art. I cite them, on the
contrary, as an evidence of artistic weakness ; they are
a very good example of the view in which a story must
have marriages and rescues in the nick of time, as a
matter of course. I must add, in fairness to George
Eliot, that the marriage of the nun-like Dinah, which
shocks the reader, who sees in it a base concession,
was a *trouvaille* of Lewes's and is a small sign of that
same faulty judgment in literary things which led
him to throw his influence on the side of her writing
verse—verse which is *all* reflection, with direct, vivifying vision, or emotion, remarkably absent.

It is a part of this same limitation of the pleasure she was capable of taking in the fact of representation for itself that the various journals and notes of her visits to the Continent are, though by no means destitute of the tempered enjoyment of foreign sights which was as near as she ever came to rapture, singularly vague in expression on the subject of the general and particular spectacle—the life and manners, the works of art. She enumerates diligently all the pictures and statues she sees, and the way she does so is a proof of her active, earnest intellectual habits ; but it is rarely apparent that they have said much to her, or that what they have said is one of their deeper secrets. She is capable of writing, after coming out of the great chapel of San Lorenzo, in Florence, that " the world-famous statues of Michael Angelo on the tombs . . . remained to us as affected and exaggerated in the original as in copies and casts." That sentence startles one, on the part of the author of *Romola*, and that Mr. Cross should have printed it is a commendable proof of his impartiality.

It was in *Romola*, precisely, that the equilibrium I spoke of just now was lost, and that reflection began to weigh down the scale. *Romola* is pre-eminently a study of the human conscience in an historical setting which is studied almost as much, and few passages in Mr. Cross's volumes are more interesting than those relating to the production of this magnificent romance. George Eliot took all her work with a noble seriousness, but into none of it did she throw herself with more passion. It drained from her as much as she gave to it, and none of her writing ploughed into her, to use her biographer's expression, so deeply. She told him that she began it a young woman and finished it an old one. More than any of her novels it was evolved, as I have said, from her moral consciousness—a moral consciousness encircled by a prodigious amount of literary research. Her literary ideal was at all times of the highest, but in the preparation of *Romola* it placed her under a control absolutely religious. She read innumerable books, some of them bearing only remotely on her subject, and consulted without stint contemporary records and documents. She neglected nothing that would enable her to live, intellectually, in the period she had undertaken to describe. We know, for the most part, I think, the result. *Romola* is on the whole the finest thing she wrote, but its defects are almost on the scale of its beauties. The great defect is that, except in the person of Tito Melema, it does not seem positively to live. It is overladen with learning, it smells of the lamp, it tastes just perceptibly of pedantry. In spite of its want of blood, however, it assuredly will survive in men's remembrance, for the finest pages in it belong to the finest part of our literature. It is on the whole a failure, but such a failure as only a great talent can produce ; and one may say of it that there are many great " hits " far

less interesting than such a mistake. A twentieth
part of the erudition would have sufficed, would have
given us the feeling and colour of the time, if there
had been more of the breath of the Florentine streets,
more of the faculty of optical evocation, a greater
saturation of the senses with the elements of the
adorable little city. The difficulty with the book,
for the most part, is that it is not Italian; it has
always seemed to me the most Germanic of the
author's productions. I cannot imagine a German
writing (in the way of a novel) anything half so
good; but if I could imagine it I should suppose
Romola to be very much the sort of picture he would
achieve—the sort of medium through which he would
show us how, by the Arno-side, the fifteenth century
came to an end. One of the sources of interest in
the book is that, more than any of its companions,
it indicates how much George Eliot proceeded by
reflection and research; how little important, comparatively, she thought that same breath of the streets.
It carries to a maximum the in-door quality.

The most definite impression produced, perhaps,
by Mr. Cross's volumes (by the second and third) is
that of simple success—success which had been the
result of no external accidents (unless her union with
Lewes be so denominated), but was involved in the
very faculties nature had given her. All the elements of an eventual happy fortune met in her
constitution. The great foundation, to begin with,
was there—the magnificent mind, vigorous, luminous,

and eminently sane. To her intellectual vigour, her
immense facility, her exemption from cerebral lassitude, her letters and journals bear the most copious
testimony. Her daily stint of arduous reading and
writing was of the largest. Her ability, as one may
express it in the most general way, was astonishing,
and it belonged to every season of her long and fruitful career. Her passion for study encountered no
impediment, but was able to make everything feed
and support it. The extent and variety of her knowledge is by itself the measure of a capacity which
triumphed wherever it wished. Add to this an
immense special talent which, as soon as it tries its
wings, is found to be adequate to the highest, longest
flights and brings back great material rewards.
George Eliot of course had drawbacks and difficulties,
physical infirmities, constant liabilities to headache,
dyspepsia, and other illness, to deep depression, to
despair about her work ; but these jolts of the
chariot were small in proportion to the impetus
acquired, and were hardly greater than was necessary for reminding her of the secret of all ambitious
workers in the field of art—that effort, effort, always
effort, is the only key to success. Her great further-
ance was that, intensely intellectual being as she
was, the life of affection and emotion was also widely
open to her. She had all the initiation of knowledge
and none of its dryness, all the advantages of judgment and all the luxuries of feeling. She had an
imagination which enabled her to sit at home with

book and pen, and yet enter into the life of other generations ; project herself into Warwickshire alehouses and Florentine symposia, reconstitute conditions utterly different from her own. Toward the end she triumphed over the great impossible ; she reconciled the greatest sensibility with the highest serenity. She succeeded in guarding her pursuits from intrusion ; in carrying out her habits ; in sacrificing her work as little as possible ; in leading, in the midst of a society united in conspiracies to interrupt and vulgarise, an independent, strenuously personal life. People who had the honour of penetrating into the sequestered precinct of the Priory— the house in London in which she lived from 1863 to 1880—remember well a kind of sanctity in the place, an atmosphere of stillness and concentration, something that suggested a literary temple.

It was part of the good fortune of which I speak that in Mr. Lewes she had found the most devoted of caretakers, the most jealous of ministers, a companion through whom all business was transacted. The one drawback of this relation was that, considering what she attempted, it limited her experience too much to itself ; but for the rest it helped her in a hundred ways—it saved her nerves, it fortified her privacy, it protected her leisure, it diminished the friction of living. His admiration of her work was of the largest, though not always, I think, truly discriminating, and he surrounded her with a sort of temperate zone of independence—independence of everything except him and her own standards. Nervous, sensitive, delicate in every way in which genius is delicate (except, indeed, that she had a robust reason), it was a great thing for her to have accident made rare and exposure mitigated; and to this result Lewes, as the administrator of her fame, admirably contributed. He filtered the stream, giving her only the clearer water. The accident of reading reviews of one's productions, especially when they are bad, is, for the artist of our day, one of the most frequent; and Mr. Lewes, by keeping these things out of her way, enabled her to achieve what was perhaps the highest form of her success—an inaccessibility to the newspaper. "It is remarkable to me," she writes in 1876, "that I have entirely lost my *personal* melancholy. I often, of course, have melancholy thoughts about the destinies of my fellow creatures, but I am never in that *mood* of sadness which used to be my frequent visitant even in the midst of external happiness." Her later years, coloured by this accumulated wisdom, when she had taken her final form before the world and had come to be regarded more and more as a teacher and philosopher, are full of suggestion to the critic, but I have exhausted my limited space. There is a certain coldness in them perhaps—the coldness that results from most of one's opinions being formed, one's mind made up, on many great subjects; from the degree, in a word, to which "culture" had taken the place of the more primitive processes of experience.

" Ah, les livres, ils nous débordent, ils nous

étouffent—nous périssons par les livres!" That cry of a distinguished French novelist (there is no harm in mentioning M. Alphonse Daudet), which fell upon the ear of the present writer some time ago, represents as little as possible the emotion of George Eliot confronted with literatures and sciences. M. Alphonse Daudet went on to say that, to his mind, the personal impression, the effort of direct observation, was the most precious source of information for the novelist; that nothing could take its place; that the effect of books was constantly to check and pervert this effort; that a second-hand, third-hand, tenth-hand, impression was constantly tending to substitute itself for a fresh perception; that we were ending by seeing everything through literature instead of through our own senses; and that in short literature was rapidly killing literature. This view has immense truth on its side, but the case would be too simple if, on one side or the other, there were only one way of finding out. The effort of the novelist is to find out, to know, or at least to see, and no one, in the nature of things, can less afford to be indifferent to side-lights. Books are themselves, unfortunately, an expression of human passions. George Eliot had no doubts, at any rate; if impressionism, before she laid down her pen, had already begun to be talked about, it would have made no difference with her—she would have had no desire to pass for an impressionist.

There is one question we cannot help asking ourselves as we close this record of her life; it is im-

possible not to let our imagination wander in the
direction of what turn her mind or her fortune
might have taken if she had never met George
Henry Lewes, or never cast her lot with his. It is
safe to say that, in one way or another, in the long
run, her novels would have got themselves written,
and it is possible they would have been more natural,
as one may call it, more familiarly and casually
human. Would her development have been less
systematic, more irresponsible, more personal, and
should we have had more of *Adam Bede* and *Silas
Marner* and less of *Romola* and *Middlemarch*? The
question, after all, cannot be answered, and I do not
push it, being myself very grateful for *Middlemarch*
and *Romola*. It is as George Eliot does actually
present herself that we must judge her—a condition
that will not prevent her from striking us as one of
the noblest, most beautiful minds of our time. This
impression bears the reader company throughout
these letters and notes. It is impossible not to feel,
as we close them, that she was an admirable being.
They are less brilliant, less entertaining, than we
might have hoped ; they contain fewer " good things "
and have even a certain grayness of tone, something
measured and subdued, as of a person talking without ever raising her voice. But there rises from
them a kind of fragrance of moral elevation ; a love
of justice, truth, and light ; a large, generous way of
looking at things ; and a constant effort to hold
high the torch in the dusky spaces of man's con-

science. That is how we see her during the latter
years of her life : frail, delicate, shivering a little,
much fatigued and considerably spent, but still
meditating on what could be acquired and imparted;
still living, in the intelligence, a freer, larger life
than probably had ever been the portion of any
woman. To her own sex her memory, her example,
will remain of the highest value ; those of them for
whom the " development " of woman is the hope of
the future ought to erect a monument to George
Eliot. She helped on the cause more than any
one, in proving how few limitations are of necessity
implied in the feminine organism. She went so far
that such a distance seems enough, and in her effort
she sacrificed no tenderness, no grace. There is
much talk to-day about things being " open to
women"; but George Eliot showed that there is
nothing that is closed. If we criticise her novels
we must remember that her nature came first and
her work afterwards, and that it is not remarkable they should not resemble the productions, say,
of Alexandre Dumas. What *is* remarkable, extraordinary—and the process remains inscrutable and
mysterious—is that this quiet, anxious, sedentary,
serious, invalidical English lady, without animal
spirits, without adventures or sensations, should
have made us believe that nothing in the world was
alien to her ; should have produced such rich, deep,
masterly pictures of the multiform life of man.

1885.

III

DANIEL DERONDA

A CONVERSATION

DANIEL DERONDA:

A CONVERSATION

THEODORA, one day early in the autumn, sat on her
verandah with a piece of embroidery, the design of
which she made up as she proceeded, being careful,
however, to have a Japanese screen before her, to
keep her inspiration at the proper altitude. Pulcheria, who was paying her a visit, sat near her with
a closed book, in a paper cover, in her lap. Pulcheria was playing with the pug-dog, rather idly,
but Theodora was stitching, steadily and meditatively.
"Well," said Theodora, at last, "I wonder what he
accomplished in the East." Pulcheria took the little
dog into her lap and made him sit on the book.
"Oh," she replied, "they had tea-parties at Jerusalem
—exclusively of ladies—and he sat in the midst and
stirred his tea and made high-toned remarks. And
then Mirah sang a little, just a little, on account of
her voice being so weak. Sit still, Fido," she continued, addressing the little dog, "and keep your
nose out of my face. But it's a nice little nose, all

the same," she pursued, "a nice little short snub nose
and not a horrid big Jewish nose. Oh, my dear,
when I think what a collection of noses there must
have been at that wedding!" At this moment Constantius steps upon the verandah from within, hat and
stick in hand and his shoes a trifle dusty. He has some
distance to come before he reaches the place where
the ladies are sitting, and this gives Pulcheria time
to murmur, "Talk of snub noses!" Constantius is
presented by Theodora to Pulcheria, and he sits down
and exclaims upon the admirable blueness of the sea,
which lies in a straight band across the green of the
little lawn ; comments too upon the pleasure of having one side of one's verandah in the shade. Soon
Fido, the little dog, still restless, jumps off Pulcheria's
lap and reveals the book, which lies title upward.
"Oh," says Constantius, "you have been finishing
Daniel Deronda?" Then follows a conversation
which it will be more convenient to present in
another form.

Theodora. Yes, Pulcheria has been reading aloud
the last chapters to me. They are wonderfully
beautiful.

Constantius (after a moment's hesitation). Yes, they
are very beautiful. I am sure you read well, Pulcheria, to give the fine passages their full value.

Theodora. She reads well when she chooses, but
I am sorry to say that in some of the fine passages of
this last book she took quite a false tone. I couldn't
have read them aloud myself ; I should have broken

down. But Pulcheria—would you really believe it?
—when she couldn't go on it was not for tears, but
for—the contrary.

Constantius. For smiles? Did you really find it
comical? One of my objections to *Daniel Deronda* is
the absence of those delightfully humorous passages
which enlivened the author's former works.

Pulcheria. Oh, I think there are some places as
amusing as anything in *Adam Bede* or *The Mill on the
Floss:* for instance where, at the last, Deronda wipes
Gwendolen's tears and Gwendolen wipes his.

Constantius. Yes, I know what you mean. I
can understand that situation presenting a slightly
ridiculous image ; that is, if the current of the story
don't swiftly carry you past.

Pulcheria. What do you mean by the current of
the story? I never read a story with less current.
It is not a river ; it is a series of lakes. I once read
of a group of little uneven ponds resembling, from a
bird's-eye view, a looking-glass which had fallen upon
the floor and broken, and was lying in fragments.
That is what *Daniel Deronda* would look like, on a
bird's-eye view.

Theodora. Pulcheria found that comparison in
a French novel. She is always reading French
novels.

Constantius. Ah, there are some very good ones.

Pulcheria (perversely). I don't know ; I think
there are some very poor ones.

Constantius. The comparison is not bad, at any

rate. I know what you mean by *Daniel Deronda*
lacking current. It has almost as little as *Romola*.

Pulcheria. Oh, *Romola* is unpardonably slow ; it
is a kind of literary tortoise.

Constantius. Yes, I know what you mean by
that. But I am afraid you are not friendly to our
great novelist.

Theodora. She likes Balzac and George Sand and
other impure writers.

Constantius. Well, I must say I understand that.

Pulcheria. My favourite novelist is Thackeray,
and I am extremely fond of Miss Austen.

Constantius. I understand that too. You read
over *The Newcomes* and *Pride and Prejudice.*

Pulcheria. No, I don't read them over now ; I
think them over. I have been making visits for a
long time past to a series of friends, and I have spent
the last six months in reading *Daniel Deronda* aloud.
Fortune would have it that I should always arrive by
the same train as the new number. I am accounted
a frivolous, idle creature ; I am not a disciple in the
new school of embroidery, like Theodora ; so I was
immediately pushed into a chair and the book thrust
into my hand, that I might lift up my voice and
make peace between all the impatiences that were
snatching at it. So I may claim at least that I have
read every word of the work. I never skipped.

Theodora. I should hope not, indeed !

Constantius. And do you mean that you really
didn't enjoy it ?

Pulcheria. I found it protracted, pretentious, pedantic.

Constantius. I see ; I can understand that.

Theodora. Oh, you understand too much ! This is the twentieth time you have used that formula.

Constantius. What will you have ? You know I must try to understand ; it's my trade.

Theodora. He means he writes reviews. Trying *not* to understand is what I call that trade !

Constantius. Say then I take it the wrong way; that is why it has never made my fortune. But I do try to understand ; it is my— my— (He pauses.)

Theodora. I know what you want to say. Your strong side.

Pulcheria. And what is his weak side ?

Theodora. He writes novels.

Constantius. I have written *one.* You can't call that a side. It's a little facet, at the most.

Pulcheria. You talk as if you were a diamond. I should like to read it—not aloud !

Constantius. You can't read it softly enough. But you, Theodora, you didn't find our book too " protracted " ?

Theodora. I should have liked it to continue indefinitely, to keep coming out always, to be one of the regular things of life.

Pulcheria. Oh, come here, little dog ! To think that *Daniel Deronda* might be perpetual when you, little short-nosed darling, can't last at the most more than nine or ten years !

Theodora. A book like *Daniel Deronda* becomes part of one's life ; one lives in it, or alongside of it. I don't hesitate to say that I have been living in this one for the last eight months. It is such a complete world George Eliot builds up ; it is so vast, so much-embracing ! It has such a firm earth and such an ethereal sky. You can turn into it and lose yourself in it.

Pulcheria. Oh, easily, and die of cold and starvation !

Theodora. I have been very near to poor Gwendolen and very near to that sweet Mirah. And the dear little Meyricks also ; I know them intimately well.

Pulcheria. The Meyricks, I grant you, are the best thing in the book.

Theodora. They are a delicious family ; I wish they lived in Boston. I consider Herr Klesmer almost Shakespearean, and his wife is almost as good. I have been near to poor grand Mordecai——

Pulcheria. Oh, reflect, my dear ; not too near !

Theodora. And as for Deronda himself I freely confess that I am consumed with a hopeless passion for him. He is the most irresistible man in the literature of fiction.

Pulcheria. He is not a man at all.

Theodora. I remember nothing more beautiful than the description of his childhood, and that picture of his lying on the grass in the abbey cloister, a beautiful seraph-faced boy, with a lovely voice, reading history and asking his Scotch tutor why the Popes had so many nephews. He must have been delightfully handsome.

Pulcheria. Never, my dear, with that nose! I am sure he had a nose, and I hold that the author has shown great pusillanimity in her treatment of it. She has quite shirked it. The picture you speak of is very pretty, but a picture is not a person. And why is he always grasping his coat-collar, as if he wished to hang himself up? The author had an uncomfortable feeling that she must make him do something real, something visible and sensible, and she hit upon that clumsy figure. I don't see what you mean by saying you have been *near* those people; that is just what one is not. They produce no illusion. They are described and analysed to death, but we don't see them nor hear them nor touch them. Deronda clutches his coat-collar, Mirah crosses her feet, Mordecai talks like the Bible; but that doesn't make real figures of them. They have no existence outside of the author's study.

Theodora. If you mean that they are nobly imaginative I quite agree with you; and if they say nothing to your own imagination the fault is yours, not theirs.

Pulcheria. Pray don't say they are Shakespearean again. Shakespeare went to work another way.

Constantius. I think you are both in a measure right; there is a distinction to be drawn. There

are in *Daniel Deronda* the figures based upon observation and the figures based upon invention.   This
distinction, I know, is rather a rough one.   There
are no figures in any novel that are pure observation,
and none that are pure invention.   But either element may preponderate, and in those cases in which
invention has preponderated George Eliot seems to
me to have achieved at the best but so many brilliant
failures.

Theodora. And are *you* turning severe ?   I thought
you admired her so much.

Constantius. I defy any one to admire her more,
but one must discriminate.   Speaking brutally, I
consider *Daniel Deronda* the weakest of her books.
It strikes me as very sensibly inferior to *Middlemarch.*   I have an immense opinion of *Middlemarch.*

Pulcheria. Not having been obliged by circumstances to read *Middlemarch* to other people, I didn't
read it at all.   I couldn't read it to myself.   I tried,
but I broke down.   I appreciated Rosamond, but I
couldn't believe in Dorothea.

Theodora (very gravely).   So much the worse for
you, Pulcheria.   I have enjoyed *Daniel Deronda*
because I had enjoyed *Middlemarch.*   Why should
you throw *Middlemarch* up against her ?   It seems
to me that if a book is fine it is fine.   I have enjoyed *Deronda* deeply, from beginning to end.

Constantius. I assure you, so have I.   I can read
nothing of George Eliot's without enjoyment.   I
even enjoy her poetry, though I don't approve of it.

In whatever she writes I enjoy her intelligence ; it has space and air, like a fine landscape. The intellectual brilliancy of *Daniel Deronda* strikes me as very great, in excess of anything the author has done. In the first couple of numbers of the book this ravished me. I delighted in its deep, rich English tone, in which so many notes seemed melted together.

Pulcheria. The tone is not English, it is German.

Constantius. I understand that—if Theodora will allow me to say so. Little by little I began to feel that I cared less for certain notes than for others. I say it under my breath—I began to feel an occasional temptation to skip. Roughly speaking, all the Jewish burden of the story tended to weary me ; it is this part that produces the poor illusion which I agree with Pulcheria in finding. Gwendolen and Grandcourt are admirable—Gwendolen is a masterpiece. She is known, felt and presented, psychologically, altogether in the grand manner. Beside her and beside her husband—a consummate picture of English brutality refined and distilled (for Grandcourt is before all things brutal), Deronda, Mordecai and Mirah are hardly more than shadows. They and their fortunes are all improvisation. I don't say anything against improvisation. When it succeeds it has a surpassing charm. But it must succeed. With George Eliot it seems to me to succeed, but a little less than one would expect of her talent. The story of Deronda's life, his mother's story, Mirah's story, are quite the sort of thing one finds

in George Sand. But they are really not so good as
they would be in George Sand. George Sand would
have carried it off with a lighter hand.

Theodora. Oh, Constantius, how can you compare
George Eliot's novels to that woman's ? It is sun-
light and moonshine.

Pulcheria. I really think the two writers are very
much alike. They are both very voluble, both
addicted to moralising and philosophising à tout bout
de champ, both inartistic.

Constantius. I see what you mean. But George
Eliot is solid, and George Sand is liquid. When
occasionally George Eliot liquefies—as in the history
of Deronda's birth, and in that of Mirah—it is not
to so crystalline a clearness as the author of *Consuelo*
and *André.* Take Mirah's long narrative of her
adventures, when she unfolds them to Mrs. Meyrick.
It is arranged, it is artificial, *ancien jeu,* quite in
the George Sand manner. But George Sand would
have done it better. The false tone would have
remained, but it would have been more persuasive.
It would have been a fib, but the fib would have
been neater.

Theodora. I don't think fibbing neatly a merit,
and I don't see what is to be gained by such com-
parisons. George Eliot is pure and George Sand is
impure ; how can you compare them ? As for the
Jewish element in Deronda, I think it a very fine
idea ; it's a noble subject. Wilkie Collins and Miss
Braddon would not have thought of it, but that does

not condemn it. It shows a large conception of what one may do in a novel. I heard you say, the other day, that most novels were so trivial— that they had no general ideas. Here is a general idea, the idea interpreted by Deronda. I have never disliked the Jews as some people do ; I am not like Pulcheria, who sees a Jew in every bush. I wish there were one; I would cultivate shrubbery. I have known too many clever and charming Jews ; I have known none that were not clever.

Pulcheria. Clever, but not charming.

Constantius. I quite agree with you as to Deronda's going in for the Jews and turning out a Jew himself being a fine subject, and this quite apart from the fact of whether such a thing as a Jewish revival be at all a possibility. If it be a possibility, so much the better—so much the better for the subject, I mean.

Pulcheria. A la bonne heure !

Constantius. I rather suspect it is not a possibility; that the Jews in general take themselves much less seriously than that. They have other fish to fry. George Eliot takes them as a person outside of Judaism—æsthetically. I don't believe that is the way they take themselves.

Pulcheria. They have the less excuse then for keeping themselves so dirty.

Theodora. George Eliot must have known some delightful Jews.

Constantius. Very likely ; but I shouldn't wonder

if the most delightful of them had smiled a trifle, here and there, over her book. But that makes nothing, as Herr Klesmer would say. The subject is a noble one. The idea of depicting a nature able to feel and worthy to feel the sort of inspiration that takes possession of Deronda, of depicting it sympathetically, minutely and intimately—such an idea has great elevation. There is something very fascinating in the mission that Deronda takes upon himself. I don't quite know what it means, I don't understand more than half of Mordecai's rhapsodies, and I don't perceive exactly what practical steps could be taken. Deronda could go about and talk with clever Jews—not an unpleasant life.

Pulcheria. All that seems to me so unreal that when at the end the author finds herself confronted with the necessity of making him start for the East by the train, and announces that Sir Hugo and Lady Mallinger have given his wife "a complete Eastern outfit," I descend to the ground with a ludicrous jump.

Constantius. Unreal, if you please ; that is no objection to it ; it greatly tickles my imagination. I like extremely the idea of Mordecai believing, without ground of belief, that if he only wait, a young man on whom nature and society have centred all their gifts will come to him and receive from his hands the precious vessel of his hopes. It is romantic, but it is not vulgar romance ; it is finely romantic. And there is something very fine in the author's own feeling about Deronda. He is a very liberal creation. He is, I think, a failure—a brilliant failure; if he had been a success I should call him a splendid creation. The author meant to do things very handsomely for him; she meant apparently to make a faultless human being.

Pulcheria. She made a dreadful prig.

Constantius. He *is* rather priggish, and one wonders that so clever a woman as George Eliot shouldn't see it.

Pulcheria. He has no blood in his body. His attitude at moments is like that of a high-priest in a *tableau vivant.*

Theodora. Pulcheria likes the little gentlemen in the French novels who take good care of their attitudes, which are always the same attitude, the attitude of "conquest"—of a conquest that tickles their vanity. Deronda has a contour that cuts straight through the middle of all that. He is made of a stuff that isn't dreamt of in their philosophy.

Pulcheria. Pulcheria likes very much a novel which she read three or four years ago, but which she has not forgotten. It was by Ivan Turgénieff, and it was called *On the Eve.* Theodora has read it, I know, because she admires Turgénieff, and Constantius has read it, I suppose, because he has read everything.

Constantius. If I had no reason but that for my reading, it would be small. But Turgénieff is my man.

Pulcheria. You were just now praising George

Eliot's general ideas. The tale of which I speak contains in the portrait of the hero very much such a general idea as you find in the portrait of Deronda. Don't you remember the young Bulgarian student, Inssaroff, who gives himself the mission of rescuing his country from its subjection to the Turks? Poor man, if he had foreseen the horrible summer of 1876! His character is the picture of a race-passion, of patriotic hopes and dreams. But what a difference in the vividness of the two figures. Inssaroff is a man ; he stands up on his feet ; we see him, hear him, touch him. And it has taken the author but a couple of hundred pages—not eight volumes—to do it.

Theodora. I don't remember Inssaroff at all, but I perfectly remember the heroine, Helena. She is certainly most remarkable, but, remarkable as she is, I should never dream of calling her as wonderful as Gwendolen.

Constantius. Turgénieff is a magician, which I don't think I should call George Eliot. One is a poet, the other is a philosopher. One cares for the aspect of things and the other cares for the reason of things. George Eliot, in embarking with Deronda, took aboard, as it were, a far heavier cargo than Turgénieff with his Inssaroff. She proposed, consciously, to strike more notes.

Pulcheria. Oh, consciously, yes !

Constantius. George Eliot wished to show the possible picturesqueness—the romance, as it were—

of a high moral tone. Deronda is a moralist, a moralist with a rich complexion.

Theodora. It is a most beautiful nature. I don't know anywhere a more complete, a more deeply analysed portrait of a great nature. We praise novelists for wandering and creeping so into the small corners of the mind. That is what we praise Balzac for when he gets down upon all fours to crawl through *Le Père Goriot* or *Les Parents Pauvres.* But I must say I think it a finer thing to unlock with as firm a hand as George Eliot some of the greater chambers of human character. Deronda is in a manner an ideal character, if you will, but he seems to me triumphantly married to reality. There are some admirable things said about him ; nothing can be finer than those pages of description of his moral temperament in the fourth book—his elevated way of looking at things, his impartiality, his universal sympathy, and at the same time his fear of their turning into mere irresponsible indifference. I remember some of it verbally : " He was ceasing to care for knowledge—he had no ambition for practice —unless they could be gathered up into one current with his emotions."

Pulcheria. Oh, there is plenty about his emotions. Everything about him is " emotive." That bad word occurs on every fifth page.

Theodora. I don't see that it is a bad word.

Pulcheria. It may be good German, but it is poor English.

Theodora. It is not German at all; it is Latin. So, my dear!

Pulcheria. As I say, then, it is not English.

Theodora. This is the first time I ever heard that George Eliot's style was bad!

Constantius. It is admirable; it has the most delightful and the most intellectually comfortable suggestions. But it is occasionally a little too long-sleeved, as I may say. It is sometimes too loose a fit for the thought, a little baggy.

Theodora. And the advice he gives Gwendolen, the things he says to her, they are the very essence of wisdom, of warm human wisdom, knowing life and feeling it. " Keep your fear as a safeguard, it may make consequences passionately present to you." What can be better than that?

Pulcheria. Nothing, perhaps. But what can be drearier than a novel in which the function of the hero—young, handsome and brilliant—is to give didactic advice, in a proverbial form, to the young, beautiful and brilliant heroine?

Constantius. That is not putting it quite fairly. The function of Deronda is to make Gwendolen fall in love with him, to say nothing of falling in love himself with Mirah.

Pulcheria. Yes, the less said about that the better. All we know about Mirah is that she has delicate rings of hair, sits with her feet crossed, and talks like an article in a new magazine.

Constantius. Deronda's function   of   adviser   to

Gwendolen does not strike me as so ridiculous.   He
is not nearly so ridiculous as if he were lovesick.   It
is a very interesting situation—that of a man with
whom a beautiful woman in trouble falls in love and
yet whose affections are so preoccupied that the most
he can do for her in return is to enter kindly and
sympathetically into her position, pity her and talk
to her.   George Eliot always gives us something
that is strikingly and ironically characteristic of
human life ; and what savours more of the essential
crookedness of our fate than the sad cross-purposes
of these two young people ?   Poor Gwendolen's
falling in love with Deronda is part of her own
luckless history, not of his.

Theodora. I do think he takes it to himself rather
too little.   No man had ever so little vanity.

Pulcheria. It is very inconsistent, therefore, as
well as being extremely impertinent and ill-mannered,
his buying back and sending to her her necklace at
Leubronn.

Constantius. Oh, you must concede that ; without
it there would have been no story.   A man writing
of him, however, would certainly have made him
more peccable.   As George Eliot lets herself go, in
that quarter, she becomes delightfully, almost touchingly, feminine.   It is like her making Romola go to
housekeeping with Tessa, after Tito Melema's death ;
like her making Dorothea marry Will Ladislaw.   If
Dorothea had married any one after her misadventure
with Casaubon, she would have married a trooper.

Theodora. Perhaps some day Gwendolen will marry Rex.

Pulcheria. Pray, who is Rex ?

Theodora. Why, Pulcheria, how can you forget ?

Pulcheria. Nay, how can I remember ? But I recall such a name in the dim antiquity of the first or second book. Yes, and then he is pushed to the front again at the last, just in time not to miss the falling of the curtain. Gwendolen will certainly not have the audacity to marry any one we know so little about.

Constantius. I have been wanting to say that there seems to me to be two very distinct elements in George Eliot—a spontaneous one and an artificial one. There is what she is by inspiration and what she is because it is expected of her. These two heads have been very perceptible in her recent writings ; they are much less noticeable in her early ones.

Theodora. You mean that she is too scientific ? So long as she remains the great literary genius that she is, how can she be too scientific ? She is simply permeated with the highest culture of the age.

Pulcheria. She talks too much about the " dynamic quality " of people's eyes. When she uses such a phrase as that in the first sentence in her book she is not a great literary genius, because she shows a want of tact. There can't be a worse limitation.

Constantius. The " dynamic quality " of Gwendolen's glance has made the tour of the world.

Theodora. It shows a very low level of culture on the world's part to be agitated by a term perfectly familiar to all decently-educated people.

Pulcheria. I don't pretend to be decently educated; pray tell me what it means.

Constantius (promptly). I think Pulcheria has hit it in speaking of a want of tact. In the manner of the book, throughout, there is something that one may call a want of tact. The epigraphs in verse are a want of tact; they are sometimes, I think, a trifle more pretentious than really pregnant; the importunity of the moral reflections is a want of tact; the very diffuseness is a want of tact. But it comes back to what I said just now about one's sense of the author writing under a sort of external pressure. I began to notice it in *Felix Holt;* I don't think I had before. She strikes me as a person who certainly has naturally a taste for general considerations, but who has fallen upon an age and a circle which have compelled her to give them an exaggerated attention. She does not strike me as naturally a critic, less still as naturally a sceptic; her spontaneous part is to observe life and to feel it, to feel it with admirable depth. Contemplation, sympathy and faith—something like that, I should say, would have been her natural scale. If she had fallen upon an age of enthusiastic assent to old articles of faith, it seems to me possible that she would have had a more perfect, a more consistent and graceful development than she has actually had. If she had cast herself into

such a current—her genius being equal—it might
have carried her to splendid distances.   But she has
chosen to go into criticism, and to the critics she
addresses her work ; I mean the critics of the universe.   Instead of feeling life itself, it is "views"
upon life that she tries to feel.

Pulcheria. She is the victim of a first-class education.   I am so glad !

Constantius. Thanks to her admirable intellect she
philosophises very sufficiently ; but meanwhile she
has given a chill to her genius.   She has come near
spoiling an artist.

Pulcheria. She has quite spoiled one.   Or rather
I shouldn't say that, because there was no artist to
spoil.   I maintain that she is not an artist.   An
artist could never have put a story together so
monstrously ill.   She has no sense of form.

Theodora. Pray, what could be more artistic than
the way that Deronda's paternity is concealed till
almost the end, and the way we are made to suppose
Sir Hugo is his father ?

Pulcheria. And Mirah his sister.   How does that
fit together ?   I was as little made to suppose he
was not a Jew as I cared when I found out he was.
And his mother popping up through a trap-door and
popping down again, at the last, in that scrambling
fashion !   His mother is very bad.

Constantius. I think Deronda's mother is one of the
unvivified characters ; she belongs to the cold half of
the book.   All the Jewish part is at bottom cold ;

that is my only objection.   I have enjoyed it because
my fancy often warms cold things ; but beside Gwendolen's history it is like the empty half of the lunar
disk beside the full one.   It is admirably studied, it
is imagined, it is understood, but it is not embodied.
One feels this strongly in just those scenes between
Deronda and his mother ; one feels that one has
been appealed to on rather an artificial ground of
interest.   To make Deronda's reversion to his native
faith more dramatic and profound, the author has
given him a mother who on very arbitrary grounds,
apparently, has separated herself from this same faith
and who has been kept waiting in the wing, as it
were, for many acts, to come on and make her speech
and say so.   This moral situation of hers we are
invited retrospectively to appreciate.   But we hardly
care to do so.

Pulcheria. I don't *see* the princess, in spite of
her flame-coloured robe.   Why should an actress
and prima - donna care so much about religious
matters ?

Theodora. It was not only that ; it was the Jewish
race she hated, Jewish manners and looks.   You, my
dear, ought to understand that.

Pulcheria. I do, but I am not a Jewish actress of
genius ; I am not what Rachel was.   If I were I
should have other things to think about.

Constantius. Think now a little about poor Gwendolen.

Pulcheria. I don't care to think about her.   She

was a second-rate English girl who got into a flutter
about a lord.

Theodora. I don't see that she is worse than if she
were a first-rate American girl who should get into
exactly the same flutter.

Pulcheria. It wouldn't be the same flutter at all ;
it wouldn't be any flutter. She wouldn't be afraid
of the lord, though she might be amused at him.

Theodora. I am sure I don't perceive whom Gwendolen was afraid of. She was afraid of her misdeed
—her broken promise—after she had committed it,
and through that fear she was afraid of her husband.
Well she might be ! I can imagine nothing more
vivid than the sense we get of his absolutely clammy
selfishness.

Pulcheria. She was not afraid of Deronda when,
immediately after her marriage and without any but
the most casual acquaintance with him, she begins to
hover about him at the Mallingers' and to drop little
confidences about her conjugal woes. That seems to
me very indelicate ; ask any woman.

Constantius. The very purpose of the author is to
give us an idea of the sort of confidence that *Deronda*
inspired—its irresistible potency.

Pulcheria. A lay father-confessor—horrid !

Constantius. And to give us an idea also of the
acuteness of Gwendolen's depression, of her haunting
sense of impending trouble.

Theodora. It must be remembered that Gwendolen
was in love with Deronda from the first, long before

she knew it.   She didn't know it, poor girl, but that was it.

Pulcheria. That makes the matter worse.   It is very disagreeable to see her hovering and rustling about a man who is indifferent to her.

Theodora. He was not indifferent to her, since he sent her back her necklace.

Pulcheria. Of all the delicate attention to a charming girl that I ever heard of, that little pecuniary transaction is the most felicitous.

Constantius. You must remember that he had been *en rapport* with her at the gaming-table.   She had been playing in defiance of his observation, and he, continuing to observe her, had been in a measure responsible for her loss.   There was a tacit consciousness of this between them.   You may contest the possibility of tacit consciousness going so far, but that is not a serious objection.   You may point out two or three weak spots in detail; the fact remains that Gwendolen's whole history is vividly told. And see how the girl is known, inside out, how thoroughly she is felt and understood.   It is the most *intelligent* thing in all George Eliot's writing, and that is saying much.   It is so deep, so true, so complete, it holds such a wealth of psychological detail, it is more than masterly.

Theodora. I don't know where the perception of character has sailed closer to the wind.

Pulcheria. The portrait may be admirable, but it has one little fault.   You don't care a straw for the

original.   Gwendolen is not an interesting girl, and
when the author tries to invest her with a deep tragic
interest she does so at the expense of consistency.
She has made her at the outset too light, too flimsy ;
tragedy has no hold on such a girl.

Theodora. You are hard to satisfy.   You said this
morning that Dorothea was too heavy, and now you
find Gwendolen too light.   George Eliot wished to
give us the perfect counterpart of Dorothea.   Having
made one portrait she was worthy to make the other.

Pulcheria. She has committed the fatal error of
making Gwendolen vulgarly, pettily, drily selfish.
She was *personally* selfish.

Theodora. I know nothing more personal than
selfishness.

Pulcheria. I am selfish, but I don't go about with
my chin out like that ; at least I hope I don't.   She
was an odious young woman, and one can't care what
becomes of her.   When her marriage turned out ill
she would have become still more hard and positive ;
to make her soft and appealing is very bad logic.
The second Gwendolen doesn't belong to the first.

Constantius. She is perhaps at the first a little
childish for the weight of interest she has to carry, a
little too much after the patttern of the unconscien-
tious young ladies of Miss Yonge and Miss Sewell.

Theodora. Since when it is forbidden to make one's
heroine young ?   Gwendolen is a perfect picture of
youthfulness—its eagerness, its presumption, its preoccupation with itself, its vanity and silliness, its

sense of its own absoluteness.   But she is extremely
intelligent and clever, and therefore tragedy *can* have
a hold upon her.   Her conscience doesn't make the
tragedy ; that is an old story and, I think, a secondary
form of suffering.   It is the tragedy that makes her
conscience, which then reacts upon it ; and I can
think of nothing more powerful than the way in
which the growth of her conscience is traced, nothing
more touching than the picture of its helpless
maturity.

Constantius. That is perfectly true.   Gwendolen's
history is admirably typical — as most things are
with George Eliot : it is the very stuff that human
life is made of.   What is it made of but the discovery by each of us that we are at the best but
a rather ridiculous fifth wheel to the coach, after we
have sat cracking our whip and believing that we are
at least the coachman in person ?   We think we are
the main hoop to the barrel, and we turn out to be
but a very incidental splinter in one of the staves.
The universe forcing itself with a slow, inexorable
pressure into a narrow, complacent, and yet after all
extremely sensitive mind, and making it ache with
the pain of the process—that is Gwendolen's story.
And it becomes completely characteristic in that her
supreme perception of the fact that the world is
whirling past her is in the disappointment not of a
base but of an exalted passion.   The very chance to
embrace what the author is so fond of calling a
" larger life " seems refused to her.   She is punished

for being narrow, and she is not allowed a chance to expand. Her finding Deronda pre-engaged to go to the East and stir up the race-feeling of the Jews strikes me as a wonderfully happy invention. The irony of the situation, for poor Gwendolen, is almost grotesque, and it makes one wonder whether the whole heavy structure of the Jewish question in the story was not built up by the author for the express purpose of giving its proper force to this particular stroke.

Theodora. George Eliot's intentions are extremely complex. The mass is for each detail and each detail is for the mass.

Pulcheria. She is very fond of deaths by drowning. Maggie Tulliver and her brother are drowned, Tito Melema is drowned, Mr. Grandcourt is drowned. It is extremely unlikely that Grandcourt should not have known how to swim.

Constantius. He did, of course, but he had a cramp. It served him right. I can't imagine a more consummate representation of the most detestable kind of Englishman—the Englishman who thinks it low to articulate. And in Grandcourt the type and the individual are so happily met : the type with its sense of the proprieties and the individual with his absence of all sense. He is the apotheosis of dryness, a human expression of the simple idea of the perpendicular.

Theodora. Mr. Casaubon, in *Middlemarch*, was very dry too ; and yet what a genius it is that can give us two disagreeable husbands who are so utterly different !

Pulcheria. You must count the two disagreeable wives too—Rosamond Vincy and Gwendolen. They are very much alike. I know the author didn't mean it ; it proves how common a type the worldly, *pincée,* selfish young woman seemed to her. They are both disagreeable ; you can't get over that.

Constantius. There is something in that, perhaps. I think, at any rate, that the secondary people here are less delightful than in *Middlemarch ;* there is nothing so good as Mary Garth and her father, or the little old lady who steals sugar, or the parson who is in love with Mary, or the country relatives of old Mr. Featherstone. Rex Gascoigne is not so good as Fred Vincy.

Theodora. Mr. Gascoigne is admirable, and Mrs. Davilow is charming.

Pulcheria. And you must not forget that you think Herr Klesmer "Shakespearean." Wouldn't "Wagnerian" be high enough praise ?

Constantius. Yes, one must make an exception with regard to the Klesmers and the Meyricks. They are delightful, and as for Klesmer himself, and Hans Meyrick, Theodora may maintain her epithet. Shakespearean characters are characters that are born of the *overflow* of observation — characters that make the drama seem multitudinous, like life. Klesmer comes in with a sort of Shakespearean "value," as a painter would say, and so, in a different

tone, does Hans Meyrick.   They spring from a much-
peopled mind.

Theodora. I think Gwendolen's confrontation with
Klesmer one of the finest things in the book.

Constantius. It is like everything in George Eliot;
it will bear thinking of.

Pulcheria. All that is very fine, but you cannot
persuade me that *Deronda* is not a very ponderous
and ill-made story.   It has nothing that one can call
a subject.   A silly young girl and a solemn, sapient
young man who doesn't fall in love with her !   That
is the *donnée* of eight monthly volumes.   I call it
very flat.   Is that what the exquisite art of Thackeray and Miss Austen and Hawthorne has come to ?
I would as soon read a German novel outright.

Theodora. There is something higher than form—
there is spirit.

Constantius. I am afraid Pulcheria is sadly æsthetic.
She had better confine herself to Mérimée.

Pulcheria. I shall certainly to-day read over *La
Double Méprise.*

Theodora. Oh, my dear, *y pensez-vous ?*

Constantius. Yes, I think there is little art in
Deronda, but I think there is a vast amount of life.
In life without art you can find your account ; but
art without life is a poor affair.   The book is full of
the world.

Theodora. It is full of beauty and knowledge, and
that is quite art enough for me.

Pulcheria (to the little dog).   We are silenced,

darling, but we are not convinced, are we? (The pug begins to bark.) No, we are not even silenced. It's a young woman with two bandboxes.

Theodora. Oh, it must be our muslins.

Constantius (rising to go). I see what you mean !

1876.

IV

ANTHONY TROLLOPE

ANTHONY TROLLOPE

WHEN, a few months ago, Anthony Trollope laid down his pen for the last time, it was a sign of the complete extinction of that group of admirable writers who, in England, during the preceding half century, had done so much to elevate the art of the novelist. The author of *The Warden*, of *Barchester Towers*, of *Framley Parsonage*, does not, to our mind, stand on the very same level as Dickens, Thackeray and George Eliot; for his talent was of a quality less fine than theirs. But he belonged to the same family—he had as much to tell us about English life; he was strong, genial and abundant. He published too much; the writing of novels had ended by becoming, with him, a perceptibly mechanical process. Dickens was prolific, Thackeray produced with a freedom for which we are constantly grateful; but we feel that these writers had their periods of gestation. They took more time to look at their subject; relatively (for to-day there is not much leisure, at best, for those who undertake to entertain a hungry public), they were able to wait for inspiration.

Trollope's fecundity was prodigious; there was no
limit to the work he was ready to do. It is not
unjust to say that he sacrificed quality to quantity.
Abundance, certainly, is in itself a great merit;
almost all the greatest writers have been abundant.
But Trollope's fertility was gross, importunate; he
himself contended, we believe, that he had given to
the world a greater number of printed pages of fiction
than any of his literary contemporaries. Not only
did his novels follow each other without visible inter-
mission, overlapping and treading on each other's
heels, but most of these works are of extraordinary
length. *Orley Farm, Can You Forgive Her? He Knew
He Was Right,* are exceedingly voluminous tales.
The Way We Live Now is one of the longest of modern
novels. Trollope produced, moreover, in the intervals
of larger labour a great number of short stories,
many of them charming, as well as various books of
travel, and two or three biographies. He was the
great *improvvisatore* of these latter years. Two distinguished story-tellers of the other sex—one in
France and one in England—have shown an extraordinary facility of composition; but Trollope's pace
was brisker even than that of the wonderful Madame
Sand and the delightful Mrs. Oliphant. He had
taught himself to keep this pace, and had reduced his
admirable faculty to a system. Every day of his life
he wrote a certain number of pages of his current
tale, a number sacramental and invariable, independent of mood and place. It was once the fortune of

the author of these lines to cross the Atlantic in his company, and he has never forgotten the magnificent example of plain persistence that it was in the power of the eminent novelist to give on that occasion. The season was unpropitious, the vessel overcrowded, the voyage detestable ; but Trollope shut himself up in his cabin every morning for a purpose which, on the part of a distinguished writer who was also an invulnerable sailor, could only be communion with the muse. He drove his pen as steadily on the tumbling ocean as in Montague Square ; and as his voyages were many, it was his practice before sailing to come down to the ship and confer with the carpenter, who was instructed to rig up a rough writing-table in his small sea-chamber. Trollope has been accused of being deficient in imagination, but in the face of such a fact as that the charge will scarcely seem just. The power to shut one's eyes, one's ears (to say nothing of another sense), upon the scenery of a pitching Cunarder and open them upon the loves and sorrows of Lily Dale or the conjugal embarrassments of Lady Glencora Palliser, is certainly a faculty which could take to itself wings. The imagination that Trollope possessed he had at least thoroughly at his command. I speak of all this in order to explain (in part) why it was that, with his extraordinary gift, there was always in him a certain infusion of the common. He abused his gift, overworked it, rode his horse too hard. As an artist he never took himself seriously ; many people will say this was why he was so delightful. The people who take themselves seriously are prigs and bores; and Trollope, with his perpetual "story," which was the only thing he cared about, his strong good sense, hearty good nature, generous appreciation of life in all its varieties, responds in perfection to a certain English ideal. According to that ideal it is rather dangerous to be explicitly or consciously an artist— to have a system, a doctrine, a form. Trollope, from the first, went in, as they say, for having as little form as possible; it is probably safe to affirm that he had no "views" whatever on the subject of novel-writing. His whole manner is that of a man who regards the practice as one of the more delicate industries, but has never troubled his head nor clogged his pen with theories about the nature of his business. Fortunately he was not obliged to do so, for he had an easy road to success; and his honest, familiar, deliberate way of treating his readers as if he were one of them, and shared their indifference to a general view, their limitations of knowledge, their love of a comfortable ending, endeared him to many persons in England and America. It is in the name of some chosen form that, of late years, things have been made most disagreeable for the novel-reader, who has been treated by several votaries of the new ex-periments in fiction to unwonted and bewildering sensations. With Trollope we were always safe; there were sure to be no new experiments.

His great, his inestimable merit was a complete

appreciation of the usual. This gift is not rare in the annals of English fiction ; it would naturally be found in a walk of literature in which the feminine mind has laboured so fruitfully. Women are delicate and patient observers ; they hold their noses close, as it were, to the texture of life. They feel and perceive the real with a kind of personal tact, and their observations are recorded in a thousand delightful volumes. Trollope, therefore, with his eyes comfortably fixed on the familiar, the actual, was far from having invented a new category ; his great distinction is that in resting there his vision took in so much of the field. And then he *felt* all daily and immediate things as well as saw them ; felt them in a simple, direct, salubrious way, with their sadness, their gladness, their charm, their comicality, all their obvious and measurable meanings. He never wearied of the pre-established round of English customs—never needed a respite or a change—was content to go on indefinitely watching the life that surrounded him, and holding up his mirror to it. Into this mirror the public, at first especially, grew very fond of looking—for it saw itself reflected in all the most credible and supposable ways, with that curiosity that people feel to know how they look when they are represented, "just as they are," by a painter who does not desire to put them into an attitude, to drape them for an effect, to arrange his light and his accessories. This exact and on the whole becoming image, projected upon a surface without a strong intrinsic tone, constitutes mainly the entertainment that Trollope offered his readers. The striking thing to the critic was that his robust and patient mind had no particular bias, his imagination no light of its own. He saw things neither pictorially and grotesquely like Dickens ; nor with that combined disposition to satire and to literary form which gives such "body," as they say of wine, to the manner of Thackeray ; nor with anything of the philosophic, the transcendental cast—the desire to follow them to their remote relations—which we associate with the name of George Eliot. Trollope had his elements of fancy, of satire, of irony ; but these qualities were not very highly developed, and he walked mainly by the light of his good sense, his clear, direct vision of the things that lay nearest, and his great natural kindness. There is something remarkably tender and friendly in his feeling about all human perplexities ; he takes the good-natured, temperate, conciliatory view—the humorous view, perhaps, for the most part, yet without a touch of pessimistic prejudice. As he grew older, and had sometimes to go farther afield for his subjects, he acquired a savour of bitterness and reconciled himself sturdily to treating of the disagreeable. A more copious record of disagreeable matters could scarcely be imagined, for instance, than *The Way We Live Now*. But, in general, he has a wholesome mistrust of morbid analysis, an aversion to inflicting pain. He has an infinite love of detail, but his details are, for the most part, the innumerable items of the expected. When the French are disposed to pay a compliment to the English mind they are so good as to say that there is in it something remarkably *honnête*. If I might borrow this epithet without seeming to be patronising, I should apply it to the genius of Anthony Trollope. He represents in an eminent degree this natural decorum of the English spirit, and represents it all the better that there is not in him a grain of the mawkish or the prudish. He writes, he feels, he judges like a man, talking plainly and frankly about many things, and is by no means destitute of a certain saving grace of coarseness. But he has kept the purity of his imagination and held fast to old-fashioned reverences and preferences. He thinks it a sufficient objection to several topics to say simply that they are unclean. There was nothing in his theory of the story-teller's art that tended to convert the reader's or the writer's mind into a vessel for polluting things. He recognised the right of the vessel to protest, and would have regarded such a protest as conclusive. With a considerable turn for satire, though this perhaps is more evident in his early novels than in his later ones, he had as little as possible of the quality of irony. He never played with a subject, never juggled with the sympathies or the credulity of his reader, was never in the least paradoxical or mystifying. He sat down to his theme in a serious, business-like way, with his elbows on the table and his eye occasionally wandering to the clock.

To touch successively upon these points is to attempt a portrait, which I shall perhaps not altogether have failed to produce. The source of his success in describing the life that lay nearest to him, and describing it without any of those artistic perversions that come, as we have said, from a powerful imagination, from a cynical humour or from a desire to look, as George Eliot expresses it, for the suppressed transitions that unite all contrasts, the essence of this love of reality was his extreme interest in character. This is the fine and admirable quality in Trollope, this is what will preserve his best works in spite of those flatnesses which keep him from standing on quite the same level as the masters. Indeed this quality is so much one of the finest (to my mind at least), that it makes me wonder the more that the writer who had it so abundantly and so naturally should not have just that distinction which Trollope lacks, and which we find in his three brilliant contemporaries. If he was in any degree a man of genius (and I hold that he was), it was in virtue of this happy, instinctive perception of human varieties. His knowledge of the stuff we are made of, his observation of the common behaviour of men and women, was not reasoned nor acquired, not even particularly studied. All human doings deeply interested him, human life, to his mind, was a perpetual story ; but he never attempted to take the so-called scientific view, the view which has lately found ingenious advocates among the countrymen and successors of Balzac.

He had no airs of being able to tell you *why* people in a given situation would conduct themselves in a particular way ; it was enough for him that he felt their feelings and struck the right note, because he had, as it were, a good ear. If he was a knowing psychologist he was so by grace ; he was just and true without apparatus and without effort. He must have had a great taste for the moral question ; he evidently believed that this is the basis of the interest of fiction. We must be careful, of course, in attributing convictions and opinions to Trollope, who, as I have said, had as little as possible of the pedantry of his art, and whose occasional chance utterances in regard to the object of the novelist and his means of achieving it are of an almost startling simplicity. But we certainly do not go too far in saying that he gave his practical testimony in favour of the idea that the interest of a work of fiction is great in proportion as the people stand on their feet. His great effort was evidently to make them stand so ; if he achieved this result with as little as possible of a flourish of the hand it was nevertheless the measure of his success. If he had taken sides on the droll, bemuddled opposition between novels of character and novels of plot, I can imagine him to have said (except that he never expressed himself in epigrams), that he preferred the former class, inasmuch as character in itself is plot, while plot is by no means character. It is more safe indeed to believe that his great good sense would have prevented him from taking an idle contro-

versy seriously.   Character, in any sense in which we
can get at it, is action, and action is plot, and any plot
which hangs together, even if it pretend to interest
us only in the fashion of a Chinese puzzle, plays upon
our emotion, our suspense, by means of personal
references.   We care what happens to people only in
proportion as we know what people are.   Trollope's
great apprehension of the real, which was what made
him so interesting, came to him through his desire to
satisfy us on this point—to tell us what certain
people were and what they did in consequence of
being so.   That is the purpose of each of his tales ;
and if these things produce an illusion it comes from
the gradual abundance of his testimony as to the
temper, the tone, the passions, the habits, the moral
nature, of a certain number of contemporary Britons.

His stories, in spite of their great length, deal very
little in the surprising, the exceptional, the complicated ; as a general thing he has no great story to
tell.   The thing is not so much a story as a picture ;
if we hesitate to call it a picture it is because the
idea of composition is not the controlling one and
we feel that the author would regard the artistic, in
general, as a kind of affectation.   There is not
even much description, in the sense which the present votaries of realism in France attach to that
word.   The painter lays his scene in a few deliberate, not especially pictorial strokes, and never
dreams of finishing the piece for the sake of enabling
the reader to hang it up.   The finish, such as it is,

comes later, from the slow and somewhat clumsy accumulation of small illustrations. These illustrations are sometimes of the commonest; Trollope turns them out inexhaustibly, repeats them freely, unfolds them without haste and without rest. But they are all of the most obvious sort, and they are none the worse for that. The point to be made is that they have no great spectacular interest (we beg pardon of the innumerable love-affairs that Trollope has described), like many of the incidents, say, of Walter Scott and of Alexandre Dumas : if we care to know about them (as repetitions of a usual case), it is because the writer has managed, in his candid, literal, somewhat lumbering way, to tell us that about the men and women concerned which has already excited on their behalf the impression of life. It is a marvel by what homely arts, by what imperturbable button-holing persistence, he contrives to excite this impression. Take, for example, such a work as *The Vicar of Bullhampton.* It would be difficult to state the idea of this slow but excellent story, which is a capital example of interest produced by the quietest conceivable means. The principal persons in it are a lively, jovial, high-tempered country clergyman, a young woman who is in love with her cousin, and a small, rather dull squire who is in love with the young woman. There is no connection between the affairs of the clergyman and those of the two other persons, save that these two are the Vicar's friends. The Vicar gives countenance, for Christian charity's

sake, to a young countryman who is suspected
(falsely, as it appears), of murder, and also to the
lad's sister, who is more than suspected of leading an
immoral life. Various people are shocked at his
indiscretion, but in the end he is shown to have
been no worse a clergyman because he is a good fellow.
A cantankerous nobleman, who has a spite against
him, causes a Methodist conventicle to be erected at
the gates of the vicarage; but afterward, finding that
he has no title to the land used for this obnoxious
purpose, causes the conventicle to be pulled down,
and is reconciled with the parson, who accepts an
invitation to stay at the castle. Mary Lowther, the
heroine of *The Vicar of Bullhampton*, is sought in
marriage by Mr. Harry Gilmore, to whose passion she
is unable to respond; she accepts him, however,
making him understand that she does not love him,
and that her affections are fixed upon her kinsman,
Captain Marrable, whom she would marry (and who
would marry her), if he were not too poor to support
a wife. If Mr. Gilmore will take her on these terms
she will become his spouse; but she gives him all
sorts of warnings. They are not superfluous; for, as
Captain Marrable presently inherits a fortune, she
throws over Mr. Gilmore, who retires to foreign lands,
heart-broken, inconsolable. This is the substance of
The Vicar of Bullhampton; the reader will see that it
is not a very tangled skein. But if the interest is
gradual it is extreme and constant, and it comes
altogether from excellent portraiture. It is essen-

tially a moral, a social interest. There is something
masterly in the large-fisted grip with which, in work
of this kind, Trollope handles his brush. The Vicar's
nature is thoroughly analysed and rendered, and his
monotonous friend the Squire, a man with limitations,
but possessed and consumed by a genuine passion,
is equally near the truth.

Trollope has described again and again the ravages
of love, and it is wonderful to see how well, in these
delicate matters, his plain good sense and good taste
serve him. His story is always primarily a love-
story, and a love-story constructed on an inveterate
system. There is a young lady who has two lovers,
or a young man who has two sweethearts; we are
treated to the innumerable forms in which this pre-
dicament may present itself and the consequences,
sometimes pathetic, sometimes grotesque, which spring
from such false situations. Trollope is not what is
called a colourist; still less is he a poet: he is seated
on the back of heavy-footed prose. But his account
of those sentiments which the poets are supposed to
have made their own is apt to be as touching as
demonstrations more lyrical. There is something
wonderfully vivid in the state of mind of the unfortunate Harry Gilmore, of whom I have just spoken;
and his history, which has no more pretensions to
style than if it were cut out of yesterday's newspaper,
lodges itself in the imagination in all sorts of classic
company. He is not handsome, nor clever, nor rich,
nor romantic, nor distinguished in any way; he is

simply rather a dense, narrow-minded, stiff, obstinate, common - place, conscientious modern Englishman, exceedingly in love and, from his own point of view, exceedingly ill-used. He is interesting because he suffers and because we are curious to see the form that suffering will take in that particular nature. Our good fortune, with Trollope, is that the person put before us will have, in spite of opportunities not to have it, a certain particular nature. The author has cared enough about the character of such a person to find out exactly what it is. Another particular nature in *The Vicar of Bullhampton* is the surly, sturdy, sceptical old farmer Jacob Brattle, who doesn't want to be patronised by the parson, and in his dumb, dusky, half-brutal, half-spiritual melancholy, surrounded by domestic troubles, financial embarrassments and a puzzling world, declines altogether to be won over to clerical optimism. Such a figure as Jacob Brattle, purely episodical though it be, is an excellent English portrait. As thoroughly English, and the most striking thing in the book, is the combination, in the nature of Frank Fenwick—the delightful Vicar—of the patronising, conventional, clerical element with all sorts of manliness and spontaneity ; the union, or to a certain extent the contradiction, of official and personal geniality. Trollope touches these points in a way that shows that he knows his man. Delicacy is not his great sign, but when it is necessary he can be as delicate as any one else.

I alighted, just now, at a venture, upon the history

of Frank Fenwick ; it is far from being a conspicuous work in the immense list of Trollope's novels. But to choose an example one must choose arbitrarily, for examples of almost anything that one may wish to say are numerous to embarrassment. In speaking of a writer who produced so much and produced always in the same way, there is perhaps a certain unfairness in choosing at all. As no work has higher pretensions than any other, there may be a certain unkindness in holding an individual production up to the light. " Judge me in the lump," we can imagine the author saying ; " I have only undertaken to entertain the British public. I don't pretend that each of my novels is an organic whole." Trollope had no time to give his tales a classic roundness ; yet there is (in spite of an extraordinary defect), something of that quality in the thing that first revealed him. *The Warden* was published in 1855. It made a great impression ; and when, in 1857, *Barchester Towers* followed it, every one saw that English literature had a novelist the more. These were not the works of a young man, for Anthony Trollope had been born in 1815. It is remarkable to reflect, by the way, that his prodigious fecundity (he had published before *The Warden* three or four novels which attracted little attention), was enclosed between his fortieth and his sixty-seventh years. Trollope had lived long enough in the world to learn a good deal about it ; and his maturity of feeling and evidently large knowledge of English life were for much in the effect pro-

duced by the two clerical tales. It was easy to see
that he would take up room. What he had picked
up, to begin with, was a comprehensive, various impression of the clergy of the Church of England and
the manners and feelings that prevail in cathedral
towns. This, for a while, was his speciality, and,
as always happens in such cases, the public was
disposed to prescribe to him that path. He knew
about bishops, archdeacons, prebendaries, precentors,
and about their wives and daughters; he knew what
these dignitaries say to each other when they are
collected together, aloof from secular ears. He even
knew what sort of talk goes on between a bishop and
a bishop's lady when the august couple are enshrouded
in the privacy of the episcopal bedroom. This knowledge, somehow, was rare and precious. No one, as
yet, had been bold enough to snatch the illuminating
torch from the very summit of the altar. Trollope
enlarged his field very speedily — there is, as I
remember that work, as little as possible of the
ecclesiastical in the tale of *The Three Clerks*, which
came after *Barchester Towers*. But he always retained
traces of his early divination of the clergy; he introduced them frequently, and he always did them
easily and well. There is no ecclesiastical figure,
however, so good as the first—no creation of this
sort so happy as the admirable Mr. Harding. *The
Warden* is a delightful tale, and a signal instance of
Trollope's habit of offering us the spectacle of a
character. A motive more delicate, more slender, as

well as more charming, could scarcely be conceived.
It is simply the history of an old man's conscience.

The good and gentle Mr. Harding, precentor of
Barchester Cathedral, also holds the post of warden
of Hiram's Hospital, an ancient charity where twelve
old paupers are maintained in comfort. The office is
in the gift of the bishop, and its emoluments are as
handsome as the duties of the place are small. Mr.
Harding has for years drawn his salary in quiet
gratitude ; but his moral repose is broken by hearing
it at last begun to be said that the wardenship is a
sinecure, that the salary is a scandal, and that a large
part, at least, of his easy income ought to go to the
pensioners of the hospital. He is sadly troubled and
perplexed, and when the great London newspapers
take up the affair he is overwhelmed with confusion
and shame. He thinks the newspapers are right—he
perceives that the warden is an overpaid and rather a
useless functionary. The only thing he can do is to
resign the place. He has no means of his own—he
is only a quiet, modest, innocent old man, with a
taste, a passion, for old church-music and the violon-
cello. But he determines to resign, and he does
resign in spite of the sharp opposition of his friends.
He does what he thinks right, and goes to live in
lodgings over a shop in the Barchester High Street.
That is all the story, and it has exceeding beauty.
The question of Mr. Harding's resignation becomes a
drama, and we anxiously wait for the catastrophe.
Trollope never did anything happier than the picture

of this sweet and serious little old gentleman, who on most of the occasions of life has shown a lamblike softness and compliance, but in this particular matter opposes a silent, impenetrable obstinacy to the arguments of the friends who insist on his keeping his sinecure—fixing his mild, detached gaze on the distance, and making imaginary passes with his fiddle-bow while they demonstrate his pusillanimity.   The subject of *The Warden*, exactly viewed, is the opposition of the two natures of Archdeacon Grantley and Mr. Harding, and there is nothing finer in all Trollope than the vividness with which this opposition is presented.   The archdeacon is as happy a portrait as the precentor—an image of the full-fed, worldly churchman, taking his stand squarely upon his rich temporalities, and regarding the church frankly as a fat social pasturage.   It required the greatest tact and temperance to make the picture of Archdeacon Grantley stop just where it does.   The type, impartially considered, is detestable, but the individual may be full of amenity.   Trollope allows his archdeacon all the virtues he was likely to possess, but he makes his spiritual grossness wonderfully natural. No charge of exaggeration is possible, for we are made to feel that he is conscientious as well as arrogant, and expansive as well as hard.   He is one of those figures that spring into being all at once, solidifying in the author's grasp.   These two capital portraits are what we carry away from *The Warden*, which some persons profess to regard as our writer's masterpiece. We remember, while it was still something of a novelty, to have heard a judicious critic say that it had much of the charm of *The Vicar of Wakefield*. Anthony Trollope would not have accepted the compliment, and would not have wished this little tale to pass before several of its successors. He would have said, very justly, that it gives too small a measure of his knowledge of life. It has, however, a certain classic roundness, though, as we said a moment since, there is a blemish on its fair face. The chapter on Dr. Pessimist Anticant and Mr. Sentiment would be a mistake almost inconceivable if Trollope had not in other places taken pains to show us that for certain forms of satire (the more violent, doubtless), he had absolutely no gift. Dr. Anticant is a parody of Carlyle, and Mr. Sentiment is an exposure of Dickens : and both these little *jeux d'esprit* are as infelicitous as they are misplaced. It was no less luckless an inspiration to convert Archdeacon Grantley's three sons, denominated respectively Charles James, Henry and Samuel, into little effigies of three distinguished English bishops of that period, whose well - known peculiarities are reproduced in the description of these unnatural urchins. The whole passage, as we meet it, is a sudden disillusionment; we are transported from the mellow atmosphere of an assimilated Barchester to the air of ponderous allegory.

I may take occasion to remark here upon a very curious fact — the fact that there are certain precautions in the way of producing that illusion dear

to the intending novelist which Trollope not only
habitually scorned to take, but really, as we may
say, asking pardon for the heat of the thing, delighted
wantonly to violate. He took a suicidal satisfaction
in reminding the reader that the story he was telling
was only, after all, a make-believe. He habitually
referred to the work in hand (in the course of that
work) as a novel, and to himself as a novelist, and
was fond of letting the reader know that this novelist
could direct the course of events according to his
pleasure.   Already, in *Barchester Towers*, he falls into
this pernicious trick.   In describing the wooing of
Eleanor Bold by Mr. Arabin he has occasion to say
that the lady might have acted in a much more
direct and natural way than the way he attributes to
her.   But if she had, he adds, "where would have
been my novel?"   The last chapter of the same
story begins with the remark, "The end of a novel,
like the end of a children's dinner party, must be
made up of sweetmeats and sugar - plums."   These
little slaps at credulity (we might give many more
specimens) are very discouraging, but they are even
more inexplicable; for they are deliberately inartistic,
even judged from the point of view of that rather
vague consideration of form which is the only canon
we have a right to impose upon Trollope.   It is
impossible to imagine what a novelist takes himself
to be unless he regard himself as an historian and
his narrative as a history.   It is only as an historian
that he has the smallest *locus standi*.   As a narrator

of fictitious events he is nowhere ; to insert into his attempt a back-bone of logic, he must relate events that are assumed to be real. This assumption permeates, animates all the work of the most solid story - tellers ; we need only mention (to select a single instance), the magnificent historical tone of Balzac, who would as soon have thought of admitting to the reader that he was deceiving him, as Garrick or John Kemble would have thought of pulling off his disguise in front of the foot-lights. Therefore, when Trollope suddenly winks at us and reminds us that he is telling us an arbitrary thing, we are startled and shocked in quite the same way as if Macaulay or Motley were to drop the historic mask and intimate that William of Orange was a myth or the Duke of Alva an invention.

It is a part of this same ambiguity of mind as to what constitutes evidence that Trollope should sometimes endow his people with such fantastic names. Dr. Pessimist Anticant and Mr. Sentiment make, as we have seen, an awkward appearance in a modern novel ; and Mr. Neversay Die, Mr. Stickatit, Mr. Rerechild and Mr. Fillgrave (the two last the family physicians), are scarcely more felicitous. It would be better to go back to Bunyan at once. There is a person mentioned in *The Warden* under the name of Mr. Quiverful—a poor clergyman, with a dozen children, who holds the living of Puddingdale. This name is a humorous allusion to his overflowing nursery, and it matters little so long as he is not brought to

the front.   But in *Barchester Towers*, which carries on
the history of Hiram's Hospital, Mr. Quiverful becomes, as a candidate for Mr. Harding's vacant place,
an important element, and the reader is made pro-
portionately unhappy by the primitive character of
this satiric note.   A Mr. Quiverful with fourteen
children (which is the number attained in *Barchester
Towers*) is too difficult to believe in.   We can believe
in the name and we can believe in the children ; but
we cannot manage the combination.   It is probably
not unfair to say that if Trollope derived half his
inspiration from life, he derived the other half from
Thackeray ; his earlier novels, in especial, suggest an
honourable emulation of the author of *The Newcomes.*
Thackeray's names were perfect ; they always had a
meaning, and (except in his absolutely jocose productions, where they were still admirable) we can
imagine, even when they are most figurative, that
they should have been borne by real people.   But in
this, as in other respects, Trollope's hand was heavier
than his master's ; though when he is content not to
be too comical his appellations are sometimes fortunate enough.   Mrs. Proudie is excellent, for Mrs.
Proudie, and even the Duke of Omnium and Gatherum
Castle rather minister to illusion than destroy it.
Indeed, the names of houses and places, throughout
Trollope, are full of colour.

I would speak in some detail of *Barchester Towers*
if this did not seem to commit me to the prodigious
task of appreciating each of Trollope's works in suc-

cession. Such an attempt as that is so far from
being possible that I must frankly confess to not
having read everything that proceeded from his pen.
There came a moment in his vigorous career (it was
even a good many years ago) when I renounced the
effort to "keep up" with him. It ceased to seem
obligatory to have read his last story; it ceased soon
to be very possible to know which was his last.
Before that, I had been punctual, devoted; and the
memories of the earlier period are delightful. It
reached, if I remember correctly, to about the publication of *He Knew He Was Right*; after which, to
my recollection (oddly enough, too, for that novel
was good enough to encourage a continuance of past
favours, as the shopkeepers say), the picture becomes
dim and blurred. The author of *Orley Farm* and
The Small House at Allington ceased to produce individual works; his activity became a huge "serial."
Here and there, in the vast fluidity, an organic
particle detached itself. *The Last Chronicle of Barset*,
for instance, is one of his most powerful things; it
contains the sequel of the terrible history of Mr.
Crawley, the starving curate—an episode full of that
literally truthful pathos of which Trollope was so
often a master, and which occasionally raised him
quite to the level of his two immediate predecessors
in the vivid treatment of English life—great artists
whose pathetic effects were sometimes too visibly
prepared. For the most part, however, he should
be judged by the productions of the first half of

his career; later the strong wine was rather too
copiously watered. His practice, his acquired facility,
were such that his hand went of itself, as it were,
and the thing looked superficially like a fresh inspiration. But it was not fresh, it was rather
stale; and though there was no appearance of effort,
there was a fatal dryness of texture. It was too
little of a new story and too much of an old one.
Some of these ultimate compositions—*Phineas Redux*
(*Phineas Finn* is much better), *The Prime Minister*, *John
Caldigate*, *The American Senator*, *The Duke's Children*—
betray the dull, impersonal rumble of the mill-wheel.
What stands Trollope always in good stead (in
addition to the ripe habit of writing), is his various
knowledge of the English world—to say nothing of
his occasionally laying under contribution the American. His American portraits, by the way (they are
several in number), are always friendly; they hit it
off more happily than the attempt to depict American
character from the European point of view is accustomed to do: though, indeed, as we ourselves have
not yet learned to represent our types very finely
—are not apparently even very sure what our types
are—it is perhaps not to be wondered at that transatlantic talent should miss the mark. The weakness
of transatlantic talent in this particular is apt to be
want of knowledge; but Trollope's knowledge has
all the air of being excellent, though not intimate.
Had he indeed striven to learn the way to the
American heart? No less than twice, and possibly

even oftener, has he rewarded the merit of a scion of the British aristocracy with the hand of an American girl. The American girl was destined sooner or later to make her entrance into British fiction, and Trollope's treatment of this complicated being is full of good humour and of that fatherly indulgence, that almost motherly sympathy, which characterises his attitude throughout toward the youthful feminine. He has not mastered all the springs of her delicate organism nor sounded all the mysteries of her conversation. Indeed, as regards these latter phenomena, he has observed a few of which he has been the sole observer. "I got to be thinking if any one of them should ask me to marry him," words attributed to Miss Boncassen, in *The Duke's Children*, have much more the note of English American than of American English. But, on the whole, in these matters Trollope does very well. His fund of acquaintance with his own country—and indeed with the world at large—was apparently inexhaustible, and it gives his novels a spacious, geographical quality which we should not know where to look for elsewhere in the same degree, and which is the sign of an extraordinary difference between such an horizon as his and the limited world-outlook, as the Germans would say, of the brilliant writers who practise the art of realistic fiction on the other side of the Channel. Trollope was familiar with all sorts and conditions of men, with the business of life, with affairs, with the great world of sport, with every component part of the

ancient fabric of English society.   He had travelled
more than once all over the globe, and for him,
therefore, the background of the human drama was
a very extensive scene.   He had none of the
pedantry of the cosmopolite ; he remained a sturdy
and sensible middle-class Englishman.   But his work
is full of implied reference to the whole arena of
modern vagrancy.   He was for many years concerned in the management of the Post-Office ; and
we can imagine no experience more fitted to impress
a man with the diversity of human relations.   It is
possibly from this source that he derived his fondness for transcribing the letters of his love-lorn
maidens and other embarrassed persons.   No contemporary story-teller deals so much in letters ; the
modern English epistle (very happily imitated, for the
most part), is his unfailing resource.

There is perhaps little reason in it, but I find
myself comparing this tone of allusion to many
lands and many things, and whatever it brings us
of easier respiration, with that narrow vision of
humanity which accompanies the strenuous, serious
work lately offered us in such abundance by the
votaries of art for art who sit so long at their desks
in Parisian *quatrièmes*.   The contrast is complete,
and it would be interesting, had we space to do so
here, to see how far it goes.   On one side a wide,
good-humoured, superficial glance at a good many
things ; on the other a gimlet-like consideration of a
few.   Trollope's plan, as well as Zola's, was to de-

scribe the life that lay near him; but the two
writers differ immensely as to what constitutes life
and what constitutes nearness. For Trollope the
emotions of a nursery-governess in Australia would
take precedence of the adventures of a depraved
femme du monde in Paris or London. They both
undertake to do the same thing — to depict
French and English manners; but the English
writer (with his unsurpassed industry) is so occasional, so accidental, so full of the echoes of voices
that are not the voice of the muse. Gustave
Flaubert, Emile Zola, Alphonse Daudet, on the other
hand, are nothing if not concentrated and sedentary.
Trollope's realism is as instinctive, as inveterate as
theirs; but nothing could mark more the difference
between the French and English mind than the
difference in the application, on one side and the
other, of this system. We say system, though on
Trollope's part it is none. He has no visible, certainly no explicit care for the literary part of the
business; he writes easily, comfortably, and pro-
fusely, but his style has nothing in common either
with the minute stippling of Daudet or the studied
rhythms of Flaubert. He accepted all the common
restrictions, and found that even within the barriers
there was plenty of material. He attaches a preface
to one of his novels—*The Vicar of Bullhampton*, before
mentioned—for the express purpose of explaining
why he has introduced a young woman who may, in
truth, as he says, be called a "castaway"; and in

relation to this episode he remarks that it is the
object of the novelist's art to entertain the young
people of both sexes.　Writers of the French school
would, of course, protest indignantly against such
a formula as this, which is the only one of the
kind that I remember to have encountered in Trollope's pages.　It is meagre, assuredly ; but Trollope's
practice was really much larger than so poor a
theory.　And indeed any theory was good which
enabled him to produce the works which he put
forth between 1856 and 1869, or later.　In spite of
his want of doctrinal richness I think he tells us, on
the whole, more about life than the " naturalists " in
our sister republic.　I say this with a full consciousness of the opportunities an artist loses in
leaving so many corners unvisited, so many topics
untouched, simply because I think his perception
of character was naturally more just and liberal
than that of the naturalists.　This has been from
the beginning the good fortune of our English pro-
viders of fiction, as compared with the French.
They are inferior in audacity, in neatness, in acuteness, in intellectual vivacity, in the arrangement of
material, in the art of characterising visible things.
But they have been more at home in the moral world ;
as people say to-day they know their way about the
conscience.　This is the value of much of the work
done by the feminine wing of the school—work
which presents itself to French taste as deplorably
thin and insipid.　Much of it is exquisitely human,

and that after all is a merit. As regards Trollope,
one may perhaps characterise him best, in opposition
to what I have ventured to call the sedentary school,
by saying that he was a novelist who hunted the fox.
Hunting was for years his most valued recreation,
and I remember that when I made in his company
the voyage of which I have spoken, he had timed his
return from the Antipodes exactly so as to be able to
avail himself of the first day on which it should be
possible to ride to hounds. He "worked" the
hunting-field largely ; it constantly reappears in his
novels ; it was excellent material.

But it would be hard to say (within the circle in
which he revolved) what material he neglected. I
have allowed myself to be detained so long by general
considerations that I have almost forfeited the
opportunity to give examples. I have spoken of
The Warden not only because it made his reputation,
but because, taken in conjunction with *Barchester
Towers*, it is thought by many people to be his highest
flight. *Barchester Towers* is admirable ; it has an
almost Thackerayan richness. Archdeacon Grantley
grows more and more into life, and Mr. Harding is as
charming as ever. Mrs. Proudie is ushered into a
world in which she was to make so great an impression. Mrs. Proudie has become classical ; of all
Trollope's characters she is the most often referred
to. She is exceedingly true ; but I do not think
she is quite so good as her fame, and as several
figures from the same hand that have not won so

much honour.   She is rather too violent, too vixenish,
too sour.   The truly awful female bully—the completely fatal episcopal spouse—would have, I think, a
more insidious form, a greater amount of superficial
padding.   The Stanhope family, in *Barchester Towers*,
are a real *trouvaille*, and the idea of transporting the
Signora Vesey-Neroni into a cathedral-town was an
inspiration.   There could not be a better example of
Trollope's manner of attaching himself to character
than the whole picture of Bertie Stanhope.   Bertie
is a delightful creation; and the scene in which, at
the party given by Mrs. Proudie, he puts this
majestic woman to rout is one of the most amusing
in all the chronicles of Barset.   It is perhaps permitted to wish, by the way, that this triumph had
been effected by means intellectual rather than
physical; though, indeed, if Bertie had not despoiled
her of her drapery we should have lost the lady's
admirable " Unhand it, sir ! "   Mr. Arabin is charming, and the henpecked bishop has painful truth ;
but Mr. Slope, I think, is a little too arrant a scamp.
He is rather too much the old game ; he goes too
coarsely to work, and his clamminess and cant are
somewhat overdone.   He is an interesting illustration, however, of the author's dislike (at that period
at least) of the bareness of evangelical piety.   In
one respect *Barchester Towers* is (to the best of our
recollection) unique, being the only one of Trollope's
novels in which the interest does not centre more or
less upon a simple maiden in her flower.   The novel

offers us nothing in the way of a girl; though we
know that this attractive object was to lose nothing
by waiting. Eleanor Bold is a charming and natural
person, but Eleanor Bold is not in her flower. After
this, however, Trollope settled down steadily to the
English girl; he took possession of her, and turned
her inside out. He never made her a subject of
heartless satire, as cynical fabulists of other lands
have been known to make the shining daughters
of those climes; he bestowed upon her the most
serious, the most patient, the most tender, the most
copious consideration. He is evidently always more
or less in love with her, and it is a wonder how
under these circumstances he should make her so
objective, plant her so well on her feet. But, as I
have said, if he was a lover, he was a paternal lover;
as competent as a father who has had fifty daughters.
He has presented the British maiden under innumerable names, in every station and in every emergency
in life, and with every combination of moral and
physical qualities. She is always definite and natural.
She plays her part most properly. She has always
health in her cheek and gratitude in her eye. She
has not a touch of the morbid, and is delightfully
tender, modest and fresh. Trollope's heroines have a
strong family likeness, but it is a wonder how finely
he discriminates between them. One feels, as one
reads him, like a man with "sets" of female cousins.
Such a person is inclined at first to lump each group
together; but presently he finds that even in the

groups there are subtle differences. Trollope's girls, for that matter, would make delightful cousins. He has scarcely drawn, that we can remember, a disagreeable damsel. Lady Alexandrina de Courcy is disagreeable, and so is Amelia Roper, and so are various provincial (and indeed metropolitan) spinsters, who set their caps at young clergymen and government clerks. Griselda Grantley was a stick; and considering that she was intended to be attractive, Alice Vavasor does not commend herself particularly to our affections. But the young women I have mentioned had ceased to belong to the blooming season; they had entered the bristling, or else the limp, period. Not that Trollope's more mature spinsters invariably fall into these extremes. Miss Thorne of Ullathorne, Miss Dunstable, Miss Mackenzie, Rachel Ray (if she may be called mature), Miss Baker and Miss Todd, in *The Bertrams*, Lady Julia Guest, who comforts poor John Eames : these and many other amiable figures rise up to contradict the idea. A gentleman who had sojourned in many lands was once asked by a lady (neither of these persons was English), in what country he had found the women most to his taste. " Well, in England," he replied. " In England ? " the lady repeated. " Oh yes," said her interlocutor; " they are so affectionate ! " The remark was fatuous, but it has the merit of describing Trollope's heroines. They are so affectionate. Mary Thorne, Lucy Robarts, Adela Gauntlet, Lily Dale, Nora Rowley, Grace Crawley, have a kind of clinging tenderness, a passive sweetness, which is quite in the old English tradition. Trollope's genius is not the genius of Shakespeare, but his heroines have something of the fragrance of Imogen and Desdemona. There are two little stories to which, I believe, his name has never been affixed, but which he is known to have written, that contain an extraordinarily touching representation of the passion of love in its most sensitive form. In *Linda Tressel* and *Nina Balatka* the vehicle is plodding prose, but the effect is none the less poignant. And in regard to this I may say that in a hundred places in Trollope the extremity of pathos is reached by the homeliest means. He often achieved a conspicuous intensity of the tragical. The long, slow process of the conjugal wreck of Louis Trevelyan and his wife (in *He Knew He Was Right*), with that rather lumbering movement which is often characteristic of Trollope, arrives at last at an impressive completeness of misery. It is the history of an accidental rupture between two stiff-necked and ungracious people—"the little rift within the lute"—which widens at last into a gulf of anguish. Touch is added to touch, one small, stupid, fatal aggravation to another; and as we gaze into the widening breach we wonder at the vulgar materials of which tragedy sometimes composes itself. I have always remembered the chapter called "Casalunga," toward the close of *He Knew He Was Right*, as a powerful picture of the insanity of stiff-neckedness. Louis Trevelyan, separated from his wife, alone, haggard, suspicious, unshaven, undressed, living in a desolate villa on a hill-top near Siena and returning doggedly to his fancied wrong, which he has nursed until it becomes an hallucination, is a picture worthy of Balzac. Here and in several other places Trollope has dared to be thoroughly logical ; he has not sacrificed to conventional optimism ; he has not been afraid of a misery which should be too much like life. He has had the same courage in the history of the wretched Mr. Crawley and in that of the much-to-be-pitied Lady Mason. In this latter episode he found an admirable subject. A quiet, charming tender-souled English gentlewoman who (as I remember the story of *Orley Farm*) forges a codicil to a will in order to benefit her son, a young prig who doesn't appreciate immoral heroism, and who is suspected, accused, tried, and saved from conviction only by some turn of fortune that I forget ; who is furthermore an object of high-bred, respectful, old-fashioned gallantry on the part of a neighbouring baronet, so that she sees herself dishonoured in his eyes as well as condemned in those of her boy : such a personage and such a situation would be sure to yield, under Trollope's handling, the last drop of their reality.

There are many more things to say about him than I am able to add to these very general observations, the limit of which I have already passed. It would be natural, for instance, for a critic who affirms that his principal merit is the portrayal of individual character, to enumerate several of the figures that he has produced. I have not done this, and I must ask the reader who is not acquainted with Trollope to take my assertion on trust; the reader who knows him will easily make a list for himself. No account of him is complete in which allusion is not made to his practice of carrying certain actors from one story to another—a practice which he may be said to have inherited from Thackeray, as Thackeray may be said to have borrowed it from Balzac. It is a great mistake, however, to speak of it as an artifice which would not naturally occur to a writer proposing to himself to make a general portrait of a society He has to construct that society, and it adds to the illusion in any given case that certain other cases correspond with it. Trollope constructed a great many things—a clergy, an aristocracy, a middle-class an administrative class, a little replica of the political world. His political novels are distinctly dull, and I confess I have not been able to read them. He evidently took a good deal of pains with his aristocracy; it makes its first appearance, if I remember right, in *Doctor Thorne*, in the person of the Lady Arabella de Courcy. It is difficult for us in America to measure the success of that picture, which is probably, however, not absolutely to the life. There is in *Doctor Thorne* and some other works a certain crudity of reference to distinctions of rank—as if people's consciousness of this matter were, on either side, rather inflated. It suggests a general state of tension. It is true that, if Trollope's conscious-

ness had been more flaccid he would perhaps not
have given us Lady Lufton and Lady Glencora
Palliser. Both of these noble persons are as living
as possible, though I see Lady Lufton, with her
terror of Lucy Robarts, the best. There is a touch
of poetry in the figure of Lady Glencora, but I think
there is a weak spot in her history. The actual
woman would have made a fool of herself to the end
with Burgo Fitzgerald; she would not have discovered the merits of Plantagenet Palliser—or if she
had, she would not have cared about them. It is an
illustration of the business-like way in which Trollope
laid out his work that he always provided a sort of
underplot to alternate with his main story—a strain
of narrative of which the scene is usually laid in a
humbler walk of life. It is to his underplot that
he generally relegates his vulgar people, his dis
agreeable young women; and I have often admired
the perseverance with which he recounts these less
edifying items. Now and then, it may be said,
as in *Ralph the Heir*, the story appears to be all
underplot and all vulgar people. These, however,
are details. As I have already intimated, it is difficult to specify in Trollope's work, on account of the
immense quantity of it; and there is sadness in the
thought that this enormous mass does not present
itself in a very portable form to posterity.

Trollope did not write for posterity; he wrote for the
day, the moment; but these are just the writers whom
posterity is apt to put into its pocket. So much of

the life of his time is reflected in his novels that we must believe a part of the record will be saved ; and the best parts of them are so sound and true and genial, that readers with an eye to that sort of entertainment will always be sure, in a certain proportion, to turn to them. Trollope will remain one of the most trustworthy, though not one of the most eloquent, of the writers who have helped the heart of man to know itself. The heart of man does not always desire this knowledge ; it prefers sometimes to look at history in another way—to look at the manifestations without troubling about the motives. There are two kinds of taste in the appreciation of imaginative literature : the taste for emotions of surprise and the taste for emotions of recognition. It is the latter that Trollope gratifies, and he gratifies it the more that the medium of his own mind, through which we see what he shows us, gives a confident direction to our sympathy. His natural rightness and purity are so real that the good things he projects must be real. A race is fortunate when it has a good deal of the sort of imagination—of imaginative feeling—that had fallen to the share of Anthony Trollope; and in this possession our English race is not poor.

1883.

V

ROBERT LOUIS STEVENSON

ROBERT LOUIS STEVENSON

I

IF there be a writer of our language at the present
moment who has the effect of making us regret the
extinction of the pleasant fashion of the literary portrait, it is certainly the bright particular genius whose
name I have written at the head of these remarks.
Mr. Stevenson fairly challenges portraiture, as we
pass him on the highway of literature (if that be the
road, rather than some wandering, sun-chequered
by-lane, that he may be said to follow), just as the
possible model, in local attire, challenges the painter
who wanders through the streets of a foreign town
looking for subjects. He gives us new ground to
wonder why the effort to fix a face and figure, to
seize a literary character and transfer it to the canvas
of the critic, should have fallen into such discredit
among us, and have given way, to the mere multiplication of little private judgment-seats, where the
scales and the judicial wig, both of them considerable
awry, and not rendered more august by the company

of a vicious-looking switch, have taken the place, as the symbols of office, of the kindly, disinterested palette and brush. It has become the fashion to be effective at the expense of the sitter, to make some little point, or inflict some little dig, with a heated party air, rather than to catch a talent in the fact, follow its line, and put a finger on its essence : so that the exquisite art of criticism, smothered in grossness, finds itself turned into a question of " sides." The critic industriously keeps his score, but it is seldom to be hoped that the author, criminal though he may be, will be apprehended by justice through the handbills given out in the case ; for it is of the essence of a happy description that it shall have been preceded by a happy observation and a free curiosity ; and desuetude, as we may say, has overtaken these amiable, uninvidious faculties, which have not the glory of organs and chairs.

We hasten to add that it is not the purpose of these few pages to restore their lustre or to bring back the more penetrating vision of which we lament the disappearance. No individual can bring it back, for the light that we look at things by is, after all, made by all of us. It is sufficient to note, in passing, that if Mr. Stevenson had presented himself in an age, or in a country, of portraiture, the painters would certainly each have had a turn at him. The easels and benches would have bristled, the circle would have been close, and quick, from the canvas to the sitter, the rising and falling of heads. It has happened to all of us to have gone into a studio, a studio of pupils, and seen the thick cluster of bent backs and the conscious model in the midst. It has happened to us to be struck, or not to be struck, with the beauty or the symmetry of this personage, and to have made some remark which, whether expressing admiration or disappointment, has elicited from one of the attentive workers the exclamation, " Character, character is what he has !" These words may be applied to Mr. Robert Louis Stevenson ; in the language of that art which depends most on direct observation, character, character is what he has. He is essentially a model, in the sense of a sitter ; I do not mean, of course, in the sense of a pattern or a guiding light. And if the figures who have a life in literature may also be divided into two great classes, we may add that he is conspicuously one of the draped : he would never, if I may be allowed the expression, pose for the nude. There are writers who present themselves before the critic with just the amount of drapery that is necessary for decency ; but Mr. Stevenson is not one of these—he makes his appearance in an amplitude of costume. His costume is part of the character of which I just now spoke ; it never occurs to us to ask how he would look without it. Before all things he is a writer with a style—a model with a complexity of curious and picturesque garments. It is by the cut and the colour of this rich and becoming frippery—I use the term endearingly, as a painter might—that he arrests the eye and solicits the brush.

That is, frankly, half the charm he has for us, that he wears a dress and wears it with courage, with a certain cock of the hat and tinkle of the supereroga- tory sword ; or in other words that he is curious of expression and regards the literary form not simply as a code of signals, but as the key-board of a piano, and as so much plastic material. He has that voice deplored, if we mistake not, by Mr. Herbert Spencer, a manner—a manner for manner's sake it may some- times doubtless be said. He is as different as possible from the sort of writer who regards words as numbers, and a page as the mere addition of them ; much more, to carry out our image, the dictionary stands for him as a wardrobe, and a proposition as a button for his coat. Mr. William Archer, in an article[1] so gracefully and ingeniously turned that the writer may almost be accused of imitating even while he deprecates, speaks of him as a votary of "lightness of touch," at any cost, and remarks that "he is not only philosophically content but deliberately resolved, that his readers shall look first to his manner, and only in the second place to his matter." I shall not attempt to gainsay this ; I cite it rather, for the present, because it carries out our own sense. Mr. Stevenson delights in a style, and his own has nothing accidental or diffident ; it is eminently

[1] "R. L. Stevenson, his Style and Thought," *Time* November 1885.

conscious of its responsibilities, and meets them with a kind of gallantry—as if language were a pretty woman, and a person who proposes to handle it had of necessity to be something of a Don Juan. This bravery of gesture is a noticeable part of his nature, and it is rather odd that at the same time a striking feature of that nature should be an absence of care for things feminine. His books are for the most part books without women, and it is not women who fall most in love with them. But Mr. Stevenson does not need, as we may say, a petticoat to inflame him : a happy collocation of words will serve the purpose, or a singular image, or the bright eye of a passing conceit, and he will carry off a pretty paradox without so much as a scuffle. The tone of letters is in him— the tone of letters as distinct from that of philosophy, or of those industries whose uses are supposed to be immediate. Many readers, no doubt, consider that he carries it too far ; they manifest an impatience for some glimpse of his moral message. They may be heard to ask what it is he proposes to demonstrate, with such a variety of paces and graces.

The main thing that he demonstrates, to our own perception, is that it is a delight to read him, and that he renews this delight by a constant variety of experiment. Of this anon, however ; and meanwhile, it may be noted as a curious characteristic of current fashions that the writer whose effort is perceptibly that of the artist is very apt to find himself thrown on the defensive. A work of literature is a form, but the author who betrays a consciousness of the responsibilities involved in this circumstance not rarely perceives himself to be regarded as an uncanny personage. The usual judgment is that he may be artistic, but that he must not be too much so ; that way, apparently, lies something worse than madness. This queer superstition has so successfully imposed itself, that the mere fact of having been indifferent to such a danger constitutes in itself an originality. How few they are in number and how soon we could name them, the writers of English prose, at the present moment, the quality of whose prose is personal, expressive, renewed at each attempt ! The state of things that one would have expected to be the rule has become the exception, and an exception for which, most of the time, an apology appears to be thought necessary.   A mill that grinds with regularity and with a certain commercial fineness—that is the image suggested by the manner of a good many of the fraternity. They turn out an article for which there is a demand, they keep a shop for a speciality, and the business is carried on in accordance with a useful, well-tested prescription. It is just because he has no speciality that Mr. Stevenson is an individual, and because his curiosity is the only receipt by which he produces.   Each of his books is an independent effort—a window opened to a different view. *Doctor Jekyll and Mr. Hyde* is as dissimilar as possible from *Treasure Island ; Virginibus Puerisque* has nothing in common with *The New Arabian Nights,* and I should never have supposed *A Child's Garden of Verses* to be from the hand of the author of *Prince Otto*.

Though Mr. Stevenson cares greatly for his phrase, as every writer should who respects himself and his art, it takes no very attentive reading of his volumes to show that it is not what he cares for most, and that he regards an expressive style only, after all, as a means. It seems to me the fault of Mr. Archer's interesting paper, that it suggests too much that the author of these volumes considers the art of expression as an end—an ingenious game of words. He finds that Mr. Stevenson is not serious, that he neglects a whole side of life, that he has no perception. and no consciousness, of suffering; that he speaks as a happy but heartless pagan, living only in his senses (which the critic admits to be exquisitely fine), and that in a world full of heaviness he is not sufficiently aware of the philosophic limitations of mere technical skill. In sketching these aberrations Mr. Archer himself, by the way, displays anything but ponderosity of hand. He is not the first reader, and he will not be the last, who shall have been irritated by Mr. Stevenson's jauntiness. That jauntiness is an essential part of his genius; but to my sense it ceases to be irritating—it indeed becomes positively touching and constitutes an appeal to sympathy and even to tenderness—when once one has perceived what lies beneath the dancing-tune to which he mostly moves. Much as he cares for his phrase, he cares more for life, and for a certain transcendently lovable part of it. He feels, as it seems to us, and that is not given to every one. This constitutes a philosophy which Mr. Archer fails to read between his lines—the respectable, desirable moral which many a reader doubtless finds that he neglects to point. He does not feel everything equally, by any manner of means ; but his feelings are always his reasons. He regards them, whatever they may be, as sufficiently honourable, does not disguise them in other names or colours, and looks at whatever he meets in the brilliant candle-light that they shed. As in his extreme artistic vivacity he seems really disposed to try everything he has tried once, by way of a change, to be inhuman, and there is a hard glitter about *Prince Otto* which seems to indicate that in this case too he has succeeded, as he has done in most of the feats that he has attempted. But *Prince Otto* is even less like his other productions than his other productions are like each other.

The part of life which he cares for most is youth, and the direct expression of the love of youth is the beginning and the end of his message. His appreciation of this delightful period amounts to a passion, and a passion, in the age in which we live, strikes us on the whole as a sufficient philosophy. It ought to satisfy Mr. Archer, and there are writers who press harder than Mr. Stevenson, on whose behalf no such moral motive can be alleged. Mingled with this almost equal love of a literary surface, it represents a real originality. This combination is the

keynote of Mr. Stevenson's faculty and the explanation of his perversities. The feeling of one's teens,
and even of an earlier period (for the delights of
crawling, and almost of the rattle, are embodied in
A Child's Garden of Verses), and the feeling for happy
turns—these, in the last analysis (and his sense of a
happy turn is of the subtlest), are the corresponding
halves of his character. If *Prince Otto* and *Doctor
Jekyll* left me a clearer field for the assertion, I would
say that everything he has written is a direct apology
for boyhood; or rather (for it must be confessed that
Mr. Stevenson's tone is seldom apologetic), a direct
rhapsody on the age of heterogeneous pockets. Even
members of the very numerous class who have held
their breath over *Treasure Island* may shrug their
shoulders at this account of the author's religion; but
it is none the less a great pleasure—the highest
reward of observation—to put one's hand on a rare
illustration, and Mr. Stevenson is certainly rare.
What makes him so is the singular maturity of the
expression that he has given to young sentiments:
he judges them, measures them, sees them from the
outside, as well as entertains them. He describes
credulity with all the resources of experience, and
represents a crude stage with infinite ripeness. In a
word, he is an artist accomplished even to sophistica-
tion, whose constant theme is the unsophisticated.
Sometimes, as in *Kidnapped*, the art is so ripe that it
lifts even the subject into the general air: the execution is so serious that the idea (the idea of a boy's

romantic adventures), becomes a matter of universal
relations.   What he prizes most in the boy's ideal is
the imaginative side of it, the capacity for successful
make-believe.   The general freshness in which this
is a part of the gloss seems to him the divinest thing
in life ; considerably more divine, for instance, than
the passion usually regarded as the supremely tender
one.   The idea of making believe appeals to him
much more than the idea of making love.   That
delightful little book of rhymes, the *Child's Garden*,
commemorates from beginning to end the picturing,
personifying, dramatising faculty of infancy—the
view of life from the level of the nursery-fender.   The
volume is a wonder for the extraordinary vividness
with which it reproduces early impressions : a child
might have written it if a child could see childhood
from the outside, for it would seem that only a child
is really near enough to the nursery floor.   And
what is peculiar to Mr. Stevenson is that it is his own
childhood he appears to delight in, and not the
personal presence of little darlings.   Oddly enough,
there is no strong implication that he is fond of
babies ; he doesn't speak as a parent, or an uncle, or
an educator—he speaks as a contemporary absorbed
in his own game.   That game is almost always a
vision of dangers and triumphs, and if emotion,
with him, infallibly resolves itself into memory,
so memory is an evocation of throbs and thrills
and suspense.   He has given to the world the
romance of boyhood, as others have produced that

of the peerage and the police and the medical profession.

This amounts to saying that what he is most curious of in life is heroism — personal gallantry, if need be with a manner, or a banner, though he is also abundantly capable of enjoying it when it is artless. The delightful exploits of Jim Hawkins, in *Treasure Island*, are unaffectedly performed ; but none the less "the finest action is the better for a piece of purple," as the author remarks in the paper on "The English Admirals" in *Virginibus Puerisque*, a paper of which the moral is, largely, that "we learn to desire a grand air in our heroes ; and such a knowledge of the human stage as shall make them put the dots on their own i's, and leave us in no suspense as to when they mean to be heroic." The love of brave words as well as brave deeds—which is simply Mr. Stevenson's essential love of style—is recorded in this little paper with a charming, slightly sophistical ingenuity. "They served their guns merrily when it came to fighting, and they had the readiest ear for a bold, honourable sentiment of any class of men the world ever produced." The author goes on to say that most men of high destinies have even high-sounding names. Alan Breck, in *Kidnapped*, is a wonderful picture of the union of courage and swagger ; the little Jacobite adventurer, a figure worthy of Scott at his best, and representing the highest point that Mr. Stevenson's talent has reached, shows us that a marked taste for tawdry finery—

tarnished and tattered, some of it indeed, by ticklish occasions—is quite compatible with a perfectly high mettle.   Alan Breck is at bottom a study of the love of glory, carried out with extreme psychological truth.   When the love of glory is of an inferior order the reputation is cultivated rather than the opportunity ; but when it is a pure passion the opportunity is cultivated for the sake of the reputation.   Mr. Stevenson's kindness for adventurers extends even to the humblest of all, the mountebank and the strolling player, or even the pedlar whom he declares that in his foreign travels he is habitually taken for, as we see in the whimsical apology for vagabonds which winds up *An Inland Voyage.*   The hungry conjurer, the gymnast whose *maillot* is loose, have something of the glamour of the hero, inasmuch as they too pay with their person.   " To be even one of the outskirters of art leaves a fine stamp on a man's countenance. . . . That is the kind of thing that reconciles me to life : a ragged, tippling, incompetent old rogue, with the manners of a gentleman and the vanity of an artist, to keep up his self-respect ! "   What reconciles Mr. Stevenson to life is the idea that in the first place it offers the widest field that we know of for odd doings, and that in the second these odd doings are the best of pegs to hang a sketch in three lines or a paradox in three pages.

As it is not odd, but extremely usual, to marry, he deprecates that course in *Virginibus Puerisque*, the collection of short essays which is most a record of his opinions—that is, largely, of his likes and dislikes. It all comes back to his sympathy with the juvenile and that feeling about life which leads him to regard women as so many superfluous girls in a boy's game. They are almost wholly absent from his pages (the main exception is *Prince Otto*, though there is a Clara apiece in *The Rajah's Diamond* and *The Pavilion on the Links*), for they don't like ships and pistols and fights, they encumber the decks and require separate apartments, and, almost worst of all, have not the highest literary standard. Why should a person marry when he might be swinging a cutlass or looking for a buried treasure? Why should he waste at the nuptial altar precious hours in which he might be polishing periods? It is one of those curious and to my sense fascinating inconsistencies that we encounter in Mr. Stevenson's mind, that though he takes such an interest in the childish life he takes no interest in the fireside. He has an indulgent glance for it in the verses of the *Garden*, but to his view the normal child is the child who absents himself from the family-circle, in fact when he can, in imagination when he cannot, in the disguise of a buccaneer. Girls don't do this, and women are only grown-up girls, unless it be the delightful maiden, fit daughter of an imperial race, whom he commemorates in *An Inland Voyage*.

"A girl at school, in France, began to describe one of our regiments on parade to her French schoolmates ; and as she went on, she told me, the recollection grew so vivid, she became

so proud to be the countrywoman of such soldiers, that her
voice failed her and she burst into tears. I have never forgotten that girl ; and I think she very nearly deserves a statue.
To call her a young lady, with all its niminy associations, would
be to offer her an insult. She may rest assured of one thing ;
although she never should marry a heroic general, never see any
great or immediate result of her life, she will not have lived in
vain for her native land."

There is something of that in Mr. Stevenson ; when
he begins to describe a British regiment on parade
(or something of that sort), he too almost breaks
down for emotion : which is why I have been careful
to traverse the insinuation that he is primarily a
chiseller of prose. If things had gone differently
with him (I must permit myself this allusion to his
personal situation, and I shall venture to follow it
with two or three others), he might have been an
historian of famous campaigns—a great painter of
battle-pieces. Of course, however, in this capacity it
would not have done for him to break down for
emotion.

Although he remarks that marriage "is a field of
battle and not a bed of roses," he points out repeatedly that it is a terrible renunciation and somehow, in strictness, incompatible even with honour—
the sort of roving, trumpeting honour that appeals
most to his sympathy. After that step,

"There are no more bye-path meadows where you may inno-
cently linger, but the road lies long and straight and dusty to
the grave. . . . You may think you had a conscience and
believed in God ; but what is a conscience to a wife ? . . . To
marry is to domesticate the Recording Angel. Once you

are married, there is nothing left for you, not even suicide, but to be good. . . . How then, in such an atmosphere of compromise, to keep honour bright and abstain from base capitulations ? . . . The proper qualities of each sex are eternally surprising to the other. Between the Latin and the Teuton races there are similar divergences, not to be bridged by the most liberal sympathy. . . . It is better to face the fact and know, when you marry, that you take into your life a creature of equal if unlike frailties ; whose weak, human heart beats no more tunefully than yours."

If there be a grimness in that it is as near as Mr. Stevenson ever comes to being grim, and we have only to turn the page to find the corrective—something delicately genial, at least, if not very much less sad.

" The blind bow-boy who smiles upon us from the end of terraces in old Dutch gardens laughingly hurls his bird-bolts among a fleeting generation. But for as fast as ever he shoots, the game dissolves and disappears into eternity from under his falling arrows ; this one is gone ere he is struck ; the other has but time to make one gesture and give one passionate cry ; and they are all the things of a moment."

That is an admission that though it is soon over, the great sentimental surrender is inevitable. And there is geniality too, still over the page (in regard to quite another matter), geniality, at least, for the profession of letters, in the declaration that there is

" One thing you can never make Philistine natures understand ; one thing which yet lies on the surface, remains as unseizable to their wit as a high flight of metaphysics—namely, that the business of life is mainly carried on by the difficult art of literature, and according to a man's proficiency in that art shall be the freedom and fulness of his intercourse with other men."

Yet it is difficult not to believe that the ideal in

which our author's spirit might most gratefully have
rested would have been the character of the pater-
familias, when the eye falls on such a charming piece
of observation as these lines about children in the
admirable paper on *Child's Play:*

"If it were not for this perpetual imitation we should be
tempted to fancy they despised us outright, or only considered
us in the light of creatures brutally strong and brutally silly,
among whom they condescended to dwell in obedience, like a
philosopher at a barbarous court."

II

WE know very little about a talent till we know where it grew up, and it would halt terribly at the start, any account of the author of *Kidnapped* which should omit to insist promptly that he is a Scot of the Scots. Two facts, to my perception, go a great way to explain his composition : the first of which is that his boyhood was passed in the shadow of Edinburgh Castle, and the second that he came of a family that had set up great lights on the coast. His grandfather, his uncle, were famous constructors of lighthouses, and the name of the race is associated above all with the beautiful and beneficent tower of Skerryvore. We may exaggerate the way in which, in an imaginative youth, the sense of the "story" of things would feed upon the impressions of Edinburgh— though I suspect it would be difficult really to do so. The streets are so full of history and poetry, of picture and song, of associations springing from strong passions and strange characters, that, for our own part, we find ourselves thinking of an urchin going and coming there as we used to think (wonderingly, enviously), of the small boys who figured as super numeraries, pages or imps, in showy scenes at the theatre : the place seems the background, the complicated "set" of a drama, and the children the mysterious little beings who are made free of the magic world. How must it not have beckoned on the imagination to pass and repass, on the way to school, under the Castle rock, conscious, acutely yet familiarly, of the gray citadel on the summit, lighted up with the tartans and bagpipes of Highland regiments ? Mr. Stevenson's mind, from an early age, was furnished with the concrete Highlander, who must have had much of the effect that we nowadays call decorative. We have encountered somewhere a fanciful paper [1] of our author's, in which there is a reflection of half-holiday afternoons and, unless our own fancy plays us a trick, of lights red, in the winter dusk, in the high-placed windows of the old town—a delightful rhapsody on the penny sheets of figures for the puppet-shows of infancy, in life-like position and awaiting the impatient yet careful scissors. "If landscapes were sold," he says in *Travels with a Donkey*, "like the sheets of characters of my boyhood, one penny plain and twopence coloured, I should go the length of twopence every day of my life."

Indeed the colour of Scotland has entered into him altogether, and though, oddly enough, he has written but little about his native country, his happiest work

[1] "A Penny Plain and Twopence Coloured." Republished, since the above was written, in *Memories and Portraits*, 1887.

shows, I think, that she has the best of his ability, the best of his ambition. *Kidnapped* (whose inadequate title I may deplore in passing) breathes in every line the feeling of moor and loch, and is the finest of his longer stories, and *Thrawn Janet*, a masterpiece in thirteen pages (lately republished in the volume of *The Merry Men*), is, among the shorter, the strongest in execution. The latter consists of a gruesome anecdote of the supernatural, related in the Scotch dialect, and the genuineness which this medium (at the sight of which, in general, the face of the reader grows long) wears in Mr. Stevenson's hands is a proof of how living the question of form always is to him, and what a variety of answers he has for it. It would never have occurred to us that the style of *Travels with a Donkey* or *Virginibus Puerisque* and the idiom of the parish of Balweary could be a conception of the same mind. If it be a good fortune for a genius to have had such a country as Scotland for its primary stuff, this is doubly the case when there has been a certain process of detachment, of extreme secularisation. Mr. Stevenson has been emancipated : he is, as we may say, a Scotchman of the world. None other, I think, could have drawn with such a mixture of sympathetic and ironical observation the character of the canny young Lowlander, David Balfour, a good boy but an exasperating. *Treasure Island, The New Arabian Nights, Prince Otto, Doctor Jekyll, and Mr. Hyde,* are not very directly founded on observation ; but that quality comes in with ex-

treme fineness as soon as the subject involves consider‧
ation of race.

I have been wondering whether there is something
more than this that our author's pages would tell us
about him, or whether that particular something is
in the mind of an admirer because he happens to
have had other lights on it.   It has been possible
for so acute a critic as Mr. William Archer to read
pure high spirits and the gospel of the young man
rejoicing in his strength and his matutinal cold bath
between the lines of Mr. Stevenson's prose.   And it
is a fact that the note of a morbid sensibility is so
absent from his pages, they contain so little reference
to infirmity and suffering, that we feel a trick has
really been played upon us on discovering by accident
the actual state of the case with the writer who has
indulged in the most enthusiastic allusion to the joy
of existence.   We must permit ourselves another
mention of his personal situation, for it adds immensely to the interest of volumes through which
there draws so strong a current of life, to know that
they are not only the work of an invalid, but that
they have largely been written in bed, in dreary
"health-resorts," in the intervals of sharp attacks.
There is almost nothing in them to lead us to guess
this : the direct evidence indeed is almost all contained in the limited compass of *The Silverado
Squatters*.   In such a case, however, it is the indirect
that is the most eloquent, and I know not where
to look for that, unless in the paper called "Ordered

South," and its companion " Aes Triplex," in *Virginibus Puerisque*.   It is impossible to read "Ordered South" attentively without feeling that it is personal: the reflections it contains are from experience, not from fancy.   The places and climates to which the invalid is carried to recover or to die are mainly beautiful, but

"In his heart of hearts he has to confess that [they are] not beautiful for him. . . . He is like an enthusiast leading about with him a stolid, indifferent tourist.   There is some one by who is out of sympathy with the scene, and is not moved up to the measure of the occasion; and that some one is himself. . . . He seems to himself to touch things with muffled hands and to see them through a veil. . . . Many a white town that sits far out on the promontory, many a comely fold of wood on the mountain side, beckons and allures his imagination day after day, and is yet as inaccessible to his feet as the clefts and gorges of the clouds.   The sense of distance grows upon him wonderfully; and after some feverish efforts and the fretful uneasiness of the first few days he falls contentedly in with the restrictions of his weakness. . . . He feels, if he is to be thus tenderly weaned from the passion of life, thus gradually inducted into the slumber of death, that when at last the end comes it will come quietly and fitly. . . . He will pray for Medea : when she comes let her either rejuvenate or slay."

The second of the short essays I have mentioned has a taste of mortality only because the purpose of it is to insist that the only sane behaviour is to leave death and the accidents that lead to it out of our calculations.   Life "is a honeymoon with us all through, and none of the longest.   Small blame to us if we give our whole hearts to this glowing bride of ours."   The person who does so "makes a very

different acquaintance with the world, keeps all his
pulses going true and fast, and gathers impetus as he
runs, until if he be running towards anything better
than wildfire, he may shoot up and become a con-
stellation in the end." Nothing can be more deplorable than to "forego all the issues of living in a
parlour with a regulated temperature." Mr. Stevenson adds that as for those whom the gods love
dying young, a man dies too young at whatever
age he parts with life. The testimony of "Aes
Triplex" to the author's own disabilities is after all
very indirect. It consists mainly in the general protest not so much against the fact of extinction as
against the theory of it. The reader only asks
himself why the hero of *Travels with a Donkey*, the
historian of Alan Breck, should think of these things.
His appreciation of the active side of life has such a
note of its own that we are surprised to find that it
proceeds in a considerable measure from an intimate
acquaintance with the passive. It seems too anom-
alous that the writer who has most cherished the
idea of a certain free exposure should also be the
one who has been reduced most to looking for it
within, and that the figures of adventurers who, at
least in our literature of to-day, are the most vivid,
should be the most vicarious. The truth is, of course,
that as the *Travels with a Donkey* and *An Inland
Voyage* abundantly show, the author has a fund of
reminiscences. He did not spend his younger years
"in a parlour with a regulated temperature." A

reader who happens to be aware of how much it has been his later fate to do so may be excused for finding an added source of interest—something indeed deeply and constantly touching—in this association of peculiarly restrictive conditions with the vision of high spirits and romantic accidents, of a kind of honourably picaresque career. Mr. Stevenson is, however, distinctly, in spite of his occasional practice of the gruesome, a frank optimist—an observer who not only loves life but does not shrink from the responsibility of recommending it. There is a systematic brightness in him which testifies to this and which is after all but one of the innumerable ingenuities of patience. What is remarkable in his case is that his productions should constitute an exquisite expression, a sort of whimsical gospel of enjoyment. The only difference between *An Inland Voyage* or *Travels with a Donkey* and *The New Arabian Nights* or *Treasure Island* or *Kidnapped*, is that in the later books the enjoyment is reflective (though it simulates spontaneity with singular art), whereas in the first two it is natural and, as it were, historical.

These little histories—the first volumes, if I mistake not, that introduced Mr. Stevenson to lovers of good writing—abound in charming illustrations of his disposition to look at the world as a not exactly refined but glorified, pacified Bohemia. They narrate the quest of personal adventure, on one occasion in a canoe on the Sambre and the Oise and on another at a donkey's tail over the hills and valleys of the

Cévennes. I well remember that when I read them
in their novelty, upwards of ten years ago, I seemed
to see the author, unknown as yet to fame, jump
before my eyes into a style. His steps in literature presumably had not been many ; yet he had
mastered his form—it had in these cases perhaps
more substance than his matter—and a singular air of
literary experience. It partly, though not completely,
explains the phenomenon, that he had already been
able to write the exquisite little story of *Will of
the Mill*, published previously to *An Inland Voyage*,
and republished to-day in the volume of *The Merry
Men*, for in *Will of the Mill* there is something exceedingly rare, poetical and unexpected, with that most
fascinating quality a work of imagination can have—
a dash of alternative mystery as to its meaning, an
air (the air of life itself), of half inviting, half defying
you to interpret. This brief but finished composition
stood in the same relation to the usual "magazine
story" that a glass of Johannisberg occupies to a
draught of table d'hôte *vin ordinaire*.

"One evening he asked the miller where the river went.
. . . 'It goes out into the lowlands, and waters the great corn
country, and runs through a sight of fine cities (so they say)
where kings live all alone in great palaces, with a sentry walking up and down before the door. And it goes under bridges,
with stone men upon them, looking down and smiling so curious
at the water, and living folks leaning on their elbows on the wall
and looking over too. And then it goes on and on, and down
through marshes and sands, until at last it falls into the sea,
where the ships are that bring tobacco and parrots from the
Indies.'"

It is impossible not to open one's eyes at such a paragraph as that, especially if one has taken a common texture for granted. Will of the Mill spends his life in the valley through which the river runs, and through which, year after year, post-chaises and waggons and pedestrians, and once an army, "horse and foot, cannon and tumbrel, drum and standard," take their way, in spite of the dreams he once had of seeing the mysterious world, and it is not till death comes that he goes on his travels. He ends by keeping an inn, where he converses with many more initiated spirits ; and though he is an amiable man he dies a bachelor, having broken off with more plainness than he would have used had he been less untravelled (of course he remains sadly provincial), his engagement to the parson's daughter. The story is in the happiest key and suggests all kinds of things : but what does it in particular represent ? The advantage of waiting, perhaps—the valuable truth that, one by one, we tide over our impatiences. There are sagacious people who hold that if one does not answer a letter it ends by answering itself. So the sub-title of Mr. Stevenson's tale might be "The Beauty of Procrastination." If you do not indulge your curiosities your slackness itself makes at last a kind of rich element, and it comes to very much the same thing in the end. When it came to the point poor Will had not even the curiosity to marry ; and the author leaves us in stimulating doubt as to whether he judges him too selfish or only too philosophic.

I find myself speaking of Mr. Stevenson's last volume (at the moment I write), before I have spoken, in any detail, of its predecessors : which I must let pass as a sign that I lack space for a full enumeration. I may mention two more of his productions as completing the list of those that have a personal reference. *The Silverado Squatters* describes a picnicking episode, undertaken on grounds of health, on a mountain-top in California; but this free sketch, which contains a hundred humorous touches, and in the figure of Irvine Lovelands one of Mr. Stevenson's most veracious portraits, is perhaps less vivid, as it is certainly less painful, than those other pages in which, some years ago, he commemorated the twelvemonth he spent in America—the history of a journey from New York to San Francisco in an emigrant train, performed as a sequel to a voyage across the Atlantic in the same severe conditions. He has never made his points better than in this half-humorous, half-tragical recital, nor given a more striking instance of his talent for reproducing the feeling of queer situations and contacts. It is much to be regretted that this little masterpiece had not been brought to light a second time, as also that he has not given the world (as I believe he came very near doing), his observations in the steerage of an Atlantic liner. If, as I say, our author has a taste for the impressions of Bohemia, he has been very consistent, and has not shrunk from going far afield in search of them. And as I have already been indiscreet, I may add that if it has been his fate to be converted in fact from the sardonic view of matrimony, this occurred under an influence which should have the particular sympathy of American readers. He went to California for his wife, and Mrs. Stevenson, as appears moreover by the title-page of his work, has had a hand—evidently a light and practised one—in *The Dynamiter*, the second series, characterised by a rich extravagance, of *The New Arabian Nights*. *The Silverado Squatters* is the history of a honeymoon, prosperous it would seem, putting Irvine Lovelands aside, save for the death of dog Chuchu " in his teens, after a life so shadowed and troubled, continually shaken with alarm and with the tear of elegant sentiment permanently in his eye."

Mr. Stevenson has a theory of composition in regard to the novel on which he is to be congratulated, as any positive and genuine conviction of this kind is vivifying so long as it is not narrow. The breath of the novelist's being is his liberty, and the incomparable virtue of the form he uses is that it lends itself to views innumerable and diverse, to every variety of illustration. There is certainly no other mould of so large a capacity. The doctrine of M. Zola himself, so jejune if literally taken, is fruitful, inasmuch as in practice he romantically departs from it. Mr. Stevenson does not need to depart, his individual taste being as much to pursue the romantic as his principle is to defend it. Fortunately, in

England to-day, it is not much attacked.   The
triumphs that are to be won in the portrayal of the
strange, the improbable, the heroic, especially as
these things shine from afar in the credulous eye of
youth, are his strongest, most constant incentive.
On one happy occasion, in relating the history of
Doctor Jekyll, he has seen them as they present themselves to a maturer vision.   *Doctor Jekyll* is not a
" boy's book," nor yet is *Prince Otto ;* the latter,
however, is not, like the former, an experiment in
mystification — it is, I think, more than anything
else, an experiment in style, conceived one summer's
day when the author had given the reins to his high
appreciation of Mr. George Meredith.   It is perhaps
the most literary of his works, but it is not the most
natural.   It is one of those coquetries, as we may
call them for want of a better word, which may be
observed in Mr. Stevenson's activity—a kind of artful
inconsequence.   It is easy to believe that if his
strength permitted him to be a more abundant writer
he would still more frequently play this eminently
literary trick—that of dodging off in a new direction
—upon those who might have fancied they knew all
about him.   I made the reflection, in speaking of
Will of the Mill, that there is a kind of anticipatory
malice in the subject of that fine story : as if the
writer had intended to say to his reader " You will
never guess, from the unction with which I describe
the life of a man who never stirred five miles from
home, that I am destined to make my greatest hits

in treating of the rovers of the deep." Even here,
however, the author's characteristic irony would have
come in ; for—the rare chances of life being what he
most keeps his eye on—the uncommon belongs as
much to the way the inquiring Will sticks to his
door-sill as to the incident, say, of John Silver and
his men, when they are dragging Jim Hawkins to his
doom, hearing in the still woods of Treasure Island
the strange hoot of the maroon.

The novelist who leaves the extraordinary out of
his account is liable to awkward confrontations, as
we are compelled to reflect in this age of newspapers
and of universal publicity. The next report of the
next divorce case (to give an instance) shall offer us
a picture of astounding combinations of circumstance
and behaviour, and the annals of any energetic race
are rich in curious anecdote and startling example.
That interesting compilation *Vicissitudes of Families*
is but a superficial record of strange accidents : the
family (taken of course in the long piece), is as a
general thing a catalogue of odd specimens and
tangled situations, and we must remember that the
most singular products are those which are not exhibited. Mr. Stevenson leaves so wide a margin for
the wonderful—it impinges with easy assurance
upon the text—that he escapes the danger of being
brought up by cases he has not allowed for. When
he allows for Mr. Hyde he allows for everything, and
one feels moreover that even if he did not wave so
gallantly the flag of the imaginative and contend

that the improbable is what has most character, he would still insist that we ought to make believe. He would say we ought to make believe that the extraordinary is the best part of life even if it were not, and to do so because the finest feelings—suspense, daring, decision, passion, curiosity, gallantry, eloquence, friendship—are involved in it, and it is of infinite importance that the tradition of these precious things should not perish. He would prefer, in a word, any day in the week, Alexandre Dumas to Honoré de Balzac, and it is indeed my impression that he prefers the author of *The Three Musketeers* to any novelist except Mr. George Meredith. I should go so far as to suspect that his ideal of the delightful work of fiction would be the adventures of Monte Cristo related by the author of *Richard Feverel*. There is some magnanimity in his esteem for Alexandre Dumas, inasmuch as in *Kidnapped* he has put into a fable worthy of that inventor a closeness of notation with which Dumas never had anything to do. He makes us say, Let the tradition live, by all means, since it was delightful; but at the same time he is the cause of our perceiving afresh that a tradition is kept alive only by something being added to it. In this particular case—in *Doctor Jekyll* and *Kidnapped*—Mr. Stevenson has added psychology.

The New Arabian Nights offer us, as the title indicates, the wonderful in the frankest, most delectable form. Partly extravagant and partly very specious, they are the result of a very happy idea, that of placing a series of adventures which are pure adventures in the setting of contemporary English life, and relating them in the placidly ingenuous tone of Scheherezade. This device is carried to perfection in *The Dynamiter*, where the manner takes on more of a kind of high-flown serenity in proportion as the incidents are more " steep." In this line *The Suicide Club* is Mr. Stevenson's greatest success, and the first two pages of it, not to mention others, live in the memory. For reasons which I am conscious of not being able to represent as sufficient, I find something ineffaceably impressive—something really haunting— in the incident of Prince Florizel and Colonel Geraldine, who, one evening in March, are " driven by a sharp fall of sleet into an Oyster Bar in the immediate neighbourhood of Leicester Square," and there have occasion to observe the entrance of a young man followed by a couple of commissionaires, each of whom carries a large dish of cream tarts under a cover—a young man who " pressed these confections on every one's acceptance with exaggerated courtesy." There is no effort at a picture here, but the imagination makes one of the lighted interior, the London sleet outside, the company that we guess, given the locality, and the strange politeness of the young man, leading on to circumstances stranger still. This is what may be called putting one in the mood for a story. But Mr. Stevenson's most brilliant stroke of that kind is the opening episode of *Treasure Island*, the arrival of the brown old seaman with the sabre-cut at the " Admiral Benbow," and the advent, not long after, of the blind sailor, with a green shade over his eyes, who comes tapping down the road, in quest of him, with his stick. *Treasure Island* is a " boy's book " in the sense that it embodies a boy's vision of the extraordinary, but it is unique in this, and calculated to fascinate the weary mind of experience, that what we see in it is not only the ideal fable but, as part and parcel of that, as it were, the young reader himself and his state of mind: we seem to read it over his shoulder, with an arm around his neck.   It is all as perfect as a well-played boy's game, and nothing can exceed the spirit and skill, the humour and the open-air feeling with which the thing is kept at the palpitating pitch.   It is not only a record of queer chances, but a study of young feelings : there is a moral side in it, and the figures are not puppets with vague faces.   If Jim Hawkins illustrates successful daring, he does so with a delightful rosy good-boyishness and a conscious, modest liability to error.   His luck is tremendous, but it does not make him proud, and his manner is refreshingly provincial and human.   So is that, even more, of the admirable John Silver, one of the most picturesque and indeed in every way most genially presented villains in the whole literature of romance. He has a singularly distinct and expressive countenance, which of course turns out to be a grimacing mask.   Never was a mask more knowingly, vividly painted.   *Treasure Island* will surely become—it must already have become and will remain—in its way a classic : thanks to this indescribable mixture of the prodigious and the human, of surprising coincidences and familiar feelings. The language in which Mr. Stevenson has chosen to tell his story is an admirable vehicle for these feelings : with its humorous braveries and quaintnesses, its echoes of old ballads and yarns, it touches all kinds of sympathetic chords.

Is *Doctor Jekyll and Mr. Hyde* a work of high philosophic intention, or simply the most ingenious and irresponsible of fictions ? It has the stamp of a really imaginative production, that we may take it in different ways ; but I suppose it would generally be called the most serious of the author's tales. It deals with the relation of the baser parts of man to his nobler, of the capacity for evil that exists in the most generous natures ; and it expresses these things in a fable which is a wonderfully happy invention. The subject is endlessly interesting, and rich in all sorts of provocation, and Mr. Stevenson is to be congratulated on having touched the core of it. I may do him injustice, but it is, however, here, not the profundity of the idea which strikes me so much as the art of the presentation—the extremely successful form. There is a genuine feeling for the perpetual moral question, a fresh sense of the difficulty of being good and the brutishness of being bad ; but what there is above all is a singular ability in holding the interest. I confess that that, to my sense, is the most edifying thing in the short, rapid, concentrated story, which

is really a masterpiece of concision. There is some·
thing almost impertinent in the way, as I have
noticed, in which Mr. Stevenson achieves his best
effects without the aid of the ladies, and *Doctor Jekyll*
is a capital example of his heartless independence.
It is usually supposed that a truly poignant impression cannot be made without them, but in the
drama of Mr. Hyde's fatal ascendency they remain
altogether in the wing. It is very obvious—I do not
say it cynically—that they must have played an
important part in his development. The gruesome
tone of the tale is, no doubt, deepened by their
absence : it is like the late afternoon light of a foggy
winter Sunday, when even inanimate objects have a
kind of wicked look. I remember few situations in
the pages of mystifying fiction more to the purpose than the episode of Mr. Utterson's going to
Doctor Jekyll's to confer with the butler when the
Doctor is locked up in his laboratory, and the old
servant, whose sagacity has hitherto encountered
successfully the problems of the sideboard and the
pantry, confesses that this time he is utterly baffled.
The way the two men, at the door of the laboratory,
discuss the identity of the mysterious personage
inside, who has revealed himself in two or three
inhuman glimpses to Poole, has those touches of
which irresistible shudders are made. The butler's
theory is that his master has been murdered, and that
the murderer is in the room, personating him with a
sort of clumsy diabolism. " Well, when that masked

thing like a monkey jumped from among the chemicals
and whipped into the cabinet, it went down my spine
like ice." That is the effect upon the reader of most
of the story. I say of most rather than of all,
because the ice rather melts in the sequel, and I have
some difficulty in accepting the business of the
powders, which seems to me too explicit and explanatory. The powders constitute the machinery
of the transformation, and it will probably have
struck many readers that this uncanny process would
be more conceivable (so far as one may speak of the
conceivable in such a case), if the author had not
made it so definite.

I have left Mr. Stevenson's best book to the last,
as it is also the last he has given (at the present
speaking) to the public—the tales comprising *The
Merry Men* having already appeared ; but I find that
on the way I have anticipated some of the remarks
that I had intended to make about it. That which
is most to the point is that there are parts of it so
fine as to suggest that the author's talent has taken
a fresh start, various as have been the impulses in
which it had already indulged, and serious the
hindrances among which it is condemned to exert
itself. There would have been a kind of perverse
humility in his keeping up the fiction that a production so literary as *Kidnapped* is addressed to imma-
ture minds, and, though it was originally given to
the world, I believe, in a " boy's paper," the story
embraces every occasion that it meets to satisfy the

higher criticism.   It has two weak spots, which need
simply to be mentioned.   The cruel and miserly
uncle, in the first chapters, is rather in the tone of
superseded tradition, and the tricks he plays upon
his ingenuous nephew are a little like those of
country conjurers.   In these pages we feel that Mr.
Stevenson is thinking too much of what a "boy's
paper" is expected to contain.   Then the history
stops without ending, as it were; but I think I may
add that this accident speaks for itself.   Mr. Stevenson has often to lay down his pen for reasons that
have nothing to do with the failure of inspiration,
and the last page of David Balfour's adventures is
an honourable plea for indulgence.   The remaining
five-sixths of the book deserve to stand by *Henry
Esmond* as a fictive autobiography in archaic form.
The author's sense of the English idiom of the last
century, and still more of the Scotch, has enabled
him to give a gallant companion to Thackeray's *tour
de force*.   The life, the humour, the colour of the
central portions of *Kidnapped* have a singular pictorial virtue: these passages read like a series of
inspired footnotes on some historic page.   The
charm of the most romantic episode in the world,
though perhaps it would be hard to say why it is
the most romantic, when it was associated with
so much stupidity, is over the whole business, and
the forlorn hope of the Stuarts is revived for us
without evoking satiety.   There could be no better
instance of the author's talent for seeing the familiar

in the heroic, and reducing the extravagant to plausible detail, than the description of Alan Breck's defence in the cabin of the ship and the really magnificent chapters of "The Flight in the Heather." Mr. Stevenson has in a high degree (and doubtless for good reasons of his own) what may be called the imagination of physical states, and this has enabled him to arrive at a wonderfully exact translation of the miseries of his panting Lowland hero, dragged for days and nights over hill and dale, through bog and thicket, without meat or drink or rest, at the tail of an Homeric Highlander. The great superiority of the book resides to my mind, however, in the fact that it puts two characters on their feet with admirable rectitude. I have paid my tribute to Alan Breck, and I can only repeat that he is a masterpiece. It is interesting to observe that though the man is extravagant, the author's touch exaggerates nothing : it is throughout of the most truthful, genial, ironical kind ; full of penetration, but with none of the grossness of moralising satire. The figure is a genuine study, and nothing can be more charming than the way Mr. Stevenson both sees through it and admires it. Shall I say that he sees through David Balfour ? This would be perhaps to underestimate the density of that medium. Beautiful, at any rate, is the expression which this unfortunate though circumspect youth gives to those qualities which combine to excite our respect and our objurgation in the Scottish character. Such a scene as the episode of the quarrel of the two men on the mountain-side is a real stroke of genius, and has the very logic and rhythm of life ; a quarrel which we feel to be inevitable, though it is about nothing, or almost nothing, and which springs from exasperated nerves and the simple shock of temperaments. The author's vision of it has a profundity which goes deeper, I think, than *Doctor Jekyll*. I know of few better examples of the way genius has ever a surprise in its pocket—keeps an ace, as it were, up its sleeve. And in this case it endears itself to us by making us reflect that such a passage as the one I speak of is in fact a signal proof of what the novel can do at its best, and what nothing else can do so well. In the presence of this sort of success we perceive its immense value. It is capable of a rare transparency— it can illustrate human affairs in cases so delicate and complicated that any other vehicle would be clumsy. To those who love the art that Mr. Stevenson practises he will appear, in pointing this incidental moral, not only to have won a particular triumph, but to have given a delightful pledge.

1887.

VI

MISS WOOLSON

MISS WOOLSON

FLOODED as we have been in these latter days with
copious discussion as to the admission of women to
various offices, colleges, functions, and privileges,
singularly little attention has been paid, by themselves at least, to the fact that in one highly important
department of human affairs their cause is already
gained—gained in such a way as to deprive them
largely of their ground, formerly so substantial, for
complaining of the intolerance of man.   In America,
in England, to-day, it is no longer a question of their
admission into the world of literature : they are there
in force ; they have been admitted, with all the
honours, on a perfectly equal footing.   In America, at
least, one feels tempted at moments to exclaim that
they are in themselves the world of literature.   In
Germany and in France, in this line of production,
their presence is less to be perceived.   To speak only
of the latter country, France has brought forth in the
persons of Madame de Sévigné, Madame de Staël, and
Madame Sand, three female writers of the first rank,
without counting a hundred ladies to whom we owe

charming memoirs and volumes of reminiscence ; but
in the table of contents of the *Revue des Deux Mondes*,
that epitome of the literary movement (as regards
everything, at least, but the famous doctrine, in fiction,
of "naturalism"), it is rare to encounter the name of a
female contributor. The covers of American and English periodicals tell a different story ; in these monthly
joints of the ladder of fame the ladies stand as thick
as on the staircase at a crowded evening party.

There are, of course, two points of view from
which this free possession of the public ear may be considered—as regards its effect upon the life of women,
and as regards its effect upon literature. I hasten to
add that I do not propose to consider either, and I
touch on the general fact simply because the writer
whose name I have placed at the head of these
remarks happens to be a striking illustration of it.
The work of Miss Constance Fenimore Woolson is
an excellent example of the way the door stands
open between the personal life of American women
and the immeasurable world of print, and what makes
it so is the particular quality that this work happens
to possess. It breathes a spirit singularly and essentially conservative—the sort of spirit which, but for
a special indication pointing the other way, would in
advance seem most to oppose itself to the introduction into the feminine lot of new and complicating
elements. Miss Woolson evidently thinks that lot
sufficiently complicated, with the sensibilities which
even in primitive ages women were acknowledged to

possess ; fenced in by the old disabilities and prejudices, they seem to her to have been by their very
nature only too much exposed, and it would never
occur to her to lend her voice to the plea for further
exposure—for a revolution which should place her
sex in the thick of the struggle for power. She sees
it in preference surrounded certainly by plenty of
doors and windows (she has not, I take it, a love of
bolts and Oriental shutters), but distinctly on the
private side of that somewhat evasive and exceedingly shifting line which divides human affairs into
the profane and the sacred. Such is the turn of
mind of the author of *Rodman the Keeper* and *East
Angels*, and if it has not prevented her from writing
books, from competing for the literary laurel, this is
a proof of the strength of the current which to-day
carries both sexes alike to that mode of expression.

Miss Woolson's first productions were two collections of short tales, published in 1875 and 1880, and
entitled respectively *Castle Nowhere* and *Rodman the
Keeper*. I may not profess an acquaintance with the
former of these volumes, but the latter is full of interesting artistic work. Miss Woolson has done nothing
better than the best pages in this succession of careful, strenuous studies of certain aspects of life, after
the war, in Florida, Georgia and the Carolinas. As
the fruit of a remarkable minuteness of observation
and tenderness of feeling on the part of one who
evidently did not glance and pass, but lingered and
analysed, they have a high value, especially when

regarded in the light of the *voicelessness* of the con-
quered and reconstructed South.   Miss Woolson
strikes the reader as having a compassionate sense of
this pathetic dumbness—having perceived that no
social revolution of equal magnitude had ever reflected
itself so little in literature, remained so unrecorded,
so unpainted and unsung.   She has attempted to
give an impression of this circumstance, among others,
and a sympathy altogether feminine has guided her
pen.   She loves the whole region, and no daughter
of the land could have handled its peculiarities more
indulgently, or communicated to us more of the sense
of close observation and intimate knowledge.   Nevertheless it must be confessed that the picture, on the
whole, is a picture of dreariness—of impressions that
may have been gathered in the course of lonely
afternoon walks at the end of hot days, when the
sunset was wan, on the edge of rice-fields, dismal
swamps, and other brackish inlets.   The author is to
be congratulated in so far as such expeditions may
have been the source of her singularly exact familiarity with the "natural objects" of the region, including the negro of reality.   She knows every plant and
flower, every vague odour and sound, the song and
flight of every bird, every tint of the sky and murmur
of the forest, and she has noted scientifically the dialect
of the freedmen.   It is not too much to say that the
negroes in *Rodman the Keeper* and in *East Angels* are a
careful philological study, and that if Miss Woolson
preceded Uncle Remus by a considerable interval, she

may have the credit of the initiative—of having been the first to take their words straight from their lips.

No doubt that if in *East Angels*, as well as in the volume of tales, the sadness of Miss Woolson's South is more striking than its high spirits, this is owing somewhat to the author's taste in the way of subject and situation, and especially to her predilection for cases of heroic sacrifice—sacrifice sometimes unsuspected and always unappreciated. She is fond of irretrievable personal failures, of people who have had to give up even the memory of happiness, who love and suffer in silence, and minister in secret to the happiness of those who look over their heads. She is interested in general in secret histories, in the "inner life" of the weak, the superfluous, the disappointed, the bereaved, the unmarried. She believes in personal renunciation, in its frequency as well as its beauty. It plays a prominent part in each of her novels, especially in the last two, and the interest of *East Angels* at least is largely owing to her success in having made an extreme case of the virtue in question credible to the reader. Is it because this element is weaker in *Anne*, which was published in 1882, that *Anne* strikes me as the least happily composed of the author's works? The early chapters are charming and full of promise, but the story wanders away from them, and the pledge is not taken up. The reader has built great hopes upon Tita, but Tita vanishes into the vague, after putting him out of countenance by an infant marriage—an accident in regard to which, on the whole, throughout her stories, Miss Woolson shows perhaps an excessive indulgence. She likes the unmarried, as I have mentioned, but she likes marriages even better, and also sometimes hurries them forward in advance of the reader's exaction. The only complaint it would occur to me to make of *East Angels* is that Garda Thorne, whom we cannot think of as anything but a little girl, discounts the projects we have formed for her by marrying twice ; and somehow the case is not bettered by the fact that nothing is more natural than that she should marry twice, unless it be that she should marry three times. We have perceived her, after all, from the first, to be peculiarly adapted to a succession of pretty widowhoods.

For the Major has an idea, a little fantastic perhaps, but eminently definite. This idea is the secret effort of an elderly woman to appear really as young to her husband as (owing to peculiar circumstances) he believed her to be when he married her. Nature helps her (she happens to preserve, late in life, the look of comparative youth), and art helps nature, and her husband's illusions, fostered by failing health and a weakened brain, help them both, so that she is able to keep on the mask till his death, when she pulls it off with a passionate cry of relief—ventures at last, gives herself the luxury, to be old. The sacrifice in this case has been the sacrifice of the maternal instinct, she having had a son, now a man grown, by a former marriage, who reappears after unsuccessful wanderings in far lands, and whom she may not permit herself openly to recognise. The sacrificial attitude is indeed repeated on the part of her step-daughter, who, being at last taken into Madam Carroll's confidence, suffers the young man—a shabby, compromising, inglorious acquaintance—to pass for her lover, thereby discrediting herself almost fatally (till the situation is straightened out), with the Rev. Frederick Owen, who has really been marked out by Providence for the character, and who cannot explain on any comfortable hypothesis her relations with the mysterious Bohemian. Miss Woolson's women in general are capable of these refinements of devotion and exaltations of conscience, and she has a singular talent for making our sympathies go with them. The conception of Madam Carroll is highly ingenious and original, and the small stippled portrait has a real fascination. It is the first time that a woman has been represented as painting her face, dyeing her hair, and "dressing young," out of tenderness for another : the effort usually has its source in tenderness for herself. But Miss Woolson has done nothing of a neater execution than this fanciful figure of the little ringleted, white-frocked, falsely juvenile lady, who has the toilet-table of an actress and the conscience of a Puritan.

The author likes a glamour, and by minute touches and gentle, conciliatory arts, she usually succeeds in producing a valid one. If I had more space I should like to count over these cumulative strokes, in which a delicate manipulation of the real is mingled with

an occasionally frank appeal to the romantic muse.
But I can only mention two of the most obvious:
one the frequency of her reference to the episcopal
church as an institution giving a tone to American
life (the sort of tone which it is usually assumed
that we must seek in civilisations more permeated
with ecclesiasticism); the other her fondness for family
histories—for the idea of perpetuation of race, especially in the backward direction. I hasten to add
that there is nothing of the crudity of sectarianism
in the former of these manifestations, or of the
dreariness of the purely genealogical passion in the
latter; but none the less is it clear that Miss Woolson likes little country churches that are dedicated
to saints not vulgarised by too much notoriety,
that are dressed with greenery (and would be with
holly if there were any), at Christmas and Easter;
that have "rectors," well connected, who are properly
garmented, and organists, slightly deformed if possible, and addicted to playing Gregorian chants in
the twilight, who are adequately artistic; likes also
generations that have a pleasant consciousness of a
few warm generations behind them, screening them
in from too bleak a past, from vulgar draughts in
the rear. I know not whether for the most part we
are either so Anglican or so long-descended as in
Miss Woolson's pages we strike ourselves as being,
but it is certain that as we read we protest but little
against the soft impeachment. She represents us at
least as we should like to be, and she does so with

such discretion and taste that we have no fear of incurring ridicule by assent.   She has a high sense of
the picturesque ; she cannot get on without a social
atmosphere.   Once, I think, she has looked for these
things in the wrong place—at the country boarding-
house denominated Caryl's, in *Anne*, where there
must have been flies and grease in the dining-room,
and the ladies must have been overdressed ; but as
a general thing her quest is remarkably happy.   She
stays at home, and yet gives us a sense of being
"abroad" ; she has a remarkable faculty of making
the new world seem ancient.   She succeeds in repre
senting Far Edgerly, the mountain village in *For the
Major*, as bathed in the precious medium I speak of.
Where is it meant to be, and where was the place
that gave her the pattern of it ?   We gather vaguely,
though there are no negroes, that it is in the south ;
but this, after all, is a tolerably indefinite part
of the United States.   It is somewhere in the midst
of forests, and yet it has as many idiosyncrasies as
Mrs. Gaskell's *Cranford*, with added possibilities of
the pathetic and the tragic.   What new town is so
composite ?   What composite town is so new ?   Miss
Woolson anticipates these questions ; that is she prevents us from asking them : we swallow Far Edgerly
whole, or say at most, with a sigh, that if it couldn't
have been like that it certainly ought to have been.

It is, however, in *East Angels* that she has been
most successful in this feat of evoking a local tone,
and this is a part of the general superiority of that

very interesting work, which to my mind represents
a long stride of her talent, and has more than the
value of all else she has done.   In *East Angels* the
attempt to create an atmosphere has had, to a considerable degree, the benefit of the actual quality of
things in the warm, rank peninsula which she has
studied so exhaustively and loves so well.   Miss
Woolson found a tone in the air of Florida, but it is
not too much to say that she has left it still more
agreeably rich — converted it into a fine golden
haze.   Wonderful is the tact with which she has
pressed it into the service of her story, draped the
bare spots of the scene with it, and hung it there
half as a curtain and half as a background.   *East
Angels* is a performance which does Miss Woolson
the highest honour, and if her talent is capable, in
another novel, of making an advance equal to that
represented by this work in relation to its predecessors, she will have made a· substantial contribution to
our new literature of fiction.   Long, comprehensive,
copious, still more elaborate than her other elabor-
ations, *East Angels* presents the interest of a large
and well-founded scheme.   The result is not flawless
at every point, but the undertaking is of a fine, high
kind, and, for the most part, the effect produced is
thoroughly worthy of it.   The author has, in other
words, proposed to give us the complete natural
history, as it were, of a group of persons collected,
in a complicated relationship, in a little winter-city
on a southern shore, and she has expended on her

subject stores of just observation and an infinite deal
of the true historical spirit. How much of this
spirit and of artistic feeling there is in the book, only
an attentive perusal will reveal. The central situation is a very interesting one, and is triumphantly
treated, but I confess that what is most substantial
to me in the book is the writer's general conception
of her task, her general attitude of watching life,
waiting upon it and trying to catch it in the fact. I
know not what theories she may hold in relation to
all this business, to what camp or league she may
belong; my impression indeed would be that she is
perfectly free—that she considers that though camps
and leagues may be useful organisations for looking
for the truth, it is not in their own bosom that it is
usually to be found. However this may be, it is
striking that, artistically, she has had a fruitful instinct in seeing the novel as a picture of the actual,
of the characteristic—a study of human types and
passions, of the evolution of personal relations. In
East Angels she has gone much farther in this direction than in either of her other novels.

The book has, to my sense, two defects, which I
may as well mention at once—two which are perhaps, however, but different faces of the same. One
is that the group on which she has bent her lens
strikes us as too detached, too isolated, too much on
a desert island. Its different members go to and
fro a good deal, to New York and to Europe, but
they have a certain shipwrecked air, as of extreme

dependence on each other, though surrounded with every convenience. The other fault is that the famous "tender sentiment" usurps among them a place even greater perhaps than that which it holds in life, great as the latter very admittedly is. I spoke just now of their complicated relationships, but the complications are almost exclusively the complications of love. Our impression is of sky and sand—the sky of azure, the sand of silver—and between them, conspicuous, immense, against the low horizon, the question of engagement and marriage. I must add that I do not mean to imply that this question is not, in the very nature of things, at any time and in any place, immense, or that in a novel it should be expected to lose its magnitude. I take it indeed that on such a simple shore as Miss Woolson has described, love (with the passions that flow from it), is almost inevitably the subject, and that the perspective is not really false. It is not that the people are represented as hanging together by that cord to an abnormal degree, but that, there being few accessories and circumstances, there is no tangle and overgrowth to disguise the effect. It is a question of effect, but it is characteristic of the feminine, as distinguished from the masculine hand, that in any portrait of a corner of human affairs the particular effect produced in *East Angels*, that of what we used to call the love-story, will be the dominant one. The love-story is a composition in which the elements are distributed in a particular proportion, and every tale

which contains a great deal of love has not necessarily a title to the name. That title depends not
upon how much love there may be, but upon how
little of other things. In novels by men other
things are there to a greater or less degree, and I
therefore doubt whether a man may be said ever to
have produced a work exactly belonging to the class
in question. In men's novels, even of the simplest
strain, there are still other references and other explanations; in women's, when they are of the category
to which I allude, there are none but that one. And
there is certainly much to be said for it.

In *East Angels* the sacrifice, as all Miss Woolson's
readers know, is the great sacrifice of Margaret
Harold, who immolates herself—there is no other
word—deliberately, completely, and repeatedly, to a
husband whose behaviour may as distinctly be held
to have absolved her. The problem was a very
interesting one, and worthy to challenge a superior
talent—that of making real and natural a transcendent, exceptional act, representing a case in which the
sense of duty is raised to exaltation. What makes
Margaret Harold's behaviour exceptional and transcendent is that, in order to render the barrier between
herself and the man who loves her, and whom she
loves, absolutely insurmountable, she does her best to
bring about his marriage, endeavours to put another
woman into the frame of mind to respond to him in
the event (possible, as she is a woman whom he has
once appeared to love) of his attempting to console

himself for a bitter failure.   The care, the ingenuity,
the precautions the author has exhibited, to make us
accept Mrs. Harold in her integrity, are perceptible on
every page, and they leave us finally no alternative
but to accept her; she remains exalted, but she
remains at the same time thoroughly sound.   For it
is not a simple question of cleverness of detail, but
a question of the larger sort of imagination, and
Margaret Harold would have halted considerably if
her creator had not taken the supreme precaution of
all, and conceived her from the germ as capable of a
certain heroism—of clinging at the cost of a grave
personal loss to an idea which she believes to be a
high one, and taking such a fancy to it that she endeavours to paint it, by a refinement of magnanimity,
with still richer hues.   She is a picture, not of a
woman indulging in a great spasmodic flight or moral
tour de force, but of a nature bent upon looking at life
from a high point of view, an attitude in which there
is nothing abnormal, and which the author illustrates,
as it were, by a test case.   She has drawn Margaret
with so close and firm and living a line that she seems
to put us in the quandary, if we repudiate her, of deny-
ing that a woman *may* look at life from a high point of
view. She seems to say to us: "Are there distinguished
natures, or are there not ?   Very well, if there are,
that's what they can do—they can try and provide for
the happiness of others (when they adore them) even
to their own injury."   And we feel that we wish to be
the first to agree that there *are* distinguished natures.

Garda Thorne is the next best thing in the book
to Margaret, and she is indeed equally good in this,
that she is conceived with an equal clearness. But
Margaret produces her impression upon us by moving
before us and doing certain things, whereas Garda is
more explained, or rather she explains herself more,
tells us more about herself. She says somewhere, or
some one says of her, that she doesn't narrate, but in
fact she does narrate a good deal, for the purpose of
making the reader understand her. This the reader
does, very constantly, and Garda is a brilliant success.
I must not, however, touch upon the different parts
of *East Angels*, because in a work of so much patience
and conscience a single example carries us too far. I
will only add that in three places in especial the
author has been so well inspired as to give a definite
pledge of high accomplishment in the future. One of
these salient passages is the description of the closing
days of Mrs. Thorne, the little starved yet ardent
daughter of the Puritans, who has been condemned
to spend her life in the land of the relaxed, and who,
before she dies, pours out her accumulations of bitterness—relieves herself in a passionate confession of
everything she has suffered and missed, of how she
has hated the very skies and fragrances of Florida,
even when, as a consistent Christian, thankful for
every mercy, she has pretended most to appreciate
them. Mrs. Thorne is the pathetic, tragic form of
the type of which Mrs. Stowe's Miss Ophelia was the
comic. In almost all of Miss Woolson's stories the

New England woman is represented as regretting the
wholesome austerities of the region of her birth. She
reverts to them, in solemn hours, even when, like
Mrs. Thorne, she may appear for a time to have been
converted to mild winters. Remarkably fine is the
account of the expedition undertaken by Margaret
Harold and Evert Winthrop to look for Lanse in the
forest, when they believe him, or his wife thinks there
may be reason to believe him, to have been lost and
overtaken by a storm. The picture of their paddling
the boat by torchlight into the reaches of the river,
more or less smothered in the pestilent jungle, with
the personal drama, in the unnatural place, reaching
an acute stage between them—this whole episode is
in a high degree vivid, strange, and powerful.
Lastly, Miss Woolson has risen altogether to the
occasion in the scene in which Margaret " has it out,"
as it were, with Evert Winthrop, parts from him and,
leaving him baffled and unsurpassably sore, gives him
the measure of her determination to accept the necessity of her fate. These three episodes are not alike,
yet they have, in the high finish of Miss Woolson's
treatment of them, a family resemblance. Moreover,
they all have the stamp which I spoke of at first—
the stamp of the author's conservative feeling, the
implication that for her the life of a woman is essentially an affair of private relations.

1887.

VII

ALPHONSE DAUDET

ALPHONSE DAUDET

I

" THE novel of manners grows thick in England, and there are many reasons for it. In the first place it was born there, and a plant always flourishes in its own country." So wrote M. Taine, the French critic, many years ago. But those were the years of Dickens and Thackeray (as a prelude to a study of the latter of whom the remark was made) ; and the branch of literature mentioned by M. Taine has no longer, in the soil of our English-speaking genius, so strong a vitality. The French may bear the palm to-day in the representation of manners by the aid of fiction. Formerly, it was possible to oppose Balzac and Madame Sand to Dickens and Thackeray ; but at present we have no one, either in England or in America, to oppose to Alphonse Daudet. The appearance of a new novel by this admirable genius is to my mind the most delightful literary event that can occur just now ; in other words Alphonse Daudet is at the head of his profession. I say of his profes-

sion advisedly, for he belongs to our modern class of
trained men of letters ; he is not an occasional or a
desultory poet ; he is a novelist to his finger-tips—
a soldier in the great army of constant producers.
But such as he is, he is a master of his art, and I
may as well say definitely that if I attempt to sketch
in a few pages his literary countenance, it will be
found that the portrait is from the hand of an admirer.   We most of us feel that among the artists
of our day certain talents have more to say to us and
others less ; we have our favourites, and we have our
objects of indifference.   The writer of these remarks
has always had a sympathy for the author of the
Lettres de mon Moulin ; he began to read his novels
with a prejudice in their favour.   This prejudice
sprang from the Letters aforesaid, which do not constitute a novel, but a volume of the lightest and
briefest tales.   They had, to my mind, an extraordinary charm ; they put me quite on the side of
Alphonse Daudet, whatever he might do in the
future.   One of the first things he did was to publish the history of *Fromont Jeune et Risler Aîné.*   It
is true that this work did not give me the pleasure
that some of its successors have done, and though it
has been crowned by the French Academy, I still
think it weaker than *Les Rois en Exil* and *Numa
Roumestan.*   But I liked it better on a second reading than on a first ; it contains some delightful
things.   After that came *Jack* and *Le Nabab,* and
the two novels I have just mentioned, and that

curious and interesting tale of *L'Evangéliste*, which appeared a few months since, and which proves that the author's genius, though on the whole he has pressed it hard, is still nervous, fresh, and young. Each of these things has been better than the last, with the exception, perhaps, of *L'Evangéliste*, which, to my taste, is not superior to *Numa Roumestan*. *Numa Roumestan* is a masterpiece ; it is really a perfect work ; it has no weakness, no roughness ; it is a compact and harmonious whole. Daudet's other works have had their inequalities, their infirmities, certain places where, if you tapped them, they sounded hollow. His danger has always been a perceptible tendency to the factitious ; sometimes he has fallen into the trap laid for him by a taste for superficial effects. In *Fromont Jeune*, for instance, it seems to me difficult to care much for the horrid little heroine herself, carefully as she is studied. She has been pursued, but she has not been caught, for she is not interesting (even for a *coquine*), not even human. She is a mechanical doll, with nothing for the imagination to take hold of. She is one more proof of the fact that it is difficult to give the air of consistency to vanity and depravity, though the portraiture of the vicious side of life would seem, from the pictorial point of view, to offer such attractions. The reader's quarrel with Sidonie Chèbe is not that she is bad, but that she is not *felt*, as the æsthetic people say. In *Jack* the hollow spot, as I have called it, is the episode of Doctor Rivals and his daughter Cécile, which reminds us of the more genial parts of Dickens. It is perhaps because to us readers of English speech the figure of the young girl, in a French novel, is almost always wanting in reality—seems to be thin and conventional; in any case poor Jack's love-affair, at the end of the book, does not produce the illusion of the rest of his touching history. In *Le Nabab* this artificial element is very considerable ; it centres about the figure of Paul de Géry and embraces the whole group of M. Joyeuse and his blooming daughters, with their pretty attitudes—taking in also the very shadowy André Maranne, so touchingly re-united to his mother, who had lived for ten years with an Irish doctor to whom she was not married. In *Les Rois en Exil*, Tom Lévis and the diabolical Séphora seem to me purely fanciful creations, without any relation to reality ; they are the inferior part of the book. They are composed by a master of composition, and the comedian Tom is described with immense spirit, an art which speaks volumes as to a certain sort of Parisian initiation. But if this artistic and malignant couple are very clever water-colour, they are not really humanity. Ruffians and rascals have a certain moral nature, as well as the better-behaved ; but in the case I have mentioned M. Daudet fails to put his finger upon it. The same with Madame Autheman, the evil genius of poor Eline Ebsen, in the *L'Evangéliste*. She seems to me terribly, almost grotesquely, void. She is an elaborate portrait of

a fanatic of Protestantism, a bigot to the point of
monstrosity, cold-blooded, implacable, cruel. The
figure is painted with Alphonse Daudet's inimitable
art; no one that handles the pen to-day is such a
pictorial artist as he. But Madame Autheman
strikes me as quite automatic; psychologically she
is a blank. One does not see the operation of her
character. She must have had a soul, and a very
curious one. It was a great opportunity for a piece
of spiritual portraiture; but we know nothing about
Madame Autheman's inner springs, and I think we
fail to believe in her. I should go so far as to say
that we get little more of an inside view, as the
phrase is, of Eline Ebsen; we are not shown the
spiritual steps by which she went over to the enemy
—vividly, admirably as the outward signs and consequences of this disaster are depicted. The logic of
the matter is absent in both cases, and it takes all
the magic of the author's legerdemain to prevent us
from missing it. These things, however, are excep-
tions, and the tissue of each of his novels is, for all
the rest, really pure gold. No one has such grace,
such lightness and brilliancy of execution; it is a
fascination to see him at work. The beauty of *Numa
Roumestan* is that it has no hollow places; the idea
and the picture melt everywhere into one. Emile
Zola, criticising the work in a very friendly spirit,
speaks of the episode of Hortense Le Quesnoy and
the Provençal *tambourinaire* as a false note, and declares that it wounds his sense of delicacy. Valma-

jour is a peasant of the south of France; he is young,
handsome, wears a costume, and is a master of the
rustic fife and tambourine—instruments that are much
appreciated in his part of the country.   Mademoiselle
Le Quesnoy, living in Paris, daughter of a distinguished member of the French judiciary—"le premier
magistrat de France "—young, charming, imaginative,
romantic, marked out for a malady of the chest, and
with a certain innocent perversity of mind, sees him
play before an applauding crowd in the old Roman
arena at Nîmes, and forthwith conceives a secret, a
singular but not, under the circumstances, an absolutely unnatural passion for him.   He comes up to
Paris to seek his fortune at the " variety " theatres,
where his feeble and primitive music quite fails to
excite enthusiasm.   The young girl, reckless and
impulsive, and full of sympathy with his mortifica-
tion, writes him in three words (upon one of her
little photographs) an assurance of her devotion ; and
this innocent missive, falling soon into the hands of
his rapacious and exasperated sister (a wonderful
figure, one of the most living that has ever come
from Daudet's pen), becomes a source of infinite
alarm to the family of Mademoiselle Le Quesnoy,
who see her compromised, calumniated and black-
mailed, and finally of complete humiliation to poor
Hortense herself, now fallen into a rapid consumption,
and cured of her foolish infatuation by a nearer view
of the vain and ignorant Valmajour.   An agent of the
family recovers the photograph (with the aid of ten

thousand francs), and the young girl, with the bitter taste of her disappointment still in her soul, dies in her flower.

This little story, as I say, is very shocking to M. Zola, who cites it as an example of the folly of a departure from consistent realism. What is observed, says M. Zola, on the whole very justly, is strong; what is invented is always weak, especially what is invented to please the ladies. "See in this case," he writes, " all the misery of invented episodes. This love of Hortense, with which the author has doubtless wished to give the impression of something touching, produces a discomfort, as if it were a violation of nature. It is therefore the pages written for the ladies that are repulsive—even to a man accustomed to the saddest dissections of the human corpse." I am not of M. Zola's opinion—delightful as it would be to be of that opinion when M. Zola's sense of propriety is ruffled. The incident of Hortense and Valmajour is not (to my sense) a blot upon *Numa Roumestan ;* on the contrary, it is perfectly conceivable, and is treated with admirable delicacy. "This romantic stuff," says M. Zola, elsewhere, "is as painful as a pollution. That a young girl should lose her head over a tenor, that may be explained, for she loves the operatic personage in the interpreter. She has before her a young man sharpened and refined by life, elegant, having at least certain appearances of talent and intelligence. But this tambourinist, with his drum and penny-whistle, this village dandy, a poor devil who doesn't even know how to speak! No, life has not such cruelties as that, I protest, I who certainly, as a general thing, am not accustomed to give ground before human aberrations!" This objection was worth making; but I should look at the matter in another way. It seems to me much more natural that a girl of the temper and breeding that M. Daudet has described should take a momentary fancy to a prepossessing young rustic, bronzed by the sun of Provence (even if it be conceded that his soul was vulgar), than that she should fasten her affections upon a "lyric artist," suspected of pomatum and paint, and illuminated by the footlights. These are points which it is vain to discuss, however, both because they are delicate and because they are details. I have come so far simply from a desire to justify my high admiration of *Numa Roumestan.* But Emile Zola, again, has expressed this feeling more felicitously than I can hope to do. "This, moreover, is a very slight blemish in a work which I regard as one of those, of all Daudet's productions, that is most personal to himself. He has put his whole nature into it, helped by his southern temperament, having only to make large draughts upon his innermost recollections and sensations. I do not think that he has hitherto reached such an intensity either of irony or of geniality. . . . Happy the books which arrive in this way, at the hour of the complete maturity of a talent! They are simply the widest unfolding of an artist's nature; they have

in happy equilibrium the qualities of observation and
the qualities of style. For Alphonse Daudet *Numa
Roumestan* will mark this interfusion of a temperament and a subject that are made for each other, the
perfect plenitude of a work which the writer exactly
fills."

II

As I say, however, these are details, and I have
touched them prematurely. Alphonse Daudet is a
charmer, and the effect of his brilliant, friendly,
indefinable genius is to make it difficult, in speaking
of him, to take things in their order or follow a plan.
In writing of him some time ago, in another place, I
so far lost my head as to remark, with levity, that
he was "a great little novelist." The diminutive
epithet then, I must now say, was nothing more than
a term of endearment, the result of an irresistible
impulse to express a sense of personal fondness. This
kind of feeling is difficult to utter in English, and
the utterance of it, so far as this is possible, is not
thought consistent with the dignity of a critic. If
we were talking French, nothing would be simpler
than to say that Alphonse Daudet is adorable, and
have done with it. But this resource is denied me,
and I must arrive at my meaning by a series of
circumlocutions. I am not able even to say that he
is very "personal"; that epithet, so valuable in the
vocabulary of French literary criticism, has, when
applied to the talent of an artist, a meaning different

from the sense in which we use it. " A novelist so
personal and so penetrating," says Emile Zola, speaking of the author of *Numa Roumestan*. That phrase,
in English, means nothing in particular; so that I
must add to it that the charm of Daudet's talent
comes from its being charged to an extraordinary
degree with his temperament, his feelings, his instincts, his natural qualities. This, of course, is a
charm, in a style, only when nature has been generous.
To Alphonse Daudet she has been exceptionally so ;
she has placed in his hand an instrument of many
chords. A delicate, nervous organisation, active and
indefatigable in spite of its delicacy, and familiar
with emotion of almost every kind, equally acquainted
with pleasure and with pain ; a light, quick, joyous,
yet reflective, imagination, a faculty of seeing images,
making images, at every turn, of conceiving everything in the visible form, in the plastic spirit ; an
extraordinary sensibility to all the impressions of
life and a faculty of language which is in perfect
harmony with his wonderful fineness of perception—
these are some of the qualities of which he is the
happy possessor, and which make his equipment for
the work he has undertaken exceedingly rich. There
are others besides ; but enumerations are ponderous,
and we should avoid that danger in speaking of a
genius whose lightness of touch never belies itself.
His elder brother, who has not his talent, has written
a little book about him in which the word *modernité*
perpetually occurs. M. Ernest Daudet, in *Mon Frère*

et Moi, insists upon his possession of the qualities expressed by this barbarous substantive, which is so indispensable to the new school. Alphonse Daudet is, in truth, very modern; he has all the newly-developed, the newly-invented, perceptions. Nothing speaks so much to his imagination as the latest and most composite things, the refinements of current civilisation, the most delicate shades of the actual. It is scarcely too much to say that (especially in the Parisian race), modern manners, modern nerves, modern wealth, and modern improvements, have engendered a new sense, a sense not easily named nor classified, but recognisable in all the most characteristic productions of contemporary art. It is partly physical, partly moral, and the shortest way to describe it is to say that it is a more analytic consideration of appearances. It is known by its tendency to resolve its discoveries into pictorial form. It sees the connection between feelings and external conditions, and it expresses such relations as they have not been expressed hitherto. It deserves to win victories, because it has opened its eyes well to the fact that the magic of the arts of representation lies in their appeal to the associations awakened by things. It traces these associations into the most unlighted corners of our being, into the most devious paths of experience. The appearance of things is constantly more complicated as the world grows older, and it needs a more and more patient art, a closer notation, to divide it into its parts. Of this art Alphonse

Daudet has a wonderfully large allowance, and that is why I say that he is peculiarly modern. It is very true that his manner is not the manner of patience —though he must always have had a great deal of that virtue in the preparation of his work. The new school of fiction in France is based very much on the taking of notes ; the library of the great Flaubert, of the brothers de Goncourt, of Emile Zola, and of the writer of whom I speak, must have been in a large measure a library of memorandum-books. This of course only puts the patience back a stage or two. In composition Daudet proceeds by quick, instantaneous vision, by the happiest divination, by catching the idea as it suddenly springs up before him with a whirr of wings. What he mainly sees is the great surface of life and the parts that lie near the surface. But life is, immensely, a matter of surface, and if our emotions in general are interesting, the *form* of those emotions has the merit of being the most definite thing about them. Like most French imaginative writers (judged, at least, from the English standpoint), he is much less concerned with the moral, the metaphysical world, than with the sensible. We proceed usually from the former to the latter, while the French reverse the process. Except in politics, they are uncomfortable in the presence of abstractions, and lose no time in reducing them to the concrete. But even the concrete, for them, is a field for poetry, which brings us to the fact that the delightful thing in Daudet's talent is the inveterate poetical touch.

This is what mainly distinguishes him from the other
lights of the realistic school—modifies so completely
in his case the hardness of consistent realism.   There
is something very hard, very dry, in Flaubert, in
Edmond de Goncourt, in the robust Zola ; but there
is something very soft in Alphonse Daudet.   " Bene-
volent nature," says Zola, " has placed him at that
exquisite point where poetry ends and reality begins."
That is happily said ; Daudet's great characteristic
is this mixture of the sense of the real with the
sense of the beautiful.   His imagination is constantly
at play with his theme ; it has a horror of the literal,
the limited ; it sees an object in all its intermingled
relations—on its sentimental, its pathetic, its comical,
its pictorial side.   Flaubert, in whom Alphonse
Daudet would probably recognise to a certain degree
a literary paternity, is far from being a simple realist ;
but he was destitute of this sense of the beautiful,
destitute of facility and grace.   He had, to take its
place, a sense of the strange, the grotesque, to which
Salammbo, La Tentation de Saint-Antoine, his indescribable posthumous novel of *Bouvard et Pécuchet,*
abundantly testify.   The talent of the brothers
Goncourt strikes us as a talent that was associated
originally with a sense of beauty ; but we receive an
impression that this feeling has been perverted and
warped.   It has ceased to be natural and free ; it
has become morbid and peevish, has turned mainly
to curiosity and mannerism.   And these two authors
are capable, during a whole book (as in *Germinie*

Lacerteux or *La Fille Elisa*), of escaping from its influence altogether. No one would probably ever think of accusing Emile Zola of having a perception of the beautiful. He has an illimitable, and at times a very valuable, sense of the ugly, of the unclean ; but when he addresses himself to the poetic aspect of things, as in *La Faute de l'Abbé Mouret*, he is apt to have terrible misadventures.

III

IT is for the expressive talents that we feel an
affection, and Daudet is eminently expressive. His
manner is the manner of talk, and if the talk is
sincere, that makes a writer touch us. Daudet
expresses many things; but he most frequently
expresses himself—his own temper in the presence
of life, his own feeling on a thousand occasions.
This personal note is especially to be observed in
his earlier productions—in the *Lettres de mon Moulin*,
the *Contes du Lundi*, *Le Petit Chose;* it is also very
present in the series of prefaces which he has undertaken to supply to the octavo edition of his works.
In these prefaces he gives the history of each successive book—relates the circumstances under which
it was written. These things are ingenuously told,
but what we are chiefly conscious of in regard to
them, is that Alphonse Daudet must express himself.
His brother informs us that he is writing his memoirs,
and this will have been another opportunity for
expression. Ernest Daudet, as well (as I have mentioned), has attempted to express him. *Mon Frère et
Moi* is one of those productions which it is difficult

for an English reader to judge in fairness: it is so much more confidential than we, in public, ever venture to be. The French have, on all occasions, the courage of their emotion, and M. Ernest Daudet's leading emotion is a boundless admiration for his junior. He lays it before us very frankly and gracefully—not, on the whole, indiscreetly; and I have no quarrel whatever with his volume, for it contains a considerable amount of information on a very interesting subject. Indirectly, indeed, as well as directly, it helps us to a knowledge of his brother. Alphonse Daudet was born in Provence; he comes of an expansive, a confidential race. His style is impregnated with the southern sunshine, and his talent has the sweetness of a fruit that has grown in the warm, open air. He has the advantage of being a Provençal converted, as it were—of having a southern temperament and a northern reason. We know what he thinks of the southern temperament—*Numa Roumestan* is a vivid exposition of that. "*Gau de carriero, doulou d'oustau,*" as the Provençal has it; "*joie de rue, douleur de maison*—joy in the street and pain in the house"—that proverb, says Alphonse Daudet, describes and formulates a whole race. It has given him the subject of an admirable story, in which he has depicted with equal force and tenderness the amiable weaknesses, the mingled violence and levity of the children of the clime of the fig and olive. He has put before us, above all, their mania for talk, their irrepressible chatter, the qualities that, with them, render all passion, all purpose, inordinately vocal. Himself a complete "*produit du Midi*," like the famille Mèfre in *Numa Roumestan*, he has achieved the feat of becoming objective to his own vision, getting outside of his ingredients and judging them. This he has done by the aid of his Parisianised conscience, his exquisite taste, and that finer wisdom which resides in the artist, from whatever soil he springs. Successfully as he has done it, however, he has not done it so well but that he too does not show a little of the heightened colour, the superabundant statement, the restless movement of his compatriots. He is nothing if not demonstrative; he is always in a state of feeling; he has not a very definite ideal of reserve. It must be added that he is a man of genius, and that genius never spends its capital; that he is an artist, and that an artist always has a certain method and order. But it remains characteristic of his origin that the author of *Numa Roumestan*, one of the happiest and most pointed of satires, should have about him the aroma of some of the qualities satirised. There are passages in his tales and in his prefaces that are genuine " produits du Midi," and his brother's account of him could only have been written by a Provençal brother.

To be *personnel* to that point, transparent, effusive, gushing, to give one's self away in one's books, has never been, and will never be, the ideal of us of English speech; but that does not prevent our enjoying immensely, when we meet it, a happy example

of this alien spirit. For myself, I am free to confess,
half my affection for Alphonse Daudet comes from
the fact that he writes in a way in which I would
not write even if I could. There are certain kinds
of feeling and observation, certain impressions and
ideas, to which we are rather ashamed to give a voice,
and yet are ashamed not to have in our scale. In
these matters Alphonse Daudet renders us a great
service: he expresses such things on our behalf. I
may add that he usually does it much better than
the cleverest of us could do even if we were to try.
I have said that he is a Provençal converted, and I
should do him a great injustice if I did not dwell
upon his conversion. His brother relates the circumstances under which he came up to Paris, at the age
of twenty (in a threadbare overcoat and a pair of
india-rubbers), to seek his literary fortune. His
beginnings were difficult, his childhood had been
hard, he was familiar with poverty and disaster. He
had no adventitious aid to success—his whole fortune
consisted in his exquisite organisation. But Paris
was to be, artistically, a mine of wealth to him, and
of all the anxious and eager young spirits who, on
the battle-field of uncarpeted *cinquièmes*, have laid
siege to the indifferent city, none can have felt more
deeply conscious of the mission to take possession of
it. Alphonse Daudet, at the present hour, is in
complete possession of Paris; he knows it, loves it,
uses it; he has assimilated it to its last particle. He
has made of it a Paris of his own—a Paris like

a vast crisp water-colour, one of the water-colours of
the school of Fortuny. The French have a great
advantage in the fact that they admire their capital
very much as if it were a foreign city. Most of
their artists, their men of letters, have come up from
the provinces, and well as they may learn to know the
metropolis, it never ceases to be a spectacle, a wonder,
a fascination for them. This comes partly from the
intrinsic brilliancy and interest of the place, partly
from the poverty of provincial life, and partly from
the degree to which the faculty of appreciation is
developed in Frenchmen of the class of which I
speak. To Daudet, at any rate, the familiar aspects
of Paris are endlessly pictorial, and part of the charm
of his novels (for those who share his relish for that
huge flower of civilisation) is in the way he recalls
it, evokes it, suddenly presents it, in parts or as a
whole, to our senses. The light, the sky, the feeling
of the air, the odours of the streets, the look of certain vistas, the silvery, muddy Seine, the cool, grey
tone of colour, the physiognomy of particular quar-
ters, the whole Parisian expression, meet you suddenly in his pages, and remind you again and again
that if he paints with a pen he writes with a brush.
I remember that when I read *Le Nabab* and *Les Rois
en Exil* for the first time, I said to myself that this
was the *article de Paris* in supreme perfection, and
that no reader could understand such productions who
had not had a copious experience of the scene. It is
certain, at any rate, that those books have their full

value only for minds more or less Parisianised; half
their meaning, their magic, their subtlety of intention is liable to be lost. It may be said that this is
a great limitation—that the works of the best novelists may be understood by all the world. There is
something in that; but I know not, all the same,
whether the fact I indicate be a great limitation.
It is certainly a very illustrative quality. Daudet
has caught the tone of a particular pitch of manners; he applies it with the lightest, surest hand,
and his picture shines and lives. The most generalised representation of life cannot do more than
that.

I shrink very much from speaking of systems, in
relation to such a genius as this: I should incline to
believe that Daudet's system is simply to be as vivid
as he can. Emile Zola has a system—at least he
says so; but I do not remember, on the part of the
author of *Numa Roumestan*, the smallest technical
profession of faith. Nevertheless, he has taken a
line, as we say, and his line is to sail as close as
possible to the actual. The life of Paris being his
subject, his attempt, most frequently, is to put his
finger upon known examples; so that he has been
accused of portraying individuals instead of portraying types. There are few of his figures to which the
name of some celebrity of the day has not been
attached. The Nabob is François Bravais; the Duc
de Mora is the Duc de Morny. The Irish Doctor
Jenkins is an English physician who flourished

in Paris from such a year to such another; people
are still living (wonderful to say), who took his little
pills *à base arsénicale*. Félicia Ruys is Mademoiselle
Sarah Bernhardt; Constance Crenmitz is Madame
Taglioni; the Queen of Illyria is the Queen of
Naples; the Prince of Axel is the Prince of Orange;
Tom Lévis is an English house-agent (*not* in the Rue
Royale, but hard by); Elysée Méraut is a well-known
journalist, and Doctor Bouchereau a well-known
surgeon.   Such is the key, we are told, to these ingenious mystifications, and to many others which I
have not the space to mention.   It matters little, to
my mind, whether in each case the cap fits the supposed model; for nothing is more evident than that
Alphonse Daudet has proposed to himself to represent not only the people but the persons of his time.
The conspicuity of certain individuals has added to
the force with which they speak to his imagination.
His taste is for salient figures, and he has said to
himself that there is no greater proof of being salient
than being known.   The temptation to "put people
into a book" is a temptation of which every writer
of fiction knows something, and I hold that to suc-
cumb to it is not only legitimate but inevitable.
Putting people into books is what the novelist lives
upon; the question in the matter is the question of
delicacy, for according to that delicacy the painter
conjures away recognition or insists upon it.   Daudet
has been accused of the impertinence of insisting,
and I believe that two or three of his por-

traits have provoked a protest. He is charged with ingratitude for having produced an effigy of the Duke of Morny, who had been his benefactor, and employed him as a secretary. Such a matter as this is between M. Daudet and his conscience, and I am far from pretending to pronounce upon it. The uninitiated reader can only say that the figure is a very striking one—such a picture as (it may be imagined) the Duc de Morny would not be displeased to have inspired. It may fairly be conceded, however, that Daudet is much more an observer than an inventor. The invented parts of his tales, like the loves of Jack and of Paul de Géry and the machinations of Madame Autheman (the theological vampire of *L'Evangéliste*, to whom I shall return for a moment), are the vague, the ineffective as well as the romantic parts. (I remember that in reading *Le Nabab*, it was not very easy to keep Paul de Géry and André Maranne apart.) It is the real—the transmuted real—that he gives us best; the fruit of a process that adds to observation what a kiss adds to a greeting. The joy, the excitement of recognition, are keen, even when the object recognised is dismal. They are part of his spirit—part of his way of seeing things. *L'Evangéliste* is the saddest story conceivable; but it is lighted, throughout, by the author's irrepressibly humorous view of the conditions in which its successive elements present themselves, and by the extraordinary vivacity with which, in his hands, narration and description proceed. His humour is of the finest; it is needless to say that it is never violent nor vulgar. It is a part of the high spirits—the animal spirits, I should say, if the phrase had not an association of coarseness—that accompany the temperament of his race; and it is stimulated by the perpetual entertainment which so rare a visual faculty naturally finds in the spectacle of life, even while encountering there a multitude of distressing things. Daudet's gaiety is a part of his poetry, and his poetry is a part of everything he touches. There is little enough gaiety in the subject of *Jack*, and yet the whole story is told with a smile. To complete the charm of the thing, the smile is full of feeling. Here and there it becomes an immense laugh, and the result is a delightful piece of drollery. *Les Aventures Prodigieuses de Tartarin de Tarascon* contains all his high spirits; it is one of his few stories in which laughter and tears are not intermingled.

This little tale, which is one of his first, is, like *Numa Roumestan*, a satire on a southern foible. Tartarin de Tarascon is an excellent man who inhabits the old town on the Rhone over which the palace of the good King René keeps guard; he has not a fault in the world except an imagination too vivid. He is liable to visions, to hallucinations; the desire that a thing shall happen speedily resolves itself into the belief that the thing will happen— then that it is happening—then that it *has* happened. Tartarin accordingly presents himself to the world (and to himself) as a gentleman to whom all wonders are familiar ; his experience blooms with supposititious flowers. The coveted thing for a man of his romantic mould is that he shall be the bravest of the brave, and he passes his life in a series of heroic exploits, in which, as you listen to him, it is impossible not to believe. He passes over from Marseilles to Algiers, where his adventures deepen to a climax, and where he has a desperate flirtation with the principal ornament of the harem of a noble Arab. The lady proves at the end to be a horribly improper little Frenchwoman, and poor Tartarin, abused and disabused, returns to Tarascon to meditate on what might have been. Nothing could be more charming than the light comicality of the sketch, which fills a small volume. This is the most mirthful, the most completely diverting of all Daudet's tales ; but the same element, in an infinitely subtler form, runs through the others. The essence of it is the wish to please, and this brings me back to the point to which I intended to return. The wish to please is the quality by which Daudet persuades his readers most; it is this that elicits from them that friendliness, that confession that they are charmed, of which I spoke at the beginning of these remarks. It gives a sociability to his manner, in spite of the fact that he describes all sorts of painful and odious things. This contradiction is a part of his originality. He has no pretension to being simple, he is perfectly conscious of being complex, and in nothing is he more modern than in this expressive and sympathetic smile—the smile of the artist, the sceptic, the man of the world—with which he shows us the miseries and cruelties of life. It is singular that we should like him for that—and doubtless many people do not, or think they do not. What they really dislike, I believe, is the things he relates, which are often lamentable.

IV

THE first of these were slight and simple, and for the most part cheerful ; little anecdotes and legends of Provence, impressions of an artist's holidays in that strange, bare, lovely land, and of wanderings further afield, in Corsica and Algeria ; sketches of Paris during the siege ; incidents of the invasion, the advent of the Prussian rule in other parts of the country. In all these things there is *la note émue*, the smile which is only a more synthetic sign of being moved. And then such grace of form, such lightness of touch, such alertness of observation! Some of the chapters of the *Lettres de mon Moulin* are such perfect vignettes, that the brief treatment of small subjects might well have seemed, at first, Alphonse Daudet's appointed work. He had almost invented a manner, and it was impossible to do better than he the small piece, or even the passage. Glimpses, reminiscences, accidents, he rendered them with the brilliancy of a violinist improvising on a sudden hint. The *Lettres de mon Moulin*, moreover, are impregnated with the light, with the fragrance of a Provençal summer ; the rosemary and thyme are

in the air as we read, the white rocks and the grey
foliage stretch away to an horizon of hills—the
Alpilles, the little Alps — on which colour is as
iridescent as the breast of a dove.　The Provence of
Alphonse Daudet is a delightful land ; even when the
mistral blows there it has a music in its whistle.
Emile Zola has protested against this ; he too is of
Provençal race, he passed his youth in the old
Languedoc, and he intimates that his fanciful friend
throws too much sweetness into the picture.　It is
beyond contradiction that Daudet, like Tartarin de
Tarascon and Numa Roumestan, exaggerates a little ;
he sees with great intensity, and is very sensitive to
agreeable impressions.　*Le Petit Chose*, his first long
story, reads to-day like the attempt of a beginner,
and of a beginner who had read and enjoyed
Dickens.　I risk this allusion to the author of
Copperfield in spite of a conviction that Alphonse
Daudet must be tired of hearing that he imitates
him.　It is not imitation ; there is nothing so gross
as imitation in the length and breadth of Daudet's
work ; but it is conscious sympathy, for there is
plenty of that.　There are pages in his tales which
seem to say to us that at one moment of his life
Dickens had been a revelation to him—pages more
particularly in *Le Petit Chose*, in *Fromont Jeune* and
in *Jack*.　The heroine of the first of these works (a
very shadowy personage) is never mentioned but as
the " black eyes " ; some one else is always spoken
of as the *dame de grand mérite ;* the heroine's father,

who keeps a flourishing china-shop, never opens his
mouth without saying "C'est le cas de le dire." These
are harmless, they are indeed sometimes very happy,
Dickensisms. We make no crime of them to M.
Daudet, who must have felt as intelligently as he
has felt everything else the fascinating form of the
English novelist's drollery. *Fromont Jeune et Risler
Aîné* is a study of life in the old quarter of the
Marais, the Paris of the seventeenth century, whose
stately *hôtels* have been invaded by the innumerable
activities of modern trade. When I say a study, I
use the word with all those restrictions with which
it must be applied to a genius who is truthful without being literal, and who has a pair of butterfly's
wings attached to the back of his observation. If
sub-titles were the fashion to-day, the right one for
Fromont Jeune would be—*or the Dangers of Partnership.*
The action takes place for the most part in a manu-
factory of wall-papers, and the persons in whom the
author seeks to interest us are engaged in this useful
industry. There are delightful things in the book,
but, as I intimated at the beginning of these remarks,
there are considerable inequalities. The pages that
made M. Daudet's fortune—for it was with *Fromont
Jeune* that his fortune began—are those which relate
to the history of M. Delobelle, the superannuated
tragedian, his long-suffering wife, and his exquisite
lame daughter, who makes butterflies and humming-
birds for ladies' head-dresses. This eccentric and
pathetic household was an immense hit, and Daudet

has never been happier than in the details of the
group.   Delobelle himself, who has not had an engagement for ten years, and who never will have one
again, but who holds none the less that it is his duty
not to leave the stage, "not to give up the theatre,"
though his platonic passion is paid for by the weary
eyesight of his wife and daughter, who sit up half
the night attaching bead-eyes to little stuffed animals
—the blooming and sonorous Delobelle, ferociously
selfish and fantastically vain, under the genial forms
of melodrama, is a beautiful representation of a
vulgarly factitious nature.   The book revealed a
painter ; all the descriptive passages, the pictorial
touches, had the truest felicity.   No one better than
Daudet gives what we call the feeling of a place.
The story illustrates, among other things, the fact
that a pretty little woman who is consumed with
the lowest form of vanity, and unimpeded in her
operations by the possession of a heart, may inflict
an unlimited amount of injury upon people about
her, if she only have the opportunity.   The case is
well demonstrated, and Sidonie Chèbe is an elaborate
study of flimsiness ; her papery quality, as I may
call it, her rustling dryness, are effectively rendered.
But I think there is a limit to the interest which the
English-speaking reader of French novels can take
to-day in the adventures of a lady who leads the life
of Madame Sidonie.   In the first place he has met
her again and again—he knows exactly what she will
do and say in every situation ; and in the second

there always seems to him to be in her vices, her disorders, an element of the conventional. There is a receipt among French novelists for making little high-heeled reprobates. However this may be, he has at least a feeling that at night all cats are grey, and that the particular tint of depravity of a woman whose nature has the shallowness of a sanded floor is not a very important *constatation.* Daudet has expended much ingenuity in endeavouring to hit the particular tint of Sidonie; he has wished to make her a type—the type of the daughter of small unsuccessful shopkeepers (narrow-minded and self-complacent to imbecility), whose corruption comes from the examples, temptations, opportunities of a great city, as well as from her impure blood and the infection of the meanest associations. But what all this illustrates was not worth illustrating.

The early chapters of *Jack* are admirable; the later ones suffer a little, I think, from the story being drawn out too much, like an accordion when it wishes to be plaintive. Jack is a kind of younger brother of the Petit Chose, though he takes the troubles of life rather more stoutly than that delicate and diminutive hero ; a poor boy with a doting and disreputable mother, whose tenderness is surpassed by her frivolity, and who sacrifices her son to the fantastic egotism of an unsuccessful man of letters with whom she passes several years of her life. She is another study of *coquinerie*—she is another shade ; but she is a more apprehensible figure than Sidonie

Chèbe—she is, indeed, a very admirable portrait.
The success of the book, however, is the figure of her
lover, that is of her protector and bully, the unrecog-
nised genius aforesaid, author of *Le Fils de Faust,* an
uncirculated dramatic poem in the manner of Goethe,
and centre of a little group of *ratés*—a collection of
dead-beats, as we say to-day, as pretentious, as im-
potent, as envious and as bilious as himself.   He
conceives a violent hatred of the offspring of his
amiable companion, and the subject of *Jack* is the
persecution of the boy by this monstrous charlatan.
This persecution is triumphantly successful ; the
youthful hero dies on the threshold of manhood,
broken down by his tribulations and miseries : he
has been thrown upon the world to earn his bread,
and among other things seeks a livelihood as a stoker
on an Atlantic steamer.   Jack has been taken
young, and though his nature is gentle and tender,
his circumstances succeed in degrading him.   He is
reduced at the end to a kind of bewildered brutishness.   The story is simply the history of a juvenile
martyrdom, pityingly, expansively told, and I am
afraid that Mr. Charles Dudley Warner, who, in
writing lately about " Modern Fiction," [1] complains of
the abuse of pathetic effects in that form of composition, would find little to commend in this brilliant
paraphrase of suffering.   Mr. Warner's complaint is
eminently just, and the fault of *Jack* is certainly the
abuse of pathos.   Mr. Warner does not mention

[1] In the *Atlantic Monthly,* for April 1883.

Alphonse Daudet by name, but it is safe to assume that in his reflections upon the perversity of those writers who will not make a novel as comfortable as one's stockings, or as pretty as a Christmas card, he was thinking of the author of so many uncompromising *dénouements*. It is true that this probability is diminished by the fact that when he remarks that surely " the main object in the novel is to entertain," he appears to imply that the writers who furnish his text are faithless to this duty. It is possible he would not have made that implication if he had had in mind the productions of a story-teller who has the great peculiarity of being " amusing," as the old-fashioned critics say, even when he touches the source of tears. The word entertaining has two or three shades of meaning; but in whatever sense it is used I may say, in parenthesis, that I do not agree with Mr. Warner's description of the main object of the novel. I should put the case differently : I should say that the main object of the novel is to represent life. I cannot understand any other motive for interweaving imaginary incidents, and I do not perceive any other measure of the value of such combinations. The *effect* of a novel—the effect of any work of art—is to entertain ; but that is a very different thing. The success of a work of art, to my mind, may be measured by the degree to which it produces a certain illusion ; that illusion makes it appear to us for the time that we have lived another life—that we have had a miraculous enlargement of

experience. The greater the art the greater the
miracle, and the more certain also the fact that we
have been entertained—in the best meaning of that
word, at least, which signifies that we have been
living at the expense of some one else. I am perfectly aware that to say the object of a novel is to
represent life does not bring the question to a point
so fine as to be uncomfortable for any one. It is of
the greatest importance that there should be a very
free appreciation of such a question, and the definition
I have hinted at gives plenty of scope for that. For,
after all, may not people differ infinitely as to what
constitutes life—what constitutes representation ?
Some people, for instance, hold that Miss Austen
deals with life, that Miss Austen represents. Others
attribute these achievements to the accomplished
Ouida. Some people find that illusion, that enlargement of experience, that miracle of living at the
expense of others, of which I have spoken, in the
novels of Alexandre Dumas. Others revel in them
in the pages of Mr. Howells.

V

M. DAUDET'S unfortunate Jack, at any rate, lives altogether at his own cost—that of his poor little juvenile constitution, and of his innocent affections and aspirations. He is sent to the horrible Gymnase Moronval, where he has no beguiling works of fiction to read. The Gymnase Moronval is a Dotheboys' Hall in a Parisian "passage"—a very special class of academy. Nothing could be more effective than Daudet's picture of this horrible institution, with its bankrupt and exasperated proprietors, the greasy penitentiary of a group of unremunerative children whose parents and guardians have found it convenient to forget them. The episode of the wretched little hereditary monarch of an African tribe who has been placed there for a royal education, and who, livid with cold, short rations, and rough usage, and with his teeth chattering with a sense of dishonour, steals away and wanders in the streets of Paris, and then, recaptured and ferociously punished, surrenders his little dusky soul in the pestilential dormitory of the establishment—all this part of the tale is a masterpiece of vivid description. We seem

to assist at the terrible soirées where the *ratés* exhibit
their talents (M. Moronval is of course a *raté*), and
where the wife of the principal, a very small woman
with a very big head and a very high forehead,
expounds the wonderful Méthode-Décostère (invented by herself and designated by her maiden
name), for pronouncing the French tongue with elegance.   My criticism of this portion of the book, and
indeed of much of the rest of it, would be that the
pathetic element is too intentional, too *voulu*, as the
French say.   And I am not sure that the reader
enters into the author's reason for making Charlotte,
Jack's mother, a woman of the class that we do not
specify in American magazines.   She is an accom-
modating idiot, but her good nature is unfortunately
not consecutive, and she consents, at the instigation
of the diabolical d'Argenton, to her child's being
brought up like a pauper.   D'Argenton, like Delobelle, is a study of egotism pushed to the grotesque ;
but the portrait is still more complete, and some
of the details are inimitable.   As regards the infatuated Charlotte, who sacrifices her child to the
malignity of her lover, I repeat that certain of the
features of her character appear to me a mistake,
judged in relation to the effect that the author wishes
to produce.   He wishes to show us all that the boy
loses in being disinherited—if I may use that term
with respect to a situation in which there is nothing
to inherit.   But his loss is not great when we consider that his mother had, after all, very little to

give him. She had divested herself of important
properties. Bernard Jansoulet, in *Le Nabab,* is not,
like the two most successful figures that Daudet has
previously created, a representation of full-blown
selfishness. The unhappy nabob is generous to a
fault; he is the most good-natured and free-handed
of men, and if he has made use of all sorts of
means to build up his enormous fortune, he knows an
equal number of ways of spending it. This voluminous tale had an immense success; it seemed to
show that Daudet had found his manner, a manner
that was perfectly new and remarkably ingenious.
As I have said, it held up the mirror to contemporary
history, and attempted to complete for us, by supple-
mentary revelations, those images which are projected
by the modern newspaper and the album of photographs. *Les Rois en Exil* is an historical novel of
this pattern, in which the process is applied with
still more spirit. In these two works Daudet
enlarged his canvas surprisingly, and showed his
ability to deal with a multitude of figures.

The distance traversed artistically from the little
anecdotes of the *Lettres de mon Moulin* to the complex
narrative of *Le Nabab* and its successor, are like the
transformation — often so rapid — of a slim and
charming young girl into a blooming and accomplished woman of the world. The author's style
had taken on bone and muscle, and become conscious
of treasures of nervous agility. I have left myself
no space to speak of these things in detail, and it

was not part of my purpose to examine Daudet's
novels piece by piece; but I may say that it is
the items, the particular touches, that make the
value of writing of this kind.   I am not concerned
to defend the process, the system, so far as there is a
system; but I cannot open either *Le Nabab* or *Les
Rois en Exil*, cannot rest my eyes upon a page, without being charmed by the brilliancy of execution.   It
is difficult to give an idea, by any general terms, of
Daudet's style — a style which defies convention,
tradition, homogeneity, prudence, and sometimes even
syntax, gathers up every patch of colour, every col-
loquial note, that will help to illustrate, and moves
eagerly, lightly, triumphantly along, like a clever
woman in the costume of an eclectic age.   There is
nothing classic in this mode of expression; it is not
the old-fashioned drawing in black and white.   It
never rests, never is satisfied, never leaves the idea
sitting half-draped, like patience on a monument; it
is always panting, straining, fluttering, trying to add
a little more, to produce the effect which shall make
the reader see with his eyes, or rather with the mar-
vellous eyes of Alphonse Daudet.   *Le Nabab* is full
of episodes which are above all pages of execution,
triumphs of translation.   The author has drawn up
a list of the Parisian solemnities and painted the
portrait — or given a summary — of each of them.
The opening day at the Salon, a funeral at Père-la-
Chaise, a debate in the Chamber of Deputies, the
première of a new play at a favourite theatre, furnish

him with so many opportunities for his gymnastics of observation. I should like to say how rich and entertaining I think the figure of Jansoulet, the robust and good - natured son of his own works (originally a dock-porter at Marseilles), who, after amassing a fabulous number of millions in selling European luxuries on commission to the Bey of Tunis, comes to Paris to try to make his social fortune as he has already made his financial, and after being a nine-days' wonder, a public joke, and the victim of his boundless hospitality; after being flattered by charlatans, rifled by adventurers, belaboured by newspapers, and "exploited" to the last penny of his coffers and the last pulsation of his vanity by every one who comes near him, dies of apoplexy in his box at the theatre, while the public hoots him for being unseated for electoral frauds in the Chamber of Deputies, where for a single mocking hour he has tasted the sweetness of political life. I should like to say, too, that however much or however little the Duc de Mora may resemble the Duc de Morny, the character depicted by Daudet is a wonderful study of that modern passion, the love of "good form." The chapter that relates the death of the Duke, and describes the tumult, the confusion, of his palace, the sudden extinction of the rapacious interests that crowd about him, and to which the collapse of his splendid security comes as the first breath of a revolution— this chapter is famous, and gives the fullest measure

of what Daudet can do when he fairly warms to
his work.

Les Rois en Exil, however, has a greater perfection ;
it is simpler, more equal, and it contains much more
of the beautiful. In *Le Nabab* there are various
lacunæ and a certain want of logic; it is not a
sustained narrative, but a series of almost diabolically
clever pictures. But the other book has more large-
ness of line—a fine tragic movement which deepens
and presses to the catastrophe. Daudet had observed
that several dispossessed monarchs had taken up
their residence in the French capital—some of them
waiting and plotting for a restoration, and chafing
under their disgrace ; others indifferent, resigned, relieved, eager to console themselves with the pleasures
of Paris. It occurred to him to suppose a drama
in which these exalted personages should be the
actors, and which, unlike either of his former productions, should have a pure and noble heroine. He
was conscious of a dauntless little imagination, the
idea of making kings and queens talk among themselves had no terror for him; he had faith in his
good taste, in his exquisite powers of divination.
The success is worthy of the spirit — the gallant
artistic spirit—in which it was invoked. *Les Rois
en Exil* is a finished picture. He has had, it is
true, to simplify his subject a good deal to make it
practicable ; the court of the king and queen of
Illyria, in the suburb of Saint-Mandé, is a little too
much like a court in a fairy-tale. But the amiable

depravity of Christian, in whom conviction, resolution, ambition, are hopelessly dead, and whose one desire is to enjoy Paris with the impunity of a young man about town ; the proud, serious, concentrated nature of Frederica, who believes ardently in her royal function, and lives with her eyes fixed on the crown, which she regards as a symbol of duty ; both of these conceptions do M. Daudet the utmost honour, and prove that he is capable of handling great situations—situations which have a depth of their own, and do not depend for their interest on amusing accidents. It takes perhaps some courage to say so, but the feelings, the passions, the view of life, of royal personages, differ essentially from those of common mortals ; their education, their companions, their traditions, their exceptional position, take sufficient care of that. Alphonse Daudet has comprehended the difference ; and I scarcely know, in the last few years, a straighter flight of imagination. The history of the queen of Illyria is a tragedy. Her husband sells his birthright for a few millions of francs, and rolls himself in the Parisian gutter ; her child perishes from poverty of blood ; she herself dries up in her despair. There is nothing finer in all Daudet than the pages, at the end of the book, which describe her visits to the great physician Bouchereau, when she takes her poor half-blind child by the hand, and (wishing an opinion unbiassed by the knowledge of her rank) goes to sit in his waiting-room like one of the vulgar multitude. Wonderful are the delicacy, the verity, the tenderness of these pages ; we always point to them to justify our pre-dilection. But we must stop pointing. We will not say more of *Numa Roumestan* than we have already said ; for it is better to pass so happy a work by than to speak of it inadequately. We will only repeat that we delight in *Numa Roumestan.* Alphonse Daudet's last book is a novelty at the time I write ; *L'Evangéliste* has been before the public but a month or two. I will say but little of it, partly because my opportunity is already over, and partly because I have found that, for a fair judgment of one of Daudet's works, the book should be read a second time, after a certain interval has elapsed. This interval has not brought round my second perusal of *L'Evangéliste.* My first suggests that with all the author's present mastery of his resources the book has a grave defect. It is not that the story is painful ; that is a defect only when the sources of this element are not, as I may say, abundant. It treats of a young girl (a Danish Protestant) who is turned to stone by a Medusa of Calvinism, the sombre and fanatical wife of a great Protestant banker. Madame Autheman persuades Eline Ebsen to wash her hands of the poor old mother with whom up to this moment she has lived in the closest affection, and go forth into strange countries to stir up the wicked to conversion. The excellent Madame Ebsen, bewildered, heart-broken, desperate, terrified at the imagined penalties of her denunciation of the rich and powerful bigot (so that she leaves her habitation and hides in a household of small mechanics to escape from them—one of the best episodes in the book), protests, struggles, goes down on her knees in vain; then, at last, stupefied and exhausted, desists, looks for the last time at her inexorable, impenetrable daughter, who has hard texts on her lips and no recognition in her eye, and who lets her pass away, without an embrace, for ever. The incident in itself is perfectly conceivable : many well-meaning persons have held human relationships cheap in the face of a religious call. But Daudet's weakness has been simply a want of acquaintance with his subject. Proposing to himself to describe a particular phase of French Protestantism, he has " got up " certain of his facts with commendable zeal ; but he has not felt nor understood the matter, has looked at it solely from the outside, sought to make it above all things grotesque and extravagant. Into these excesses it doubtless frequently falls ; but there is a general humar verity which regulates even the most stubborn wills, the most perverted lives ; and of this saving principle the author, in quest of striking pictures, has rather lost his grasp. His pictures are striking, as a matter of course ; but to us readers of Protestant race, familiar with the large, free, salubrious life which the children of that faith have carried with them over the globe, there is almost a kind of drollery in these fearsome pictures of the Protestant temperament. The fact is that M. Daudet has not

(to my belief) any natural understanding of the
religious passion ; he has a quick perception of
many things, but that province of the human mind
cannot be *fait de chic*—experience, there, is the only
explorer.   Madame Autheman is not a real bigot ;
she is simply a dusky effigy, she is undemonstrated.
Eline Ebsen is not a victim, inasmuch as she is but
half alive, and victims are victims only in virtue of
being thoroughly sentient.   I do not easily perceive
her spiritual joints.   All the human part of the book,
however, has the author's habitual felicity ; and the
reader of these remarks knows what I hold that to
be.   It may seem to him, indeed, that in making the
concession I made just above—in saying that Alphonse
Daudet's insight fails him when he begins to take
the soul into account—I partly retract some of the
admiration I have expressed for him.   For that
amounts, after all, to saying that he has no high
imagination, and, as a consequence, no ideas.   It is
very true, I am afraid, that he has not a great
number of ideas.   There are certain things he does
not conceive—certain forms that never appear to him.
Imaginative writers of the first order always give us
an impression that they have a kind of philosophy.
We should be embarrassed to put our finger on
Daudet's philosophy.   " And yet you have praised
him so much," we fancy we hear it urged ; " you
have praised him as if he were one of the very first."
All that is very true, and yet we take nothing back.
Determinations of rank are a delicate matter, and it

is sufficient priority for an author that one likes him immensely.   Daudet is bright, vivid, tender ; he has an intense artistic life.   And then he is so free. For the spirit that moves slowly, going carefully from point to point, not sure whether this or that or the other will " do," the sight of such freedom is delightful.

1883.

VIII

GUY DE MAUPASSANT

GUY DE MAUPASSANT

I

THE first artists, in any line, are doubtless not those whose general ideas about their art are most often on their lips—those who most abound in precept, apology, and formula and can best tell us the reasons and the philosophy of things. We know the first usually by their energetic practice, the constancy with which they apply their principles, and the serenity with which they leave us to hunt for their secret in the illustration, the concrete example. None the less it often happens that a valid artist utters his mystery, flashes upon us for a moment the light by which he works, shows us the rule by which he holds it just that he should be measured. This accident is happiest, I think, when it is soonest over; the shortest explanations of the products of genius are the best, and there is many a creator of living figures whose friends, however full of faith in his inspiration, will do well to pray for him when he sallies forth into the dim wilderness of theory. The doctrine is apt to be so much less inspired than the work, the work is often so much more intelligent than the doctrine. M. Guy de Maupassant has lately traversed with a firm and rapid step a literary crisis of this kind ; he has clambered safely up the bank at the further end of the morass. If he has relieved himself in the preface to *Pierre et Jean,* the last-published of his tales, he has also rendered a service to his friends ; he has not only come home in a recognisable plight, escaping gross disaster with a success which even his extreme good sense was far from making in advance a matter of course, but he has expressed in intelligible terms (that by itself is a ground of felicitation) his most general idea, his own sense of his direction. He has arranged, as it were, the light in which he wishes to sit. If it is a question of attempting, under however many disadvantages, a sketch of him, the critic's business therefore is simplified : there will be no difficulty in placing him, for he himself has chosen the spot, he has made the chalk-mark on the floor.

I may as well say at once that in dissertation M. de Maupassant does not write with his best pen ; the philosopher in his composition is perceptibly inferior to the story-teller. I would rather have written half a page of *Boule de Suif* than the whole of the introduction to Flaubert's *Letters to Madame Sand ;* and his little disquisition on the novel in general, attached to that particular example of it which he has just put forth,[1] is considerably less to the point than the

---

[1] *Pierre et Jean.*   Paris : Ollendorff, 1888.

masterpiece which it ushers in. In short, as a commentator M. de Maupassant is slightly common, while as an artist he is wonderfully rare. Of course we must, in judging a writer, take one thing with another, and if I could make up my mind that M. de Maupassant is weak in theory, it would almost make me like him better, render him more approachable, give him the touch of softness that he lacks, and show us a human flaw. The most general quality of the author of *La Maison Tellier* and *Bel-Ami*, the impression that remains last, after the others have been accounted for, is an essential hardness—hardness of form, hardness of nature ; and it would put us more at ease to find that if the fact with him (the fact of execution) is so extraordinarily definite and adequate, his explanations, after it, were a little vague and sentimental. But I am not sure that he must even be held foolish to have noticed the race of critics : he is at any rate so much less foolish than several of that fraternity. He has said his say concisely and as if he were saying it once for all. In fine, his readers must be grateful to him for such a passage as that in which he remarks that whereas the public at large very legitimately says to a writer, " Console me, amuse me, terrify me, make me cry, make me dream, or make me think," what the sincere critic says is, " Make me something fine in the form that shall suit you best, according to your temperament." This seems to me to put into a nutshell the whole question of the different classes of fiction, concerning which there has recently been so much discourse. There are simply as many different kinds as there are persons practising the art, for if a picture, a tale, or a novel be a direct impression of life (and that surely constitutes its interest and value), the impression will vary according to the plate that takes it, the particular structure and mixture of the recipient.

I am not sure that I know what M. de Maupassant means when he says, "The critic shall appreciate the result only according to the nature of the effort; he has no right to concern himself with tendencies." The second clause of that observation strikes me as rather in the air, thanks to the vagueness of the last word. But our author adds to the definiteness of his contention when he goes on to say that any form of the novel is simply a vision of the world from the standpoint of a person constituted after a certain fashion, and that it is therefore absurd to say that there is, for the novelist's use, only one reality of things. This seems to me commendable, not as a flight of metaphysics, hovering over bottomless gulfs of controversy, but, on the contrary, as a just indication of the vanity of certain dogmatisms. The particular way we see the world is our particular illusion about it, says M. de Maupassant, and this illusion fits itself to our organs and senses; our receptive vessel becomes the furniture of *our* little plot of the universal consciousness.

"How childish, moreover, to believe in reality, since we each carry our own in our thought and in our organs. Our eyes, our ears, our sense of smell, of taste, differing from one person to another, create as many truths as there are men upon earth. And our minds, taking instruction from these organs, so diversely impressed, understand, analyse, judge, as if each of us belonged to a different race. Each one of us, therefore, forms for himself an illusion of the world, which is the illusion poetic, or sentimental, or joyous, or melancholy, or unclean, or dismal, according to his nature. And the writer has no other mission than to reproduce faithfully this illusion, with all the contrivances of art that he has learned and has at his command. The illusion of beauty, which is a human convention! The illusion of ugliness, which is a changing opinion! The illusion of truth, which is never immutable! The illusion of the ignoble, which attracts so many! The great artists are those who make humanity accept their particular illusion. Let us, therefore, not get angry with any one theory, since every theory is the generalised expression of a temperament asking itself questions."

What is interesting in this is not that M. de Maupassant happens to hold that we have no universal measure of the truth, but that it is the last word on a question of art from a writer who is rich in experience and has had success in a very rare degree. It is of secondary importance that our impression should be called, or not called, an illusion; what is excellent is that our author has stated more neatly than we have lately seen it done that the value of the artist resides in the clearness with which he gives forth that impression. His particular organism constitutes a *case*, and the critic is intelligent in proportion as he apprehends and enters into that case. To quarrel with it because it is not another, which it could not possibly have been without a wholly different outfit, appears to M. de Maupassant a deplorable waste of time.   If this appeal to our disinterestedness may strike some readers as chilling (through their inability to conceive of any other form than the one they like—a limitation excellent for a reader but poor for a judge), the occasion happens to be none of the best for saying so, for M. de Maupassant himself precisely presents all the symptoms of a " case" in the most striking way, and shows us how far the consideration of them may take us. Embracing such an opportunity as this, and giving ourselves to it freely, seems to me indeed to be a course more fruitful in valid conclusions, as well as in entertainment by the way, than the more common method of establishing one's own premises.   To make clear to ourselves those of the author of *Pierre et Jean*—those to which he is committed by the very nature of his mind — is an attempt that will both stimulate and repay curiosity.   There is no way of looking at his work less dry, less academic, for as we proceed from one of his peculiarities to another, the whole horizon widens, yet without our leaving firm ground, and we see ourselves landed, step by step, in the most general questions — those explanations of things which reside in the race, in the society.   Of course there are cases and cases, and it is the salient ones that the disinterested critic is delighted to meet.

What makes M. de Maupassant salient is two

facts : the first of which is that his gifts are remarkably strong and definite, and the second that he
writes directly *from* them, as it were : holds the
fullest, the most uninterrupted — I scarcely know
what to call it — the boldest communication with
them. A case is poor when the cluster of the artist's
sensibilities is small, or they themselves are wanting
in keenness, or else when the personage fails to
admit them—either through ignorance, or diffidence,
or stupidity, or the error of a false ideal—to what
may be called a legitimate share in his attempt. It
is, I think, among English and American writers
that this latter accident is most liable to occur ·
more than the French we are apt to be misled by
some convention or other as to the sort of feeler
we *ought* to put forth, forgetting that the best one
will be the one that nature happens to have given
us. We have doubtless often enough the courage of
our opinions (when it befalls that we have opinions),
but we have not so constantly that of our perceptions. There is a whole side of our perceptive
apparatus that we in fact neglect, and there are
probably many among us who would erect this
tendency into a duty. M. de Maupassant neglects
nothing that he possesses ; he cultivates his garden
with admirable energy ; and if there is a flower you
miss from the rich parterre, you may be sure that
it could not possibly have been raised, his mind not
containing the soil for it. He is plainly of the
opinion that the first duty of the artist, and the

thing that makes him most useful to his fellow-men, is to master his instrument, whatever it may happen to be.

His own is that of the senses, and it is through them alone, or almost alone, that life appeals to him; it is almost alone by their help that he describes it, that he produces brilliant works. They render him this great assistance because they are evidently, in his constitution, extraordinarily alive; there is scarcely a page in all his twenty volumes that does not testify to their vivacity. Nothing could be further from his thought than to disavow them and to minimise their importance. He accepts them frankly, gratefully, works them, rejoices in them. If he were told that there are many English writers who would be sorry to go with him in this, he would, I imagine, staring, say that that is about what was to have been expected of the Anglo-Saxon race, or even that many of them probably could not go with him if they would. Then he would ask how our authors can be so foolish as to sacrifice such a *moyen*, how they can afford to, and exclaim, "They must be pretty works, those they produce, and give a fine, true, complete account of life, with such omissions, such lacunæ!" M. de Maupassant's productions teach us, for instance, that his sense of smell is exceptionally acute—as acute as that of those animals of the field and forest whose subsistence and security depend upon it. It might be thought that he would, as a student of the human race, have found an abnormal development of this

faculty embarrassing, scarcely knowing what to do
with it, where to place it. But such an apprehension
betrays an imperfect conception of his directness and
resolution, as well as of his constant economy of
means. Nothing whatever prevents him from representing the relations of men and women as largely
governed by the scent of the parties. Human life in
his pages (would this not be the most general description he would give of it ?) appears for the most part
as a sort of concert of odours, and his people are
perpetually engaged, or he is engaged on their behalf,
in sniffing up and distinguishing them, in some
pleasant or painful exercise of the nostril. "If everything in life speaks to the nostril, why on earth
shouldn't we say so ?" I suppose him to inquire;
"and what a proof of the empire of poor conventions
and hypocrisies, *chez vous autres*, that you should pretend to describe and characterise, and yet take no
note (or so little that it comes to the same thing) of
that essential sign ! "

Not less powerful is his visual sense, the quick,
direct discrimination of his eye, which explains the
singularly vivid concision of his descriptions. These
are never prolonged nor analytic, have nothing of
enumeration, of the quality of the observer, who
counts the items to be sure he has made up the sum.
His eye *selects* unerringly, unscrupulously, almost
impudently—catches the particular thing in which
the character of the object or the scene resides, and,
by expressing it with the artful brevity of a master,

leaves a convincing, original picture. If he is inveterately synthetic, he is never more so than in the way he brings this hard, short, intelligent gaze to bear. His vision of the world is for the most part a vision of ugliness, and even when it is not, there is in his easy power to generalise a certain absence of love, a sort of bird's-eye-view contempt. He has none of the superstitions of observation, none of our English indulgences, our tender and often imaginative superficialities. If he glances into a railway carriage bearing its freight into the Parisian suburbs of a summer Sunday, a dozen dreary lives map themselves out in a flash.

"There were stout ladies in farcical clothes, those middle-class goodwives of the *banlieue* who replace the distinction they don't possess by an irrelevant dignity; gentlemen weary of the office, with sallow faces and twisted bodies, and one of their shoulders a little forced up by perpetual bending at work over a table. Their anxious, joyless faces spoke moreover of domestic worries, incessant needs for money, old hopes finally shattered; for they all belonged to the army of poor threadbare devils who vegetate frugally in a mean little plaster house, with a flower-bed for a garden." . . .

Even in a brighter picture, such as the admirable vignette of the drive of Madame Tellier and her companions, the whole thing is an impression, as painters say nowadays, in which the figures are cheap. The six women at the station clamber into a country cart and go jolting through the Norman landscape to the village.

"But presently the jerky trot of the nag shook the vehicle so terribly that the chairs began to dance, tossing up the travellers to right, to left, with movements like puppets, scared grimaces, cries of dismay suddenly interrupted by a more violent bump. They clutched the sides of the trap, their bonnets turned over on to their backs, or upon the nose or the shoulder; and the white horse continued to go, thrusting out his head and straightening the little tail, hairless like that of a rat, with which from time to time he whisked his buttocks Joseph Rivet, with one foot stretched upon the shaft, the other leg bent under him, and his elbows very high, held the reins and emitted from his throat every moment a kind of cluck which caused the animal to prick up his ears and quicken his pace. On either side of the road the green country stretched away. The colza, in flower, produced in spots a great carpet of undulating yellow, from which there rose a strong, wholesome smell, a smell penetrating and pleasant, carried very far by the breeze. In the tall rye the cornflowers held up their little azure heads, which the women wished to pluck; but M. Rivet refused to stop. Then, in some place, a whole field looked as if it were sprinkled with blood, it was so crowded with poppies. And in the midst of the great level, taking colour in this fashion from the flowers of the soil, the trap passed on with the jog of the white horse, seeming itself to carry a nosegay of richer hues; it disappeared behind the big trees of a farm, to come out again where the foliage stopped and parade afresh through the green and yellow crops, pricked with red or blue, its blazing cartload of women, which receded in the sunshine."

As regards the other sense, the sense *par excellence*, the sense which we scarcely mention in English fiction, and which I am not very sure I shall be allowed to mention in an English periodical, M. de Maupassant speaks for that, and of it, with extraordinary distinctness and authority. To say that it occupies the first place in his picture is to say too little; it covers in truth the whole canvas, and his work is little else but a report of its innumerable manifestations. These manifestations are not, for him, so many incidents of life; they are life itself, they represent the standing answer to any question that we may ask about it. He describes them in detail, with a familiarity and a frankness which leave nothing to be added; I should say with singular truth, if I did not consider that in regard to this article he may be taxed with a certain exaggeration. M. de Maupassant would doubtless affirm that where the empire of the sexual sense is concerned, no exaggeration is possible: nevertheless it may be said that whatever depths may be discovered by those who dig for them, the impression of the human spectacle for him who takes it as it comes has less analogy with that of the monkeys' cage than this admirable writer's account of it. I speak of the human spectacle as we Anglo-Saxons see it—as we Anglo-Saxons pretend we see it, M. de Maupassant would possibly say.

At any rate, I have perhaps touched upon this peculiarity sufficiently to explain my remark that his point of view is almost solely that of the senses. If he is a very interesting case, this makes him also an embarrassing one, embarrassing and mystifying for the moralist. I may as well admit that no writer of the day strikes me as equally so. To find M. de Maupassant 'a lion in the path—that may seem to some people a singular proof of want of courage; but I think the obstacle will not be made light of by

those who have really taken the measure of the
animal. We are accustomed to think, we of the
English faith, that a cynic is a living advertisement
of his errors, especially in proportion as he is a
thorough-going one; and M. de Maupassant's cynicism,
unrelieved as it is, will not be disposed of off-hand by
a critic of a competent literary sense. Such a critic
is not slow to perceive, to his no small confusion,
that though, judging from usual premises, the author
of *Bel-Ami* ought to be a warning, he somehow is
not. His baseness, as it pervades him, ought to be
written all over him ; yet somehow there are there
certain aspects — and those commanding, as the
house-agents say—in which it is not in the least to
be perceived. It is easy to exclaim that if he judges
life only from the point of view of the senses, many
are the noble and exquisite things that he must leave
out. What he leaves out has no claim to get itself
considered till after we have done justice to what he
takes in. It is this positive side of M. de Maupassant
that is most remarkable—the fact that his literary
character is so complete and edifying. " Auteur à peu
près irréprochable dans un genre qui ne l'est pas,"as that
excellent critic M. Jules Lemaître says of him, he dis-
turbs us by associating a conscience and a high standard
with a temper long synonymous, in our eyes, with an
absence of scruples. The situation would be simpler
certainly if he were a bad writer ; but none the less it
is possible, I think, on the whole, to circumvent him,
even without attempting to prove that after all he is one.

The latter part of his introduction to *Pierre et Jean* is less felicitous than the beginning, but we learn from it—and this is interesting—that he regards the analytic fashion of telling a story, which has lately begotten in his own country some such remarkable experiments (few votaries as it has attracted among ourselves), as very much less profitable than the simple epic manner which "avoids with care all complicated explanations, all dissertations upon motives, and confines itself to making persons and events pass before our eyes." M. de Maupassant adds that in his view "psychology should be hidden in a book, as it is hidden in reality under the facts of existence. The novel conceived in this manner gains interest, movement, colour, the bustle of life." When it is a question of an artistic process, we must always mistrust very sharp distinctions, for there is surely in every method a little of every other method. It is as difficult to describe an action without glancing at its motive, its moral history, as it is to describe a motive without glancing at its practical consequence. Our history and our fiction are what we do; but it surely is not more easy to determine where what we do begins than to determine where it ends— notoriously a hopeless task. Therefore it would take a very subtle sense to draw a hard and fast line on the borderland of explanation and illustration. If psychology be hidden in life, as, according to M. de Maupassant, it should be in a book, the question immediately comes up, "From whom is it hidden?" From some people, no doubt, but very much less from others; and all depends upon the observer, the nature of one's observation, and one's curiosity. For some people motives, reasons, relations, explanations, are a part of the very surface of the drama, with the footlights beating full upon them. For me an act, an incident, an attitude, may be a sharp, detached, isolated thing, of which I give a full account in saying that in such and such a way it came off. For you it may be hung about with implications, with relations, and conditions as necessary to help you to recognise it as the clothes of your friends are to help you know them in the street. You feel that they would seem strange to you without petticoats and trousers.

M. de Maupassant would probably urge that the right thing is to know, or to guess, how events come to pass, but to say as little about it as possible. There are matters in regard to which he feels the importance of being explicit, but that is not one of them. The contention to which I allude strikes me as rather arbitrary, so difficult is it to put one's finger upon the reason why, for instance, there should be so little mystery about what happened to Christiane Andermatt, in *Mont-Oriol*, when she went to walk on the hills with Paul Brétigny, and so much, say, about the forces that formed her for that gentleman's convenience, or those lying behind any other odd collapse that our author may have related. The

rule misleads, and the best rule certainly is the tact
of the individual writer, which will adapt itself to
the material as the material comes to him. The
cause we plead is ever pretty sure to be the cause of
our idiosyncrasies, and if M. de Maupassant thinks
meanly of "explanations," it is, I suspect, that they
come to him in no great affluence. His view of the
conduct of man is so simple as scarcely to require
them; and indeed so far as they are needed he *is*,
virtually, explanatory. He deprecates reference to
motives, but there is one, covering an immense
ground in his horizon, as I have already hinted, to
which he perpetually refers. If the sexual impulse
be not a moral antecedent, it is none the less the wire
that moves almost all M. de Maupassant's puppets,
and as he has not hidden it, I cannot see that he has
eliminated analysis or made a sacrifice to discretion.
His pages are studded with that particular analysis;
he is constantly peeping behind the curtain, telling
us what he discovers there. The truth is that the
admirable system of simplification which makes his
tales so rapid and so concise (especially his shorter
ones, for his novels in some degree, I think, suffer
from it), strikes us as not in the least a conscious
intellectual effort, a selective, comparative process.
He tells us all he knows, all he suspects, and if
these things take no account of the moral nature of
man, it is because he has no window looking in that
direction, and not because artistic scruples have compelled him to close it up. The very compact

mansion in which he dwells presents on that side a perfectly dead wall.

This is why, if his axiom that you produce the effect of truth better by painting people from the outside than from the inside has a large utility, his example is convincing in a much higher degree. A writer is fortunate when his theory and his limitations so exactly correspond, when his curiosities may be appeased with such precision and promptitude. M. de Maupassant contends that the most that the analytic novelist can do is to put himself—his own peculiarities—into the costume of the figure analysed. This may be true, but if it applies to one manner of representing people who are not ourselves, it applies also to any other manner. It is the limitation, the difficulty of the novelist, to whatever clan or camp he may belong. M. de Maupassant is remarkably objective and impersonal, but he would go too far if he were to entertain the belief that he has kept himself out of his books. They speak of him eloquently, even if it only be to tell us how easy—how easy, given his talent of course—he has found this impersonality. Let us hasten to add that in the case of describing a character it is doubtless more difficult to convey the impression of something that is not one's self (the constant effort, however delusive at bottom, of the novelist), than in the case of describing some object more immediately visible. The operation is more delicate, but that circumstance only increases the beauty of the problem.

On the question of style our author has some
excellent remarks ; we may be grateful indeed for
every one of them, save an odd reflection about the
way to "become original" if we happen not to be so.
The recipe for this transformation, it would appear,
is to sit down in front of a blazing fire, or a tree in
a plain, or any object we encounter in the regular
way of business, and remain there until the tree, or
the fire, or the object, whatever it be, become different for us from all other specimens of the same class.
I doubt whether this system would always answer,
for surely the resemblance is what we wish to discover, quite as much as the difference, and the best
way to preserve it is not to look for something
opposed to it. Is not this indication of the road
to take to become, as a writer, original touched
with the same fallacy as the recommendation about
eschewing analysis ? It is the only *naïveté* I have
encountered in M. de Maupassant's many volumes.
The best originality is the most unconscious, and the
best way to describe a tree is the way in which it
has struck us.   "Ah, but we don't always know how
it has struck us," the answer to that may be, "and it
takes some time and ingenuity—much fasting and
prayer—to find out."   If we do not know, it probably
has not struck us very much: so little indeed that our
inquiry had better be relegated to that closed chamber
of an artist's meditations, that sacred back kitchen,
which no *a priori* rule can light up.   The best thing
the artist's adviser can do in such a case is to trust

him and turn away, to let him fight the matter out
with his conscience.   And be this said with a full
appreciation of the degree in which M. de Maupassant's observations on the whole question of a writer's
style, at the point we have come to to-day, bear the
stamp of intelligence and experience.   His own style
is of so excellent a tradition that the presumption is
altogether in favour of what he may have to say.

He feels oppressively, discouragingly, as many
another of his countrymen must have felt—for the
French have worked their language as no other
people have done — the penalty of coming at the
end of three centuries of literature, the difficulty of
dealing with an instrument of expression so worn
by friction, of drawing new sounds from the old
familiar pipe.   "When we read, so saturated with
French writing as we are that our whole body gives
us the impression of being a paste made of words,
do we ever find a line, a thought, which is not
familiar to us, and of which we have not had at least
a confused presentiment?"   And he adds that the
matter is simple enough for the writer who only
seeks to amuse the public by means already known ;
he attempts little, and he produces " with confidence,
in the candour of his mediocrity," works which answer
no question and leave no trace.   It is he who wants
to do more than this that has less and less an easy
time of it.   Everything seems to him to have been
done, every effect produced, every combination already
made.   If he be a man of genius, his trouble is

lightened, for mysterious ways are revealed to him,
and new combinations spring up for him even after
novelty is dead. It is to the simple man of taste
and talent, who has only a conscience and a will,
that the situation may sometimes well appear desperate; he judges himself as he goes, and he can
only go step by step over ground where every step
is already a footprint.

If it be a miracle whenever there is a fresh tone,
the miracle has been wrought for M. de Maupassant.
Or is he simply a man of genius to whom short cuts
have been disclosed in the watches of the night? At
any rate he has had faith—religion has come to his
aid; I mean the religion of his mother tongue, which
he has loved well enough to be patient for her sake.
He has arrived at the peace which passeth understanding, at a kind of conservative piety. He has
taken his stand on simplicity, on a studied sobriety,
being persuaded that the deepest science lies in that
direction rather than in the multiplication of new
terms, and on this subject he delivers himself with
superlative wisdom. "There is no need of the queer,
complicated, numerous, and Chinese vocabulary which
is imposed on us to-day under the name of artistic
writing, to fix all the shades of thought; the right
way is to distinguish with an extreme clearness all
those modifications of the value of a word which
come from the place it occupies. Let us have fewer
nouns, verbs and adjectives of an almost imperceptible sense, and more different phrases variously con-

structed, ingeniously cast, full of the science of sound and rhythm. Let us have an excellent general form rather than be collectors of rare terms." M. de Maupassant's practice does not fall below his exhortation (though I must confess that in the foregoing passage he makes use of the detestable expression "stylist," which I have not reproduced). Nothing can exceed the masculine firmness, the quiet force of his own style, in which every phrase is a close sequence, every epithet a paying piece, and the ground is completely cleared of the vague, the ready-made and the second-best. Less than any one to-day does he beat the air ; more than any one does he hit out from the shoulder.

II

HE has produced a hundred short tales and only four regular novels; but if the tales deserve the first place in any candid appreciation of his talent it is not simply because they are so much the more numerous: they are also more characteristic; they represent him best in his originality, and their brevity, extreme in some cases, does not prevent them from being a collection of masterpieces. (They are very unequal, and I speak of the best.) The little story is but scantily relished in England, where readers take their fiction rather by the volume than by the page, and the novelist's idea is apt to resemble one of those old-fashioned carriages which require a wide court to turn round. In America, where it is associated pre-eminently with Hawthorne's name, with Edgar Poe's, and with that of Mr. Bret Harte, the short tale has had a better fortune. France, however, has been the land of its great prosperity, and M. de Maupassant had from the first the advantage of addressing a public accustomed to catch on, as the modern phrase is, quickly. In some respects, it may be said, he encountered prejudices too friendly, for he found a tradition of indecency ready made to his hand. I say indecency with plainness, though my indication would perhaps please better with another word, for we suffer in English from a lack of roundabout names for the *conte leste*—that element for which the French, with their *grivois*, their *gaillard*, their *égrillard*, their *gaudriole*, have so many convenient synonyms. It is an honoured tradition in France that the little story, in verse or in prose, should be liable to be more or less obscene (I can think only of that alternative epithet), though I hasten to add that among literary forms it does not monopolise the privilege. Our uncleanness is less producible—at any rate it is less produced.

For the last ten years our author has brought forth with regularity these condensed compositions, of which, probably, to an English reader, at a first glance, the most universal sign will be their licentiousness. They really partake of this quality, however, in a very differing degree, and a second glance shows that they may be divided into numerous groups. It is not fair, I think, even to say that what they have most in common is their being extremely *lestes*. What they have most in common is their being extremely strong, and after that their being extremely brutal. A story may be obscene without being brutal, and *vice versâ*, and M. de Maupassant's contempt for those interdictions which are supposed to be made in the interest of good morals is but an incident—a very large one indeed—

of his general contempt.   A pessimism so great that
its alliance with the love of good work, or even with
the calculation of the sort of work that pays best in
a country of style, is, as I have intimated, the most
puzzling of anomalies (for it would seem in the light
of such sentiments that nothing is worth anything),
this cynical strain is the sign of such gems of
narration as *La Maison Tellier L'Histoire d'une Fille de
Ferme, L'Ane, Le Chien, Mademoiselle Fifi, Monsieur
Parent, L'Héritage, En Famille, Le Baptême, Le Père
Amable.*   The author fixes a hard eye on some small
spot of human life, usually some ugly, dreary, shabby,
sordid one, takes up the particle, and squeezes it
either till it grimaces or till it bleeds.   Sometimes
the grimace is very droll, sometimes the wound is
very horrible ; but in either case the whole thing is
real, observed, noted, and represented, not an invention
or a castle in the air.   M. de Maupassant sees human
life as a terribly ugly business relieved by the
comical, but even the comedy is for the most part the
comedy of misery, of avidity, of ignorance, helpless-
ness, and grossness.   When his laugh is not for these
things, it is for the little *saletés* (to use one of his own
favourite words) of luxurious life, which are intended
to be prettier, but which can scarcely be said to
brighten the picture.   I like *La Bête à Maître Bel-
homme, La Ficelle, Le Petit Fût, Le Cas de Madame
Luneau, Tribuneaux Rustiques,* and many others of this
category much better than his anecdotes of the
mutual confidences of his little *marquises* and *baronnes.*

Not counting his novels for the moment, his tales may be divided into the three groups of those which deal with the Norman peasantry, those which deal with the *petit employé* and small shopkeeper, usually in Paris, and the miscellaneous, in which the upper walks of life are represented, and the fantastic, the whimsical, the weird, and even the supernatural, figure as well as the unexpurgated. These last things range from *Le Horla* (which is not a specimen of the author's best vein—the only occasion on which he has the weakness of imitation is when he strikes us as emulating Edgar Poe) to *Miss Harriet*, and from *Boule de Suif* (a triumph) to that almost inconceivable little growl of Anglophobia, *Découverte*—inconceivable I mean in its irresponsibility and ill-nature on the part of a man of M. de Maupassant's distinction ; passing by such little perfections as *Petit Soldat, L'Abandonné, Le Collier* (the list is too long for complete enumeration), and such gross imperfections (for it once in a while befalls our author to go woefully astray), as *La Femme de Paul, Châli, Les Sœurs Rondoli.* To these might almost be added as a special category the various forms in which M. de Maupassant relates adventures in railway carriages. Numerous, to his imagination, are the pretexts for enlivening fiction afforded by first, second, and third class compartments ; the accidents (which have nothing to do with the conduct of the train) that occur there constitute no inconsiderable part of our earthly transit.

It is surely by his Norman peasant that his tales
will live ; he knows this worthy as if he had made
him, understands him down to the ground, puts him
on his feet with a few of the freest, most plastic
touches.   M. de Maupassant does not admire him,
and he is such a master of the subject that it would
ill become an outsider to suggest a revision of judgment.   He is a part of the contemptible furniture of
the world, but on the whole, it would appear, the
most grotesque part of it.   His caution, his canniness,
his natural astuteness, his stinginess, his general
grinding sordidness, are as unmistakable as that
quaint and brutish dialect in which he expresses
himself, and on which our author plays like a virtuoso.
It would be impossible to demonstrate with a finer
sense of the humour of the thing the fatuities and
densities of his ignorance, the bewilderments of his
opposed appetites, the overreachings of his caution.
His existence has a gay side, but it is apt to be the
barbarous gaiety commemorated in *Farce Normande*,
an anecdote which, like many of M. de Maupassant's
anecdotes, it is easier to refer the reader to than to
repeat.   If it is most convenient to place *La Maison
Tellier* among the tales of the peasantry, there is no
doubt that it stands at the head of the list.   It is
absolutely unadapted to the perusal of ladies and
young persons, but it shares this peculiarity with
most of its fellows, so that to ignore it on that
account would be to imply that we must forswear M.
de Maupassant altogether, which is an incongruous

and insupportable conclusion. Every good story is of course both a picture and an idea, and the more they are interfused the better the problem is solved. In *La Maison Tellier* they fit each other to perfection ; the capacity for sudden innocent delights latent in natures which have lost their innocence is vividly illustrated by the singular scenes to which our acquaintance with Madame and her staff (little as it may be a thing to boast of), successively introduces us. The breadth, the freedom, and brightness of all this give the measure of the author's talent, and of that large, keen way of looking at life which sees the pathetic and the droll, the stuff of which the whole piece is made, in the queerest and humblest patterns. The tone of *La Maison Tellier* and the few compositions which closely resemble it, expresses M. de Maupassant's nearest approach to geniality. Even here, however, it is the geniality of the showman exhilarated by the success with which he feels that he makes his mannikins (and especially his woman-kins) caper and squeak, and who after the performance tosses them into their box with the irreverence of a practised hand. If the pages of the author of *Bel-Ami* may be searched almost in vain for a manifestation of the sentiment of respect, it is naturally not by Mme. Tellier and her charges that we must look most to see it called forth ; but they are among the things that please him most.

Sometimes there is a sorrow, a misery, or even a little heroism, that he handles with a certain tenderness (*Une Vie* is the capital example of this), without insisting on the poor, the ridiculous, or, as he is fond of saying, the bestial side of it. Such an attempt, admirable in its sobriety and delicacy, is the sketch, in *L'Abandonné*, of the old lady and gentleman, Mme. de Cadour and M. d'Apreval, who, staying with the husband of the former at a little watering-place on the Normandy coast, take a long, hot walk on a summer's day, on a straight, white road, into the interior, to catch a clandestine glimpse of a young farmer, their illegitimate son. He has been pensioned, he is ignorant of his origin, and is a commonplace and unconciliatory rustic. They look at him, in his dirty farmyard, and no sign passes between them; then they turn away and crawl back, in melancholy silence, along the dull French road. The manner in which this dreary little occurrence is related makes it as large as a chapter of history. There is tenderness in *Miss Harriet*, which sets forth how an English old maid, fantastic, hideous, sentimental, and tract-distributing, with a smell of india-rubber, fell in love with an irresistible French painter, and drowned herself in the well because she saw him kissing the maid-servant; but the figure of the lady grazes the farcical. Is it because we know Miss Harriet (if we are not mistaken in the type the author has had in his eye) that we suspect the good spinster was not so weird and desperate, addicted though her class may be, as he says, to "haunting all the *tables d'hôte* in Europe, to spoiling Italy, poisoning

Switzerland, making the charming towns of the Mediterranean uninhabitable, carrying everywhere their queer little manias, their *mœurs de vestales pétrifiées*, their indescribable garments, and that odour of india-rubber which makes one think that at night they must be slipped into a case?" What would Miss Harriet have said to M. de Maupassant's friend, the hero of the *Découverte*, who, having married a little Anglaise because he thought she was charming when she spoke broken French, finds she is very flat as she becomes more fluent, and has nothing more urgent than to denounce her to a gentleman he meets on the steamboat, and to relieve his wrath in ejaculations of "Sales Anglais"?

M. de Maupassant evidently knows a great deal about the army of clerks who work under government, but it is a terrible tale that he has to tell of them and of the *petit bourgeois* in general. It is true that he has treated the *petit bourgeois* in *Pierre et Jean* without holding him up to our derision, and the effort has been so fruitful, that we owe to it the work for which, on the whole, in the long list of his successes, we are most thankful. But of *Pierre et Jean*, a production neither comic nor cynical (in the degree, that is, of its predecessors), but serious and fresh, I will speak anon. In *Monsieur Parent*, *L'Héritage*, *En Famille*, *Une Partie de Campagne*, *Promenade*, and many other pitiless little pieces, the author opens the window wide to his perception of everything mean, narrow, and sordid. The subject is ever the struggle for existence in hard conditions, lighted up simply by more or less *polissonnerie.* Nothing is more strik-ing to an Anglo-Saxon reader than the omission of all the other lights, those with which our imagination, and I think it ought to be said our observation, is familiar, and which our own works of fiction at any rate do not permit us to forget : those of which the most general description is that they spring from a certain mixture of good-humour and piety—piety, I mean, in the civil and domestic sense quite as much as in the religious. The love of sport, the sense of decorum, the necessity for action, the habit of respect, the absence of irony, the pervasiveness of childhood, the expansive tendency of the race, are a few of the qualities (the analysis might, I think, be pushed much further) which ease us off, mitigate our tension and irritation, rescue us from the nervous exasperation which is almost the commonest element of life as depicted by M. de Maupassant. No doubt there is in our literature an immense amount of conventional blinking, and it may be questioned whether pessi-mistic representation in M. de Maupassant's manner do not follow his particular original more closely than our perpetual quest of pleasantness (does not Mr. Rider Haggard make even his African carnage pleasant ?) adheres to the lines of the world we our-selves know.

Fierce indeed is the struggle for existence among even our pious and good-humoured millions, and it is attended with incidents as to which after all little testimony is to be extracted from our literature of fiction. It must never be forgotten that the optimism of that literature is partly the optimism of women and of spinsters; in other words the optimism of ignorance as well as of delicacy. It might be supposed that the French, with their mastery of the *arts d'agrément*, would have more consolations than we, but such is not the account of the matter given by the new generation of painters. To the French we seem superficial, and we are certainly open to the reproach; but none the less even to the infinite majority of readers of good faith there will be a wonderful want of correspondence between the general picture of *Bel-Ami*, of *Mont-Oriol*, of *Une Vie*, *Yvette* and *En Famille*, and our own vision of reality. It is an old impression of course that the satire of the French has a very different tone from ours; but few English readers will admit that the feeling of life is less in ours than in theirs. The feeling of life is evidently, *de part et d'autre*, a very different thing. If in ours, as the novel illustrates it, there are superficialities, there are also qualities which are far from being negatives and omissions: a large imagination and (is it fatuous to say?) a large experience of the positive kind. Even those of our novelists whose manner is most ironic pity life more and hate it less than M. de Maupassant and his great initiator Flaubert. It comes back I suppose to our good-humour (which may apparently also be an artistic force); at any rate, we have reserves about our shames and our

sorrows, indulgences and tolerances about our Philistinism, forbearances about our blows, and a general
friendliness of conception about our possibilities,
which take the cruelty from our self-derision and
operate in the last resort as a sort of tribute to our
freedom.   There is a horrible, admirable scene in
Monsieur Parent, which is a capital example of trium-
phant ugliness.   The harmless gentleman who gives
his name to the tale has an abominable wife, one of
whose offensive attributes is a lover (unsuspected
by her husband), only less impudent than herself.
M. Parent comes in from a walk with his little boy,
at dinner-time, to encounter suddenly in his abused,
dishonoured, deserted home, convincing proof of her
misbehaviour.   He waits and waits dinner for her,
giving her the benefit of every doubt ; but when at
last she enters, late in the evening, accompanied by
the partner of her guilt, there is a tremendous
domestic concussion.   It is to the peculiar vividness
of this scene that I allude, the way we hear it and
see it, and its most repulsive details are evoked for
us : the sordid confusion, the vulgar noise, the dis-
ordered table and ruined dinner, the shrill insolence
of the wife, her brazen mendacity, the scared in-
feriority of the lover, the mere momentary heroics
of the weak husband, the scuffle and somersault, the
eminently unpoetic justice with which it all ends.

When Thackeray relates how Arthur Pendennis
goes home to take pot-luck with the insolvent Newcomes at Boulogne, and how the dreadful Mrs.

Mackenzie receives him, and how she makes a scene, when the frugal repast is served, over the diminished mutton-bone, we feel that the notation of that order of misery goes about as far as we can bear it. But this is child's play to the history of M. and Mme. Caravan and their attempt, after the death (or supposed death) of the husband's mother, to transfer to their apartment before the arrival of the other heirs certain miserable little articles of furniture belonging to the deceased, together with the frustration of the manœuvre not only by the grim resurrection of the old woman (which is a sufficiently fantastic item), but by the shock of battle when a married daughter and her husband appear. No one gives us like M. de Maupassant the odious words exchanged on such an occasion as that: no one depicts with so just a hand the feelings of small people about small things. These feelings are very apt to be "fury"; that word is of strikingly frequent occurrence in his pages. *L'Héritage* is a drama of private life in the little world of the Ministère de la Marine—a world, according to M. de Maupassant, of dreadful little jealousies and ineptitudes. Readers of a robust complexion should learn how the wretched M. Lesable was handled by his wife and her father on his failing to satisfy their just expectations, and how he comported himself in the singular situation thus prepared for him. The story is a model of narration, but it leaves our poor average humanity dangling like a beaten rag.

Where does M. de Maupassant find the great multitude of his detestable women? or where at least does he find the courage to represent them in such colours? Jeanne de Lamare, in *Une Vie*, receives the outrages of fate with a passive fortitude : and there is something touching in Mme. Roland's *âme tendre de caissière*, as exhibited in *Pierre et Jean*. But for the most part M. de Maupassant's heroines are a mixture of extreme sensuality and extreme mendacity. They are a large element in that general disfigurement, that *illusion de l'ignoble, qui attire tant d'êtres*, which makes the perverse or the stupid side of things the one which strikes him first, which leads him, if he glances at a group of nurses and children sunning themselves in a Parisian square, to notice primarily the *yeux de brute* of the nurses ; or if he speaks of the longing for a taste of the country which haunts the shopkeeper fenced in behind his counter, to identify it as the *amour bête de la nature ;* or if he has occasion to put the boulevards before us on a summer's evening, to seek his effect in these terms : "The city, as hot as a stew, seemed to sweat in the suffocating night. The drains puffed their pestilential breath from their mouths of granite, and the underground kitchens poured into the streets, through their low windows, the infamous miasmas of their dishwater and old sauces." I do not contest the truth of such indications, I only note the particular selection and their seeming to the writer the most *àpropos*.

Is it because of the inadequacy of these indications when applied to the long stretch that M. de Maupassant's novels strike us as less complete, in proportion to the talent expended upon them, than his *contes* and *nouvelles?* I make this invidious distinction in spite of the fact that *Une Vie* (the first of the novels in the order of time) is a remarkably interesting experiment, and that *Pierre et Jean* is, so far as my judgment goes, a faultless production. *Bel-Ami* is full of the bustle and the crudity of life (its energy and expressiveness almost bribe one to like it), but it has the great defect that the physiological explanation of things here too visibly contracts the problem in order to meet it. The world represented is too special, too little inevitable, too much to take or to leave as we like—a world in which every man is a cad and every woman a harlot. M. de Maupassant traces the career of a finished blackguard who succeeds in life through women, and he represents him primarily as succeeding in the profession of journalism. His colleagues and his mistresses are as depraved as himself, greatly to the injury of the ironic idea, for the real force of satire would have come from seeing him engaged and victorious with natures better than his own. It may be remarked that this was the case with the nature of Mme. Walter; but the reply to that is—hardly! Moreover the author's whole treatment of the episode of Mme. Walter is the thing on which his admirers have least to congratulate him. The taste of it is so

atrocious, that it is difficult to do justice to the way
it is made to stand out.   Such an instance as this
pleads with irresistible eloquence, as it seems to me,
the cause of that salutary diffidence or practical
generosity which I mentioned on a preceding page.
I know not the English or American novelist who
could have written this portion of the history of *Bel-
Ami* if he would.   But I also find it impossible to
conceive of a member of that fraternity who would
have written it if he could.   The subject of *Mont-
Oriol* is full of queerness to the English mind.   Here
again the picture has much more importance than
the idea, which is simply that a gentleman, if he
happen to be a low animal, is liable to love a lady
very much less if she presents him with a pledge of
their affection.   It need scarcely be said that the
lady and gentleman who in M. de Maupassant's
pages exemplify this interesting truth are not united
in wedlock—that is with each other.

M. de Maupassant tells us that he has imbibed
many of his principles from Gustave Flaubert, from
the study of his works as well as, formerly, the enjoyment of his words.   It is in *Une Vie* that Flaubert's
influence is most directly traceable, for the thing has
a marked analogy with *L'Education Sentimentale.*
That is, it is the presentation of a simple piece of a
life (in this case a long piece), a series of observations
upon an episode *quelconque*, as the French say, with
the minimum of arrangement of the given objects.
It is an excellent example of the way the impression

of truth may be conveyed by that form, but it would
have been a still better one if in his search for the
effect of dreariness (the effect of dreariness may be
said to be the subject of *Une Vie*, so far as the
subject is reducible) the author had not eliminated
excessively. He has arranged, as I say, as little as
possible ; the necessity of a " plot " has in no degree
imposed itself upon him, and his effort has been to
give the uncomposed, unrounded look of life, with its
accidents, its broken rhythm, its queer resemblance
to the famous description of " Bradshaw "—a compound of trains that start but don't arrive, and trains
that arrive but don't start. It is almost an arrangement of the history of poor Mme. de Lamare to have
left so many things out of it, for after all she is
described in very few of the relations of life. The
principal ones are there certainly ; we see her as a
daughter, a wife, and a mother, but there is a certain
accumulation of secondary experience that marks
any passage from youth to old age which is a wholly
absent element in M. de Maupassant's narrative, and
the suppression of which gives the thing a tinge of
the arbitrary. It is in the power of this secondary
experience to make a great difference, but nothing
makes any difference for Jeanne de Lamare as M. de
Maupassant puts her before us. Had she no other
points of contact than those he describes ?—no friends,
no phases, no episodes, no chances, none of the miscellaneous *remplissage* of life ? No doubt M. de Maupassant would say that he has had to select, that the

most comprehensive enumeration is only a condensation, and that, in accordance with the very just principles enunciated in that preface to which I have perhaps too repeatedly referred, he has sacrificed what is uncharacteristic to what is characteristic. It characterises the career of this French country lady of fifty years ago that its long gray expanse should be seen as peopled with but five or six figures. The essence of the matter is that she was deceived in almost every affection, and that essence is given if the persons who deceived her are given.

The reply is doubtless adequate, and I have only intended my criticism to suggest the degree of my interest. What it really amounts to is that if the subject of this artistic experiment had been the existence of an English lady, even a very dull one, the air of verisimilitude would have demanded that she should have been placed in a denser medium. *Une Vie* may after all be only a testimony to the fact of the melancholy void of the coast of Normandy, even within a moderate drive of a great seaport, under the Restoration and Louis Philippe. It is especially to be recommended to those who are interested in the question of what constitutes a " story," offering as it does the most definite sequences at the same time that it has nothing that corresponds to the usual idea of a plot, and closing with an implication that finds us prepared. The picture again in this case is much more dominant than the idea, unless it be an idea that loneliness and grief are terrible. The picture, at any rate, is full of truthful touches, and the work has the merit and the charm that it is the most delicate of the author's productions and the least hard. In none other has he occupied himself so continuously with so innocent a figure as his soft, bruised heroine ; in none other has he paid our poor blind human history the compliment (and this is remarkable, considering the flatness of so much of the particular subject) of finding it so little *bête*. He may think it, here, but comparatively he does not say it. He almost betrays a sense of moral things. Jeanne is absolutely passive, she has no moral spring, no active moral life, none of the edifying attributes of character (it costs her apparently as little as may be in the way of a shock, a complication of feeling, to discover, by letters, after her mother's death, that this lady has not been the virtuous woman she has supposed); but her chronicler has had to handle the immaterial forces of patience and renunciation, and this has given the book a certain purity, in spite of two or three "physiological" passages that come in with violence—a violence the greater as we feel it to be a result of selection. It is very much a mark of M. de Maupassant that on the most striking occasion, with a single exception, on which his picture is not a picture of libertinage it is a picture of unmitigated suffering. Would he suggest that these are the only alternatives ?

The exception that I here allude to is for *Pierre et Jean*, which I have left myself small space to speak

of.   Is it because in this masterly little novel there
is a show of those immaterial forces which I just
mentioned, and because Pierre Roland is one of the
few instances of operative character that can be re-
called from so many volumes, that many readers will
place M. de Maupassant's latest production altogether
at the head of his longer ones?   I am not sure, inasmuch as after all the character in question is not
extraordinarily distinguished, and the moral problem
not presented in much complexity.   The case is only
relative.   Perhaps it is not of importance to fix the
reasons of preference in respect to a piece of writing
so essentially a work of art and of talent.   *Pierre et
Jean* is the best of M. de Maupassant's novels mainly
because M. de Maupassant has never before been so
clever.   It is a pleasure to see a mature talent able
to renew itself, strike another note, and appear still
young.   This story suggests the growth of a perception that everything has not been said about the
actors on the world's stage when they are represented
either as helpless victims or as mere bundles of
appetites.   There is an air of responsibility about
Pierre Roland, the person on whose behalf the tale
is mainly told, which almost constitutes a pledge.
An inquisitive critic may ask why in this particular
case M. de Maupassant should have stuck to the *petit
bourgeois*, the circumstances not being such as to
typify that class more than another.   There are
reasons indeed which on reflection are perceptible ;
it was necessary that his people should be poor, and

necessary even that to attenuate Madame Roland's misbehaviour she should have had the excuse of the contracted life of a shopwoman in the Rue Montmartre. Were the inquisitive critic slightly malicious as well, he might suspect the author of a fear that he should seem to give way to the *illusion du beau* if in addition to representing the little group in *Pierre et Jean* as persons of about the normal conscience he had also represented them as of the cultivated class. If they belong to the humble life this belittles and— I am still quoting the supposedly malicious critic— M. de Maupassant *must*, in one way or the other, belittle. To the English reader it will appear, I think, that Pierre and Jean are rather more of the cultivated class than two young Englishmen in the same social position. It belongs to the drama that the struggle of the elder brother—educated, proud, and acute—should be partly with the pettiness of his opportunities. The author's choice of a *milieu*, moreover, will serve to English readers as an example of how much more democratic contemporary French fiction is than that of his own country. The greater part of it — almost all the work of Zola and of Daudet, the best of Flaubert's novels, and the best of those of the brothers De Goncourt—treat of that vast, dim section of society which, lying between those luxurious walks on whose behalf there are easy presuppositions and that darkness of misery which, in addition to being picturesque, brings philanthropy also to the writer's aid, constitutes really, in extent

and expressiveness, the substance of any nation.   In
England, where the fashion of fiction still sets mainly
to the country house and the hunting-field, and yet
more novels are published than anywhere else in the
world, that thick twilight of mediocrity of condition
has been little explored.   May it yield triumphs in
the years to come !

It may seem that I have claimed little for M. de
Maupassant, so far as English readers are concerned
with him, in saying that after publishing twenty
improper volumes he has at last published a twenty-
first, which is neither indecent nor cynical.   It is not
this circumstance that has led me to dedicate so
many pages to him, but the circumstance that in
producing all the others he yet remained, for those
who are interested in these matters, a writer with
whom it was impossible not to reckon.   This is why
I called him, to begin with, so many ineffectual names :
a rarity, a "case," an embarrassment, a lion in the
path.   He is still in the path as I conclude these
observations, but I think that in making them we
have discovered a legitimate way round.   If he is
a master of his art and it is discouraging to find
what low views are compatible with mastery, there is
satisfaction, on the other hand in learning on what
particular condition he holds his strange success.
This condition, it seems to me, is that of having
totally omitted one of the items of the problem, an
omission which has made the problem so much easier
that it may almost be described as a short cut to a

solution. The question is whether it be a fair cut
M. de Maupassant has simply skipped the whole
reflective part of his men and women—that reflective
part which governs conduct and produces character.
He may say that he does not see it, does not know it;
to which the answer is, " So much the better for you,
if you wish to describe life without it. The strings
you pull are by so much the less numerous, and you
can therefore pull those that remain with greater
promptitude, consequently with greater firmness, with
a greater air of knowledge." Pierre Roland, I repeat,
shows a capacity for reflection, but I cannot think
who else does, among the thousand figures who com-
pete with him—I mean for reflection addressed to
anything higher than the gratification of an instinct.
We have an impression that M. d'Apreval and
Madame de Cadour reflect, as they trudge back from
their mournful excursion, but that indication is not
pushed very far. An aptitude for this exercise is a
part of disciplined manhood, and disciplined manhood M. de Maupassant has simply not attempted to
represent. I can remember no instance in which he
sketches any considerable capacity for conduct, and
his women betray that capacity as little as his men.
I am much mistaken if he has once painted a gentleman, in the English sense of the term. His gentlemen, like Paul Brétigny and Gontran de Ravenel,
are guilty of the most extraordinary deflections. For
those who are conscious of this element in life, look
for it and like it, the gap will appear to be immense.

It will lead them to say, "No wonder you have a contempt if that is the way you limit the field. No wonder you judge people roughly if that is the way you see them. Your work, on your premises, remains the admirable thing it is, but is your 'case' not adequately explained?"

The erotic element in M. de Maupassant, about which much more might have been said, seems to me to be explained by the same limitation, and explicable in a similar way wherever else its literature occurs in excess. The carnal side of man appears the most characteristic if you look at it a great deal; and you look at it a great deal if you do not look at the other, at the side by which he reacts against his weaknesses, his defeats. The more you look at the other, the less the whole business to which French novelists have ever appeared to English readers to give a disproportionate place—the business, as I may say, of the senses—will strike you as the only typical one. Is not this the most useful reflection to make in regard to the famous question of the morality, the decency, of the novel? It is the only one, it seems to me, that will meet the case as we find the case to-day. Hard and fast rules, *a priori* restrictions, mere interdictions (you shall not speak of this, you shall not look at that), have surely served their time, and will in the nature of the case never strike an energetic talent as anything but arbitrary. A healthy, living and growing art, full of curiosity and fond of exercise, has an indefeasible mistrust of rigid prohibitions

Let us then leave this magnificent art of the novelist to itself and to its perfect freedom, in the faith that one example is as good as another, and that our fiction will always be decent enough if it be sufficiently general.   Let us not be alarmed at this prodigy (though prodigies are alarming) of M. de Maupassant, who is at once so licentious and so impeccable, but gird ourselves up with the conviction that another point of view will yield another perfection.

1888.

IX

IVAN TURGÉNIEFF

IVAN TURGÉNIEFF

WHEN the mortal remains of Ivan Turgénieff were about to be transported from Paris for interment in his own country, a short commemorative service was held at the Gare du Nord. Ernest Renan and Edmond About, standing beside the train in which his coffin had been placed, bade farewell in the name of the French people to the illustrious stranger who for so many years had been their honoured and grateful guest. M. Renan made a beautiful speech, and M. About a very clever one, and each of them characterised, with ingenuity, the genius and the moral nature of the most touching of writers, the most lovable of men. "Turgénieff," said M. Renan, "received by the mysterious decree which marks out human vocations the gift which is noble beyond all others : he was born essentially impersonal." The passage is so eloquent that one must repeat the whole of it. "His conscience was not that of an individual to whom nature had been more or less generous : it was in some sort the conscience of a people. Before he was born he had lived for thousands of years ;

infinite successions of reveries had amassed themselves in the depths of his heart. No man has been
as much as he the incarnation of a whole race:
generations of ancestors, lost in the sleep of centuries,
speechless, came through him to life and utterance."

I quote these lines for the pleasure of quoting
them; for while I see what M. Renan means by
calling Turgénieff impersonal, it has been my wish
to devote to his delightful memory a few pages
written under the impression of contact and intercourse. He seems to us impersonal, because it is from
his writings almost alone that we of English, French
and German speech have derived our notions—even
yet, I fear, rather meagre and erroneous—of the
Russian people. His genius for us is the Slav genius;
his voice the voice of those vaguely-imagined multi-
tudes whom we think of more and more to-day as
waiting their turn, in the arena of civilisation, in the
grey expanses of the North. There is much in his
writings to encourage this view, and it is certain that
he interpreted with wonderful vividness the temperament of his fellow-countrymen. Cosmopolite that he
had become by the force of circumstances, his roots
had never been loosened in his native soil. The
ignorance with regard to Russia and the Russians
which he found in abundance in the rest of Europe
—and not least in the country he inhabited for ten
years before his death—had indeed the effect, to a
certain degree, to throw him back upon the deep
feelings which so many of his companions were unable

to share with him, the memories of his early years, the sense of wide Russian horizons, the joy and pride of his mother-tongue. In the collection of short pieces, so deeply interesting, written during the last few years of his life, and translated into German under the name of *Senilia*, I find a passage—it is the last in the little book—which illustrates perfectly this reactionary impulse : "In days of doubt, in days of anxious thought on the destiny of my native land, thou alone art my support and my staff, O great powerful Russian tongue, truthful and free ! If it were not for thee how should man not despair at the sight of what is going on at home ? But it is inconceivable that such a language has not been given to a great people." This Muscovite, home-loving note pervades his productions, though it is between the lines, as it were, that we must listen for it. None the less does it remain true that he was not a simple conduit or mouthpiece ; the inspiration was his own as well as the voice. He was an individual, in other words, of the most unmistakable kind, and those who had the happiness to know him have no difficulty to-day in thinking of him as an eminent, responsible figure. This pleasure, for the writer of these lines, was as great as the pleasure of reading the admirable tales into which he put such a world of life and feeling : it was perhaps even greater, for it was not only with the pen that nature had given Turgénieff the power to express himself. He was the richest, the most delightful, of talkers, and his

face, his person, his temper, the thoroughness with
which he had been equipped for human intercourse,
make in the memory of his friends an image which
is completed, but not thrown into the shade, by his
literary distinction. The whole image is tinted with
sadness : partly because the element of melancholy
in his nature was deep and constant—readers of his
novels have no need to be told of that ; and partly
because, during the last years of his life, he had been
condemned to suffer atrociously. Intolerable pain
had been his portion for too many months before he
died ; his end was not a soft decline, but a deepen-
ing distress. But of brightness, of the faculty of
enjoyment, he had also the large allowance usually
made to first-rate men, and he was a singularly complete human being. The author of these pages had
greatly admired his writings before having the fortune
to make his acquaintance, and this privilege, when it
presented itself, was highly illuminating. The man
and the writer together occupied from that moment
a very high place in his affection. Some time
before knowing him I committed to print certain
reflections which his tales had led me to make ; and
I may perhaps, therefore, without impropriety give
them a supplement which shall have a more vivifying
reference. It is almost irresistible to attempt to say,
from one's own point of view, what manner of man
he was.

It was in consequence of the article I just mentioned that I found reason to meet him, in Paris,

where he was then living, in 1875. I shall never forget the impression he made upon me at that first interview. I found him adorable; I could scarcely believe that he would prove—that any man could prove—on nearer acquaintance so delightful as that. Nearer acquaintance only confirmed my hope, and he remained the most approachable, the most practicable, the least unsafe man of genius it has been my fortune to meet. He was so simple, so natural, so modest, so destitute of personal pretension and of what is called the consciousness of powers, that one almost doubted at moments whether he were a man of genius after all. Everything good and fruitful lay near to him; he was interested in everything; and he was absolutely without that eagerness of self-reference which sometimes accompanies great, and even small, reputations. He had not a particle of vanity; nothing whatever of the air of having a part to play or a reputation to keep up. His humour exercised itself as freely upon himself as upon other subjects, and he told stories at his own expense with a sweetness of hilarity which made his peculiarities really sacred in the eyes of a friend. I remember vividly the smile and tone of voice with which he once repeated to me a figurative epithet which Gustave Flaubert (of whom he was extremely fond) had applied to him —an epithet intended to characterise a certain expansive softness, a comprehensive indecision, which pervaded his nature, just as it pervades so many of the characters he has painted. He enjoyed Flaubert's use of this term, good-naturedly opprobrious, more even than Flaubert himself, and recognised perfectly the element of truth in it. He was natural to an extraordinary degree; I do not think I have ever seen his match in this respect, certainly not among people who bear, as he did, at the same time, the stamp of the highest cultivation. Like all men of a large pattern, he was composed of many different pieces; and what was always striking in him was the mixture of simplicity with the fruit of the most various observation. In the little article in which I had attempted to express my admiration for his works, I had been moved to say of him that he had the aristocratic temperament: a remark which in the light of further knowledge seemed to me singularly inane. He was not subject to any definition of that sort, and to say that he was democratic would be (though his political ideal was a democracy), to give an equally superficial account of him. He felt and understood the opposite sides of life; he was imaginative, speculative, anything but literal. He had not in his mind a grain of prejudice as large as the point of a needle, and people (there are many) who think this a defect would have missed it immensely in Ivan Serguéitch. (I give his name, without attempting the Russian orthography, as it was uttered by his friends when they addressed him in French.) Our Anglo-Saxon, Protestant, moralistic, conventional standards were far away from him, and he judged things with a freedom and spontaneity in which I found a perpetual refreshment. His sense of beauty, his love of truth and right, were the foundation of his nature; but half the charm of conversation with him was that one breathed an air in which cant phrases and arbitrary measurements simply sounded ridiculous.

I may add that it was not because I had written a laudatory article about his books that he gave me a friendly welcome; for in the first place my article could have very little importance for him, and in the second it had never been either his habit or his hope to bask in the light of criticism. Supremely modest as he was, I think he attached no great weight to what might happen to be said about him; for he felt that he was destined to encounter a very small amount of intelligent appreciation, especially in foreign countries. I never heard him even allude to any judgment which might have been passed upon his productions in England. In France he knew that he was read very moderately; the "demand" for his volumes was small, and he had no illusions whatever on the subject of his popularity. He had heard with pleasure that many intelligent persons in the United States were impatient for everything that might come from his pen; but I think he was never convinced, as one or two of the more zealous of these persons had endeavoured to convince him, that he could boast of a "public" in America. He gave me the impression of thinking of criticism as most serious workers think of it—that it is the amusement, the exercise, the subsistence of the critic (and, so far as this goes,

of immense use) ; but that though it may often concern other readers, it does not much concern the artist
himself.　In comparison with all those things which
the production of a considered work forces the artist
little by little to say to himself, the remarks of the
critic are vague and of the moment ; and yet, owing
to the large publicity of the proceeding, they have a
power to irritate or discourage which is quite out of
proportion to their use to the person criticised.　It
was not, moreover (if this explanation be not more
gross than the spectre it is meant to conjure away),
on account of any esteem which he accorded to my
own productions (I used regularly to send them to
him) that I found him so agreeable, for to the best
of my belief he was unable to read them.　As regards
one of the first that I had offered him he wrote me
a little note to tell me that a distinguished friend,
who was his constant companion, had read three or
four chapters aloud to him the evening before and
that one of them was written *de main de maître !*
This gave me great pleasure, but it was my first and
last pleasure of the kind.　I continued, as I say, to
send him my fictions, because they were the only
thing I had to give ; but he never alluded to the rest
of the work in question, which he evidently did not
finish, and never gave any sign of having read its
successors.　Presently I quite ceased to expect this,
and saw why it was (it interested me much), that my
writings could not appeal to him.　He cared, more
than anything else, for the air of reality, and my

reality was not to the purpose. I do not think my stories struck him as quite meat for men. The manner was more apparent than the matter; they were too *tarabiscoté*, as I once heard him say of the style of a book—had on the surface too many little flowers and knots of ribbon. He had read a great deal of English, and knew the language remarkably well—too well, I used often to think, for he liked to speak it with those to whom it was native, and, successful as the effort always was, it deprived him of the facility and raciness with which he expressed himself in French.

I have said that he had no prejudices, but perhaps after all he had one. I think he imagined it to be impossible to a person of English speech to converse in French with complete correctness. He knew Shakespeare thoroughly, and at one time had wandered far and wide in English literature. His opportunities for speaking English were not at all frequent, so that when the necessity (or at least the occasion) presented itself, he remembered the phrases he had encountered in books. This often gave a charming quaintness and an unexpected literary turn to what he said. " In Russia, in spring, if you enter a beechen grove "—those words come back to me from the last time I saw him. He continued to read English books and was not incapable of attacking the usual Tauchnitz novel. The English writer (of our day) of whom I remember to have heard him speak with most admiration was Dickens, of whose faults he was conscious, but whose power of presenting to the eye a vivid, salient figure he rated very high. In the young French school he was much interested ; I mean, in the new votaries of realism, the grandsons of Balzac. He was a good friend of most of them, and with Gustave Flaubert, the most singular and most original of the group, he was altogether intimate. He had his reservations and discriminations, and he had, above all, the great back-garden of his Slav imagination and his Germanic culture, into which the door constantly stood open, and the grandsons of Balzac were not, I think, particularly free to accompany him. But he had much sympathy with their experiment, their general movement, and it was on the side of the careful study of life as the best line of the novelist that, as may easily be supposed, he ranged himself. For some of the manifestations of the opposite tradition he had a great contempt. This was a kind of emotion he rarely expressed, save in regard to certain public wrongs and iniquities ; bitterness and denunciation seldom passed his mild lips. But I remember well the little flush of conviction, the seriousness, with which he once said, in allusion to a novel which had just been running through the *Revue des Deux Mondes*, " If I had written anything so bad as that, I should blush for it all my life."

His was not, I should say, predominantly, or even in a high degree, the artistic nature, though it was deeply, if I may make the distinction, the poetic.

But during the last twelve years of his life he lived much with artists and men of letters, and he was eminently capable of kindling in the glow of discussion. He cared for questions of form, though not in the degree in which Flaubert and Edmond de Goncourt cared for them, and he had very lively sympathies. He had a great regard for Madame George Sand, the head and front of the old romantic tradition ; but this was on general grounds, quite independent of her novels, which he never read, and which she never expected him, or apparently any one else, to read. He thought her character remarkably noble and sincere. He had, as I have said, a great affection for Gustave Flaubert, who returned it ; and he was much interested in Flaubert's extraordinary attempts at bravery of form and of matter, knowing perfectly well when they failed. During those months which it was Flaubert's habit to spend in Paris, Turgénieff went almost regularly to see him on Sunday afternoon, and was so good as to introduce me to the author of *Madame Bovary*, in whom I saw many reasons for Turgénieff's regard. It was on these Sundays, in Flaubert's little salon, which, at the top of a house at the end of the Faubourg Saint-Honoré, looked rather bare and provisional, that, in the company of the other familiars of the spot, more than one of whom [1] have commemorated these occasions, Turgénieff's beautiful faculty of talk showed at its best. He was easy, natural, abundant, more than I

[1] Maxime Du Camp, Alphonse Daudet, Emile Zola.

can describe, and everything that he said was touched with the exquisite quality of his imagination. What was discussed in that little smoke-clouded room was chiefly questions of taste, questions of art and form; and the speakers, for the most part, were in æsthetic matters, radicals of the deepest dye. It would have been late in the day to propose among them any discussion of the relation of art to morality, any question as to the degree in which a novel might or might not concern itself with the teaching of a lesson. They had settled these preliminaries long ago, and it would have been primitive and incongruous to recur to them. The conviction that held them together was the conviction that art and morality are two perfectly different things, and that the former has no more to do with the latter than it has with astronomy or embryology. The only duty of a novel was to be well written; that merit included every other of which it was capable. This state of mind was never more apparent than one afternoon when *ces messieurs* delivered themselves on the subject of an incident which had just befallen one of them. *L'Assommoir* of Emile Zola had been discontinued in the journal through which it was running as a serial, in consequence of repeated protests from the subscribers. The subscriber, as a type of human imbecility, received a wonderful dressing, and the Philistine in general was roughly handled. There were gulfs of difference between Turgénieff and Zola, but Turgénieff, who, as I say, understood everything, understood Zola too, and rendered perfect justice to the high solidity of much of his work. His attitude, at such times, was admirable, and I could imagine nothing more genial or more fitted to give an idea of light, easy, human intelligence. No one could desire more than he that art should be art; always, ever, incorruptibly, art. To him this proposition would have seemed as little in need of proof, or susceptible of refutation, as the axiom that law should always be law or medicine always medicine. As much as any one he was prepared to take note of the fact that the demand for abdications and concessions never comes from artists themselves, but always from purchasers, editors, subscribers. I am pretty sure that his word about all this would have been that he could not quite see what was meant by the talk about novels being moral or the reverse; that a novel could no more propose to itself to be moral than a painting or a symphony, and that it was arbitrary to lay down a distinction between the numerous forms of art. He was the last man to be blind to their unity. I suspect that he would have said, in short, that distinctions were demanded in the interest of the moralists, and that the demand was indelicate, owing to their want of jurisdiction. Yet at the same time that I make this suggestion as to his state of mind I remember how little he struck me as bound by mere neatness of formula, how little there was in him of the partisan or the pleader. What he thought of the relation of art to life his stories, after all, show better than anything else. The immense variety of life was ever present to his mind, and he would never have argued the question I have just hinted at in the interest of particular liberties—the liberties that were apparently the dearest to his French *confrères*. It was this air that he carried about with him of feeling all the variety of life, of knowing strange and far-off things, of having an horizon in which the Parisian horizon—so familiar, so wanting in mystery, so perpetually *exploité*—easily lost itself, that distinguished him from these companions. He was not all there, as the phrase is; he had something behind, in reserve. It was Russia, of course, in a large measure; and, especially before the spectacle of what is going on there to-day, that was a large quantity. But so far as he was on the spot, he was an element of pure sociability.

I did not intend to go into these details immediately, for I had only begun to say what an impression of magnificent manhood he made upon me when I first knew him. That impression, indeed, always remained with me, even after it had been brought home to me how much there was in him of the quality of genius. He was a beautiful intellect, of course, but above all he was a delightful, mild, masculine figure. The combination of his deep, soft, lovable spirit, in which one felt all the tender parts of genius, with his immense, fair Russian physique, was one of the most attractive things conceivable. He had a frame which would have made it perfectly lawful, and even becoming, for him to be brutal; but there was not a grain of brutality in his composition. He had always been a passionate sportsman ; to wander in the woods or the steppes, with his dog and gun, was the pleasure of his heart.   Late in life he continued to shoot, and he had a friend in Cambridge-shire for the sake of whose partridges, which were famous, he used sometimes to cross the Channel.   It would have been impossible to imagine a better representation of a Nimrod of the north.   He was exceedingly tall, and broad and robust in proportion. His head was one of the finest, and though the line of his features was irregular, there was a great deal of beauty in his face.   It was eminently of the Russian type—almost everything in it was wide. His expression had a singular sweetness, with a touch of Slav languor, and his eye, the kindest of eyes, was deep and melancholy.   His hair, abundant and straight, was as white as silver, and his beard, which he wore trimmed rather short, was of the colour of his hair.   In all his tall person, which was very striking wherever it appeared, there was an air of neglected strength, as if it had been a part of his modesty never to remind himself that he was strong. He used sometimes to blush like a boy of sixteen. He had very few forms and ceremonies, and almost as little manner as was possible to a man of his natural *prestance*.   His noble appearance was in itself a manner ; but whatever he did he did very simply, and he had not the slightest pretension to not being subject to rectification.   I never saw any one receive it with less irritation. Friendly, candid, unaffectedly benignant, the impression that he produced most strongly and most generally was, I think, simply that of goodness.

When I made his acquaintance he had been living, since his removal from Baden-Baden, which took place in consequence of the Franco-Prussian war, in a large detached house on the hill of Montmartre, with his friends of many years, Madame Pauline Viardot and her husband, as his fellow-tenants. He occupied the upper floor, and I like to recall, for the sake of certain delightful talks, the aspect of his little green sitting-room, which has, in memory, the consecration of irrecoverable hours. It was almost entirely green, and the walls were not covered with paper, but draped in stuff. The *portières* were green, and there was one of those immense divans, so indispensable to Russians, which had apparently been fashioned for the great person of the master, so that smaller folk had to lie upon it rather than sit. I remember the white light of the Paris street, which came in through windows more or less blinded in their lower part, like those of a studio. It rested, during the first years that I went to see Turgénieff, upon several choice pictures of the modern French school, especially upon a very fine specimen of Théodore Rousseau, which he valued exceedingly. He had a great love of painting, and was an excellent critic of a picture. The last time I saw him—it was at his house in the country— he showed me half a dozen large copies of Italian

works, made by a young Russian in whom he was
interested, which he had, with characteristic kindness,
taken into his own apartments in order that he
might bring them to the knowledge of his friends.
He thought them, as copies, remarkable ; and they
were so, indeed, especially when one perceived that
the original work of the artist had little value.
Turgénieff warmed to the work of praising them, as
he was very apt to do ; like all men of imagination
he had frequent and zealous admirations. As a
matter of course there was almost always some
young Russian in whom he was interested, and
refugees and pilgrims of both sexes were his natural
clients. I have heard it said by persons who had
known him long and well that these enthusiasms
sometimes led him into error, that he was apt to *se
monter la tête* on behalf of his protégés. He was prone
to believe that he had discovered the coming Russian
genius ; he talked about his discovery for a month,
and then suddenly one heard no more of it. I
remember his once telling me of a young woman who
had come to see him on her return from America,
where she had been studying obstetrics at some
medical college, and who, without means and without
friends, was in want of help and of work. He
accidentally learned that she had written something,
and asked her to let him see it. She sent it to him,
and it proved to be a tale in which certain phases
of rural life were described with striking truthful-
ness. He perceived in the young lady a great

natural talent; he sent her story off to Russia to be
printed, with the conviction that it would make a
great impression, and he expressed the hope of being
able to introduce her to French readers. When I
mentioned this to an old friend of Turgénieff he
smiled, and said that we should not hear of her again,
that Ivan Serguéitch had already discovered a great
many surprising talents, which, as a general thing,
had not borne the test. There was apparently some
truth in this, and Turgénieff's liability to be deceived was
too generous a weakness for me to hesitate to allude to
it, even after I have insisted on the usual certainty of
his taste. He was deeply interested in his young
Russians; they were what interested him most in
the world. They were almost always unhappy, in
want and in rebellion against an order of things
which he himself detested. The study of the Russian
character absorbed and fascinated him, as all readers
of his stories know. Rich, unformed, undeveloped,
with all sorts of adumbrations, of qualities in a state
of fusion, it stretched itself out as a mysterious
expanse in which it was impossible as yet to perceive
the relation between gifts and weaknesses. Of its
weaknesses he was keenly conscious, and I once heard
him express himself with an energy that did him
honour and a frankness that even surprised me (considering that it was of his countrymen that he spoke),
in regard to a weakness which he deemed the greatest
of all—a weakness for which a man whose love of
veracity was his strongest feeling would have least

toleration. His young compatriots, seeking their fortune in foreign lands, touched his imagination and his pity, and it is easy to conceive that under the circumstances the impression they often made upon him may have had great intensity. The Parisian background, with its brilliant sameness, its absence of surprises (for those who have known it long), threw them into relief and made him see them as he saw the figures in his tales, in relations, in situations which brought them out. There passed before him in the course of time many wonderful Russian types. He told me once of his having been visited by a religious sect. The sect consisted of but two persons, one of whom was the object of worship and the other the worshipper. The divinity apparently was travelling about Europe in company with his prophet. They were intensely serious but it was very handy, as the term is, for each. The god had always his altar and the altar had (unlike some altars) always its god.

In his little green salon nothing was out of place; there were none of the odds and ends of the usual man of letters, which indeed Turgénieff was not; and the case was the same in his library at Bougival, of which I shall presently speak. Few books even were visible; it was as if everything had been put away. The traces of work had been carefully removed. An air of great comfort, an immeasurable divan and several valuable pictures—that was the effect of the place. I know not exactly at what hours Turgénieff did his work; I think he had no regular times and seasons, being in this respect as different as possible from Anthony Trollope, whose autobiography, with its candid revelation of intellectual economies, is so curious. It is my impression that in Paris Turgénieff wrote little; his times of production being rather those weeks of the summer that he spent at Bougival, and the period of that visit to Russia which he supposed himself to make every year. I say "supposed himself," because it was impossible to see much of him without discovering that he was a man of delays. As on the part of some other Russians whom I have known, there was something Asiatic in his faculty of procrastination. But even if one suffered from it a little one thought of it with kindness, as a part of his general mildness and want of rigidity. He went to Russia, at any rate, at intervals not infrequent, and he spoke of these visits as his best time for production. He had an estate far in the interior, and here, amid the stillness of the country and the scenes and figures which give such a charm to the *Memoirs of a Sportsman*, he drove his pen without interruption.

It is not out of place to allude to the fact that he possessed considerable fortune; this is too important in the life of a man of letters. It had been of great value to Turgénieff, and I think that much of the fine quality of his work is owing to it. He could write according to his taste and his mood; he was never pressed nor checked (putting the Russian censorship aside) by considerations foreign to his plan, and never was in danger of becoming a hack. Indeed, taking into consideration the absence of a pecuniary spur and that complicated indolence from which he was not exempt, his industry is surprising, for his tales are a long list. In Paris, at all events, he was always open to proposals for the midday breakfast. He liked to breakfast *au cabaret*, and freely consented to an appointment. It is not unkind to add that, at first, he never kept it. I may mention without reserve this idiosyncrasy of Turgénieff's, because in the first place it was so inveterate as to be very amusing—it amused not only his friends but himself ; and in the second, he was as sure to come in the end as he was sure not to come in the beginning. After the appointment had been made or the invitation accepted, when the occasion was at hand, there arrived a note or a telegram in which Ivan Serguéitch excused himself, and begged that the meeting might be deferred to another date, which he usually himself proposed. For this second date still another was sometimes substituted ; but if I remember no appointment that he exactly kept, I remember none that he completely missed. His friends waited for him frequently, but they never lost him. He was very fond of that wonderful Parisian *déjeûner*—fond of it I mean as a feast of reason. He was extremely temperate, and often ate no breakfast at all ; but he found it a good hour

for talk, and little, on general grounds, as one might
be prepared to agree with him, if he was at the table
one was speedily convinced.   I call it wonderful, the
déjeûner of Paris, on account of the assurance with
which it plants itself in the very middle of the
morning.   It divides the day between rising and
dinner so unequally, and opposes such barriers of
repletion to any prospect of ulterior labours, that
the unacclimated stranger wonders when the fertile
French people do their work.   Not the least wonderful part of it is that the stranger himself likes it, at
last, and manages to piece together his day with the
shattered fragments that survive.   It was not, at
any rate, when one had the good fortune to breakfast
at twelve o'clock with Turgénieff that one was struck
with its being an inconvenient hour.   Any hour was
convenient for meeting a human being who conformed
so completely to one's idea of the best that human
nature is capable of.   There are places in Paris
which I can think of only in relation to some occasion
on which he was present, and when I pass them the
particular things I heard him say there come back to
me.   There is a café in the Avenue de l'Opéra—a
new, sumptuous establishment, with very deep settees,
on the right as you leave the Boulevard—where I
once had a talk with him, over an order singularly
moderate, which was prolonged far into the afternoon, and in the course of which he was extraordinarily suggestive and interesting, so that my
memory now reverts affectionately to all the circum-

stances. It evokes the grey damp of a Parisian December, which made the dark interior of the café look more and more rich and hospitable, while the light faded, the lamps were lit, the habitués came in to drink absinthe and play their afternoon game of dominoes, and we still lingered over our morning meal. Turgénieff talked almost exclusively about Russia, the nihilists, the remarkable figures that came to light among them, the curious visits he received, the dark prospects of his native land. When he was in the vein, no man could speak more to the imagination of his auditor. For myself, at least, at such times, there was something extraordinarily vivifying and stimulating in his talk, and I always left him in a state of "intimate" excitement, with a feeling that all sorts of valuable things had been suggested to me ; the condition in which a man swings his cane as he walks, leaps lightly over gutters, and then stops, for no reason at all, to look, with an air of being struck, into a shop window where he sees nothing. I remember another symposium, at a restaurant on one of the corners of the little *place* in front of the Opéra Comique, where we were four, including Ivan Serguéitch, and the two other guests were also Russian, one of them uniting to the charm of this nationality the merit of a sex that makes the combination irresistible. The establishment had been a discovery of Turgénieff's—a discovery, at least, as far as our particular needs were concerned— and I remember that we hardly congratulated him on it. The dinner, in a low entresol, was not what it had been intended to be, but the talk was better even than our expectations. It was not about nihilism but about some more agreeable features of life, and I have no recollection of Turgénieff in a mood more spontaneous and charming. One of our friends had, when he spoke French, a peculiar way of sounding the word *adorable*, which was frequently on his lips, and I remember well his expressive prolongation of the *a* when, in speaking of the occasion afterwards, he applied this term to Ivan Serguéitch. I scarcely know, however, why I should drop into the detail of such reminiscences, and my excuse is but the desire that we all have, when a human relationship is closed, to save a little of it from the past—to make a mark which may stand for some of the happy moments of it.

Nothing that Turgénieff had to say could be more interesting than his talk about his own work, his manner of writing. What I have heard him tell of these things was worthy of the beautiful results he produced; of the deep purpose, pervading them all, to show us life itself. The germ of a story, with him, was never an affair of plot—that was the last thing he thought of: it was the representation of certain persons. The first form in which a tale appeared to him was as the figure of an individual, or a combination of individuals, whom he wished to see in action, being sure that such people must do something very special and interesting. They stood before him definite, vivid, and he wished to know, and to show, as much as possible of their nature. The first thing was to make clear to himself what he did know, to begin with; and to this end, he wrote out a sort of biography of each of his characters, and everything that they had done and that had happened to them up to the opening of the story. He had their *dossier*, as the French say, and as the police has of that of every conspicuous criminal. With this material in his hand he was able to proceed; the story all lay in the question, What shall I make them do? He always made them do things that showed them completely; but, as he said, the defect of his manner and the reproach that was made him was his want of "architecture"— in other words, of composition. The great thing, of course, is to have architecture as well as precious material, as Walter Scott had them, as Balzac had them. If one reads Turgénieff's stories with the knowledge that they were composed—or rather that they came into being—in this way, one can trace the process in every line. Story, in the conventional sense of the word—a fable constructed, like Wordsworth's phantom, "to startle and waylay"—there is as little as possible. The thing consists of the motions of a group of selected creatures, which are not the result of a preconceived action, but a consequence of the qualities of the actors. Works of art are produced from every possible point of view, and stories, and very good ones, will continue to be written in which the evolution is that of a dance—a series of steps the more complicated and lively the better, of course, determined from without and forming a figure. This figure will always, probably, find favour with many readers, because it reminds them enough, without reminding them too much, of life. On this opposition many young talents in France are ready to rend each other, for there is a numerous school on either side. We have not yet in England and America arrived at the point of treating such questions with passion, for we have not yet arrived at the point of feeling them intensely, or indeed, for that matter, of understanding them very well. It is not open to us as yet to discuss whether a novel had better be an excision from life or a structure built up of picture-cards, for we have not made up our mind as to whether life in general may be described. There is evidence of a good deal of shyness on this point—a tendency rather to put up fences than to jump over them. Among us, therefore, even a certain ridicule attaches to the consideration of such alternatives. But individuals may feel their way, and perhaps even pass unchallenged, if they remark that for them the manner in which Turgénieff worked will always seem the most fruitful. It has the immense recommendation that in relation to any human occurrence it begins, as it were, further back. It lies in its power to tell us the most about men and women. Of course it will but slenderly satisfy those numerous readers among whom the answer to this would be, "Hang it, we don't care a straw about men and women: we want a good story!"

And yet, after all, *Elena* is a good story, and *Lisa* and *Virgin Soil* are good stories. Reading over lately several of Turgénieff's novels and tales, I was struck afresh with their combination of beauty and reality. One must never forget, in speaking of him, that he was both an observer and a poet. The poetic element was constant, and it had great strangeness and power. It inspired most of the short things that he wrote during the last few years of his life, since the publication of *Virgin Soil*, things that are in the highest degree fanciful and exotic. It pervades the frequent little reveries, visions, epigrams of the *Senilia*. It was no part of my intention, here, to criticise his writings, having said my say about them, so far as possible, some years ago. But I may mention that in re-reading them I find in them all that I formerly found of two other elements—their richness and their sadness. They give one the impression of life itself, and not of an arrangement, a *réchauffé* of life. I remember Turgénieff's once saying in regard to Homais, the little Norman country apothecary, with his pedantry of "enlightened opinions," in *Madame Bovary*, that the great strength of such a portrait consisted in its being at once an individual, of the most concrete sort, and a type. This is the great strength of his own representations of character; they are so strangely, fascinatingly particular, and yet

they are so recognisably general. Such a remark as
that about Homais makes me wonder why it was that
Turgénieff should have rated Dickens so high, the
weakness of Dickens being in regard to just that
point. If Dickens fail to live long, it will be because
his figures are particular without being general;
because they are individuals without being types;
because we do not feel their continuity with the rest
of humanity—see the matching of the pattern with
the piece out of which all the creations of the novelist
and the dramatist are cut. I often meant, but
accidentally neglected, to put Turgénieff on the subject of Dickens again, and ask him to explain his
opinion. I suspect that his opinion was in a large
measure merely that Dickens diverted him, as well
he might. That complexity of the pattern was in
itself fascinating. I have mentioned Flaubert, and I
will return to him simply to say that there was some
thing very touching in the nature of the friendship
that united these two men. It is much to the honour
of Flaubert, to my sense, that he appreciated Ivan
Turgénieff. There was a partial similarity between
them. Both were large, massive men, though the
Russian reached to a greater height than the Norman;
both were completely honest and sincere, and both
had the pessimistic element in their composition.
Each had a tender regard for the other, and I think
that I am neither incorrect nor indiscreet in saying
that on Turgénieff's part this regard had in it a strain
of compassion. There was something in Gustave

Flaubert that appealed to such a feeling. He had failed, on the whole, more than he had succeeded, and the great machinery of erudition,—the great polishing process,—which he brought to bear upon his productions, was not accompanied with proportionate results. He had talent without having cleverness, and imagination without having fancy. His effort was heroic, but except in the case of *Madame Bovary*, a masterpiece, he imparted something to his works (it was as if he had covered them with metallic plates) which made them sink rather than sail. He had a passion for perfection of form and for a certain splendid suggestiveness of style. He wished to produce perfect phrases, perfectly interrelated, and as closely woven together as a suit of chain-mail. He looked at life altogether as an artist, and took his work with a seriousness that never belied itself. To write an admirable page—and his idea of what constituted an admirable page was transcendent—seemed to him something to live for. He tried it again and again, and he came very near it ; more than once he touched it, for *Madame Bovary* surely will live. But there was something ungenerous in his genius. He was cold, and he would have given everything he had to be able to glow. There is nothing in his novels like the passion of Elena for Inssaroff, like the purity of Lisa, like the anguish of the parents of Bazaroff, like the hidden wound of Tatiana ; and yet Flaubert yearned, with all the accumulations of his vocabulary, to touch the chord of pathos. There were some parts

of his mind that did not "give," that did not render a
sound.   He had had too much of some sorts of experience and not enough of others.   And yet this failure
of an organ, as I may call it, inspired those who knew
him with a kindness.   If Flaubert was powerful and
limited, there is something human, after all, and even
rather august in a strong man who has not been able
completely to express himself.

After the first year of my acquaintance with Turgénieff I saw him much less often.   I was seldom in
Paris, and sometimes when I was there he was absent.
But I neglected no opportunity of seeing him, and
fortune frequently assisted me.   He came two or
three times to London, for visits provokingly brief.
He went to shoot in Cambridgeshire, and he passed
through town in arriving and departing.   He liked
the English, but I am not sure that he liked London,
where he had passed a lugubrious winter in 1870-71.
I remember some of his impressions of that period,
especially a visit that he had paid to a "bishopess"
surrounded by her daughters, and a description of the
cookery at the lodgings which he occupied.   After
1876 I frequently saw him as an invalid.   He was
tormented by gout, and sometimes terribly besieged ;
but his account of what he suffered was as charming
—I can apply no other word to it—as his description
of everything else.   He had so the habit of observation, that he perceived in excruciating sensations all
sorts of curious images and analogies, and analysed
them to an extraordinary fineness.   Several times I

found him at Bougival, above the Seine, in a very
spacious and handsome chalet—a little unsunned, it
is true—which he had built alongside of the villa
occupied by the family to which, for years, his life
had been devoted.   The place is delightful; the two
houses are midway up a long slope, which descends,
with the softest inclination, to the river, and behind
them the hill rises to a wooded crest.   On the left,
in the distance, high up and above an horizon of
woods, stretches the romantic aqueduct of Marly.   It
is a very pretty domain.   The last time I saw him,
in November 1882, it was at Bougival.   He had
been very ill, with strange, intolerable symptoms, but
he was better, and he had good hopes.   They were
not justified by the event.   He got worse again, and
the months that followed were cruel.   His beautiful
serene mind should not have been darkened and
made acquainted with violence ; it should have been
able to the last to take part, as it had always done,
in the decrees and mysteries of fate.   At the moment
I saw him, however, he was, as they say in London,
in very good form, and my last impression of him was
almost bright.   He was to drive into Paris, not being
able to bear the railway, and he gave me a seat in
the carriage.   For an hour and a half he constantly
talked, and never better.   When we got into the
city I alighted on the boulevard extérieur, as we
were to go in different directions.   I bade him good-
bye at the carriage window, and never saw him
again.   There was a kind of fair going on, near by,

in the chill November air, beneath the denuded little
trees of the Boulevard, and a Punch and Judy show,
from which nasal sounds proceeded. I almost regret
having accidentally to mix up so much of Paris
with this perhaps too complacent enumeration of
occasions, for the effect of it may be to suggest that
Ivan Turgénieff had been Gallicised. But this was not
the case ; the French capital was an accident for him,
not a necessity. It touched him at many points, but it
let him alone at many others, and he had, with that
great tradition of ventilation of the Russian mind,
windows open into distances which stretched far
beyond the *banlieue*. I have spoken of him from the
limited point of view of my own acquaintance with
him, and unfortunately left myself little space to
allude to a matter which filled his existence a good
deal more than the consideration of how a story
should be written—his hopes and fears on behalf of
his native land. He wrote fictions and dramas, but
the great drama of his life was the struggle for a
better state of things in Russia. In this drama he
played a distinguished part, and the splendid obse-
quies that, simple and modest as he was, have un-
folded themselves over his grave, sufficiently attest
the recognition of it by his countrymen. His
funeral, restricted and officialised, was none the less
a magnificent " manifestation." I have read the
accounts of it, however, with a kind of chill, a feeling
in which assent to the honours paid him bore less
part than it ought. All this pomp and ceremony

seemed to lift him out of the range of familiar recollection, of valued reciprocity, into the majestic position of a national glory. And yet it is in the presence of this obstacle to social contact that those who knew and loved him must address their farewell to him now. After all, it is difficult to see how the obstacle can be removed. He was the most generous, the most tender, the most delightful, of men ; his large nature overflowed with the love of justice : but he also was of the stuff of which glories are made.

1884.

X

GEORGE DU MAURIER

GEORGE DU MAURIER

MANY years ago a small American child, who lived in
New York and played in Union Square, which was
then inclosed by a high railing and governed by a
solitary policeman—a strange, superannuated, dilapi-
dated functionary, carrying a little cane and wear-
ing, with a very copious and very dirty shirt-front,
the costume of a man of the world—a small American
child was a silent devotee of *Punch*. Half an hour
spent to-day in turning over the early numbers
transports him quite as much to old New York as to
the London of the first Crystal Palace and the years
that immediately followed it. From about 1850 to
1855 he lived, in imagination, no small part of his
time, in the world represented by the pencil of
Leech. He pored over the pictures of the people
riding in the Row, of the cabmen and the costermongers, of the little pages in buttons, of the bathing-
machines at the sea-side, of the small boys in tall hats
and Eton jackets, of the gentlemen hunting the fox,
of the pretty girls in striped petticoats and coiffures
of the shape of the mushroom. These things were

the features of a world which he longed so to behold, that the familiar woodcuts (they were not so good in those days as they have become since) grew at last as real to him as the furniture of his home ; and when he at present looks at the *Punch* of thirty years ago he finds in it an odd association of mediæval New York.   He remembers that it was in such a locality, in that city, that he first saw such a picture : he recalls the. fading light of the winter dusk, with the red fire and the red curtains in the background, in which more than once he was bidden to put down the last numbers of the humorous sheet and come to his tea.   *Punch* was England ; *Punch* was London ; and England and London were at that time words of multifarious suggestion to this small American child.   He liked much more to think of the British Empire than to indulge in the sports natural to his tender age, and many of his hours were spent in making mental pictures of the society of which the recurrent woodcuts offered him speci- mens and revelations.   He had from year to year the prospect of really beholding this society (he heard every spring, from the earliest period, that his parents would go to Europe, and then he heard that they would not), and he had measured the value of the prospect with a keenness possibly premature.   He knew the names of the London streets, of the theatres, of many of the shops : the dream of his young life was to take a walk in Kensington Gardens and go to Drury Lane to see a pantomime.   There

was a great deal in the old *Punch* about the panto-
mimes, and harlequins and columbines peopled the
secret visions of this perverted young New Yorker.
It was a mystic satisfaction to him that he had lived
in Piccadilly when he was a baby; he remembered
neither the period nor the place, but the name of
the latter had a strange delight for him. It had been
promised him that he should behold once more that
romantic thoroughfare, and he did so by the time he
was twelve years old. Then he found that if *Punch*
had been London (as he lay on the hearth-rug inhaling the exotic fragrance of the freshly-arrived journal),
London was *Punch* and something more. He remembers to-day vividly his impression of the London
streets in the summer of 1855; they had an extraordinary look of familiarity, and every figure, every
object he encountered, appeared to have been drawn
by Leech. He has learned to know these things
better since then; but his childish impression is
subject to extraordinary revivals. The expansive
back of an old lady getting into an omnibus, the
attitude of a little girl bending from her pony in the
park, the demureness of a maid-servant opening a
street-door in Brompton, the top-heavy attitude of
the small " Ameliar-Ann," as she stands planted with
the baby in her arms on the corner of a Westminster
slum, the coal-heavers, the cabmen, the publicans,
the butcher-boys, the flunkeys, the guardsmen, the
policemen (in spite of their change of uniform), are
liable at this hour, in certain moods, to look more

like sketchy tail-pieces than natural things. (There
are moments indeed—not identical with those we
speak of—in which certain figures, certain episodes,
in the London streets, strike an even stranger, deeper
note of reminiscence. They remind the American
traveller of Hogarth : he may take a walk in Oxford
Street—on some dirty winter afternoon—and find
everything he sees Hogarthian.)

We know not whether the form of infantine nos-
talgia of which we speak is common, or was then
common, among small Americans ; but we are sure
that, when fortune happens to favour it, it is a very
delightful pain. In those days, in America, the
manufacture of children's picture-books was an
undeveloped industry ; the best things came from
London, and brought with them the aroma of a
richer civilisation. The covers were so beautiful and
shining, the paper and print so fine, the coloured
illustrations so magnificent, that it was easy to see
that over there the arts were at a very high point.
The very name of the publisher on the title-page
(the small boy we speak of always looked at that)
had a thrilling and mystifying effect. But, above
all, the contents were so romantic and delectable !
There were things in the English story-books that
one read as a child, just as there were things in
Punch, that one couldn't have seen in New York,
even if one had been fifty years old. The age had
nothing to do with it ; one had a conviction that they
were not there to be seen—we can hardly say why.

It is, perhaps, because the plates in the picture-books were almost always coloured; but it was evident that there was a great deal more colour in that other world. We remember well the dazzling tone of a little Christmas book by Leech, which was quite in the spirit of *Punch*, only more splendid, for the plates were plastered with blue and pink. It was called *Young Troublesome; or, Master Jacky's Holidays*, and it has probably become scarce to-day. It related the mischievous pranks of an Eton school-boy while at home for his Christmas vacation, and the exploit we chiefly recollect was his blacking with a burnt stick the immaculate calves of the footman who is carrying up some savoury dish to the banquet from which (in consequence of his age and his habits), Master Jacky is excluded. Master Jacky was so handsome, so brilliant, so heroic, so regardless of dangers and penalties, so fertile in resources; and those charming young ladies, his sisters, his cousins —the innocent victims of his high spirits—had such golden ringlets, such rosy cheeks, such pretty shoulders, such delicate blue sashes over such fresh muslin gowns. Master Jacky seemed to lead a life all illumined with rosy Christmas fire. A little later came Richard Doyle's delightful volume, giving the history of *Brown, Jones, and Robinson*, and it would be difficult to exaggerate the action of these remarkable designs in forming the taste of our fantastic little amateur. They told him, indeed, much less about England than about the cities of the continent; but that was not

a drawback, for he could take in the continent too
Moreover, he felt that these three travellers were
intensely British; they looked at everything from
the London point of view, and it gave him an immense feeling of initiation to be able to share their
susceptibilities. Was there not also a delightful
little picture at the end, which represented them as
restored to British ground, each holding up a tankard
of foaming ale, with the boots, behind them, rolling
their battered portmanteaux into the inn? This
seemed somehow to commemorate one's own possible
arrival in old England, even though it was not likely
that overflowing beer would be a feature of so modest
an event; just as all the rest of it was a foretaste of
Switzerland, of the Rhine, of North Italy, which
after this would find one quite prepared. We are
sorry to say that when, many years later, we ascended, for the first time, to the roof of Milan
Cathedral, what we first thought of was not the
"waveless plain of Lombardy" nor the beauty of the
edifice, but the "little London snob" whom Brown,
Jones, and Robinson saw writing his name on one of
the pinnacles of the church. We had our preferences
in this genial trio. We adored little Jones, the
artist—if memory doesn't betray us (we haven't seen
the book for twenty years), and Jones *was* the
artist. It is difficult to say why we adored him, but
it was certainly the dream of our life at that foolish
period to make his acquaintance. We did so, in
fact, not very long after. We were taken in due

course to Europe, and we met him on a steamboat on the Lake of Geneva. There was no introduction, we had no conversation, but he was the Jones we had prefigured and loved. Thackeray's Christmas books (*The Rose and the Ring* apart—it dates from 1854) came before this: we remember them in our earliest years. They, too, were of the family of *Punch*—which is my excuse for this superfluity of preface—and they were a revelation of English manners. "English manners," for a child, could of course only mean certain individual English figures —the figures in *Our Street*, in *Doctor Birch and his Young Friends* (we were glad we were not of the number), in *Mrs. Perkins's Ball*. In the first of these charming little volumes there is a pictorial exposition of the reason why the nurse-maids in *Our Street* like Kensington Gardens. When in the course of time we were taken to walk in those lovely shades, we looked about us for a simpering young woman and an insinuating soldier on a bench, with a bawling baby sprawling on the path hard by, and we were not slow to discover the group.

Many people in the United States, and doubtless in other countries, have gathered their knowledge of English life almost entirely from *Punch*, and it would be difficult to imagine a more abundant, and on the whole a more accurate, informant. The accumulated volumes of this periodical contain evidence on a multitude of points of which there is no mention in the serious works—not even in the novels—of the day. The smallest details of social habit are depicted there, and the oddities of a race of people in whom oddity is strangely compatible with the dominion of convention. That the ironical view of these things is given does not injure the force of the testimony, for the irony of *Punch*, strangely enough, has always been discreet, even delicate. It is a singular fact that, though taste is not supposed to be the strong point of the English mind, this eminently representative journal has rarely been guilty of a violation of decorum. The taste of *Punch*, like its good-humour, has known very few lapses. *The London Charivari*—we remember how difficult it was (in 1853) to arrive at the right pronunciation—has in this respect very little to envy its Parisian original. English comedy is coarse, French comedy is fine— that would be the general assumption, certainly, on the part of a French critic. But a comparison between the back volumes of the *Charivari* and the back volumes of *Punch* would make it necessary to modify this formula. English humour is simple, innocent, plain, a trifle insipid, apt to sacrifice to the graces, to the proprieties ; but if *Punch* be our witness English humour is not coarse. We are fortunately not obliged to declare just now what French humour appears to be—in the light of the *Charivari*, the *Journal Amusant*, the *Journal Pour Rire*. A Frenchman may say, in perfect good faith, that (to his sense) English drollery has doubtless every merit but that of being droll. French drollery, he may say, is salient, saltatory ; whereas the English comic effort has little freedom of wing. The French, in these matters, like a great deal of salt ; whereas the English, who spice their food very highly and have a cluster of sharp condiments on the table, take their caricatures comparatively mild. *Punch*, in short, is for the family—*Punch* may be sent up to the nursery. This surely may be admitted ; and it is the fact that *Punch* is for the family that constitutes its high value. The family is, after all, the people ; and a satirical sheet which holds up the mirror to this institution can hardly fail to be instructive. "Yes, if it hold the mirror up impartially," we can imagine the foreign critic to rejoin ; " but in these matters the British caricaturist is not to be trusted. He slurs over a great deal—he omits a great deal more. He must, above all things, be proper ; and there is a whole side of life which, in spite of his Juvenalian pretensions, he never touches at all." We must allow the foreign critic his supposed retort, without taking space to answer back—we may imagine him to be a bit of a "naturalist"—and admit that it is perhaps because they are obliged to be proper that Leech and Du Maurier give us, on the whole, such a cleanly, healthy, friendly picture of English manners. Such sustained and inveterate propriety is in itself a great force ; it takes in a good deal, as well as leaves out. The general impression that we derive from the long series of *Punch* is a very cheerful and favourable one ; it speaks of a vigorous, good-humoured, much-civilised people. The good-humour is, perhaps, the most striking point—not only the good-humour of the artist who represents the scene, but that of the figures engaged in it. The difference is remarkable in this respect between *Punch* and the French comic papers. The wonderful Cham, who for so many years contributed to those sheets, had an extraordinary sense of the ludicrous and a boundless stock of facetious invention. He was strangely expressive ; he could place a figure before you, in the most violent action, with half a dozen strokes of his pencil. But his people were like wild-cats and scorpions. The temper of the French *bourgeoisie*, as represented by Cham, is a thing to make one take to one's heels. They perpetually tear and rend each other, show their teeth and their claws, kick each other down-stairs, and pitch each other from windows. All this is in the highest degree farcical and grotesque ; but at bottom it is almost horrible. (It must be admitted that Cham and his wonderful colleague, Daumier, are much more horrible than Gavarni, who was admirably real, and at the same time capable of beauty and grace. Gavarni's women are charming ; those of Cham and Daumier are monsters.) There is nothing, or almost nothing, of the horrible in *Punch*. The author of these remarks has a friend whom he has heard more than once maintain the too-ingenious thesis that the caricatures of Cham prove the French to be a cruel people ; the same induction could, at least, never be made, even in an equal spirit of paradox, from the genial pages of *Punch*. " If *Punch* is never horrible, it is because *Punch* is always superficial, for life is full of the horrible "—so we may imagine our naturalistic objector to go on. However this may be, *Punch* is fortunate in having fallen on so smooth a surface. English life, as depicted by Leech and Du Maurier, and by that admirable Charles Keene—the best-humoured perhaps of the three, whose talent is so great that we have always wondered why it is not more comprehensive—is a compound of several very wholesome tastes : the love of the country, the love of action, the love of a harmless joke within the limits of due reverence, the love of sport, of horses and dogs, of family life, of children, of horticulture. With this there are a few other tastes of a less innocent kind—the love of ardent spirits, for instance, or of punching people's heads— or even the love of a lord. In Leech's drawings, country life plays a great part ; his landscapes, in their extreme sketchiness, are often admirable. He gave in a few strokes the look of the hunting-field in winter—the dark damp slopes, the black dense hedges, the low thick sky. He was very general ; he touched on everything, sooner or later ; but he enjoyed his sporting subjects more than anything else. In this he was thoroughly English. No close observer of that people can fail to perceive that the love of sport is the thing that binds them most closely together, and in which they have the greatest number of feelings in common. Leech depicted, with

infinite vividness, the accidents of the chase and of
the fishing-season; and his treatment of the horse
in especial contributed greatly to his popularity. He
understood the animal, he knew him intimately, he
loved him; and he drew him as if he knew how to
ride as well as to draw. The English forgive a great
deal to those who ride well; and this is doubtless
why the badness of some of the sporting subjects
that have appeared in *Punch* since Leech's death has
been tolerated : the artist has been presumed to have
a good seat. Leech never made a mistake; he did
well whatever he did; and it must be remembered
that for many years he furnished the political cartoon
to *Punch*, as well as the smaller drawings. He was
always amusing, always full of sense and point, always
intensely English. His foreigner is always an inferior
animal—his Frenchman is the Frenchman of Leicester
Square, the Frenchman whom the Exhibition of 1851
revealed to the people of London. His point is perfectly perceptible — it is never unduly fine. His
children are models of ruddy, chubby, shy yet sturdy
British babyhood; and nothing could be nicer than his
young women. The English maiden, in Leech, is
emphatically a nice girl; modest and fresh, simple
and blooming, and destined evidently for use as much
as for ornament. In those early days to which we
referred at the beginning of this article we were
deeply in love with the young ladies of Leech, and
we have never ceased to admire the simple art with
which he made these hastily designed creatures con-

form unerringly to the English type. They have English eyes and English cheeks, English figures, English hands and feet, English ringlets, English petticoats. Leech was extremely observant, but he had not a strong imagination; he had a sufficient, but not a high sense of beauty; his ideal of the beautiful had nothing of the unattainable; it was simply a *résumé* of the fresh faces he saw about him. The great thing, however, was that he was a natural, though not in the least an analytic or an exact, draughtsman; his little figures live and move; many of his little scenes are stamped on the memory. I have spoken of his representations of the country, but his town-pictures are numerous and capital. He knew his London, and his sketches of the good people of that metropolis are as happy as his episodes in the drawing-room and the hunting-field. He was admirably broad and free; and no one in his line has had more than he the knack of giving what is called a general effect. He conveys at times the look of the London streets — the colour, the temperature, the damp blackness. He does the winter weather to perfection. Long before I had seen it I was acquainted, through his sketches, with the aspect of Baker Street in December. Out of such a multitude of illustrations it is difficult to choose; the two volumes of *Sketches of Life and Character*, transferred from *Punch*, are a real museum. But I recall, for instance, the simple little sketch of the worthy man up to his neck in bed on a January morning, to

whom, on the other side of the door, the prompt
housemaid, with her hammer in her hand, announces
that "I have just broken the ice in your bath, sir."
The black cold dawn, the very smell of the early
chill, that raw sootiness of the London winter air, the
red nose of the housemaid, the unfashionable street
seen through the window—impart a peculiar vividness to the small inky-looking woodcut.

We have said too much about Leech, however,
and the purpose of these remarks is not to commemorate his work. *Punch*, for the last fifteen years,
has been, artistically speaking, George du Maurier.
(We ought, perhaps, before this, to have said that
none of our observations are to be taken as applying
to the letterpress of the comic journal, which has probably never been fully appreciated in America.) It
has employed other talents than his—notably Charles
Keene, who is as broad, as jovial, as English (half his
jokes are against Scotchmen) as Leech, but whose sense
of the beautiful, the delicate, is inferior even to Leech's.
But for a great many people, certainly in America,
Du Maurier has long been, as I say, the successor of
Leech, the embodiment of the pictorial spirit of
Punch. Shut up in the narrow limits of black and
white, without space, without colour, without the
larger opportunities, Du Maurier has nevertheless
established himself as an exquisite talent and a
genuine artist. He is not so much of a laugher as
Leech—he deals in the smile rather than the laugh
—but he is a much deeper observer, and he carries

his drawing infinitely further. He has not Leech's
animal spirits ; a want of boyishness, a tendency to
reflection, to lowness of tone, as his own Postlethwaite would say, is perhaps his limitation. But
his seriousness—if he be too serious—is that of the
satirist as distinguished from the simple joker; and
if he reflects, he does so in the literal sense of the
word—holds up a singularly polished and lucid
mirror to the drama of English society. More than
twenty years ago, when he began to draw in *Once a
Week*—that not very long-lived periodical which set
out on its career with a high pictorial standard—it
was apparent that the careful young artist who
finished his designs very highly and signed them
with a French name, stood very much upon his own
feet. The earliest things of his that we know have
the quality which has made him distinguished to-day
—the union of a great sense of beauty with a great
sense of reality. It was apparent from the first that
this was not a simple and uniform talent, but a gift
that had sprung from a combination of sources. It
is important to remember, in speaking of Du Maurier
—who is one of the pillars of the British journal *par
excellence*—that he has French blood in his veins.
George du Maurier, as we understand his history,
was born in England, of a French father and an
English mother, but was removed to France in his
early years and educated according to the customs
of that country. Later, however, he returned to
England ; and it would not be difficult for a careful

student of his drawings to guess that England is the land of his predilection.   He has drawn a great many French figures, but he has drawn them as one who knows them rather than as one who loves them.   He has perhaps been, as the phrase is, a little hard upon the French ; at any rate, he has been decidedly easy for the English.   The latter are assuredly a very handsome race ; but if we were to construct an image of them from the large majority of Du Maurier's drawings we should see before us a people of gods and goddesses.   This does not alter the fact that there is a very Gallic element in some of Du Maurier's gifts—his fineness of perception, his remarkable power of specifying types, his taste, his grace, his lightness, a certain refinement of art.   It is hard to imagine that a talent so remarkable should not have given early evidences ; but in spite of such evidences Du Maurier was, on the threshold of manhood, persuaded by those to whom it was his duty to listen to turn his attention, as Mrs. Micawber says, to chemistry. He pursued this science without enthusiasm, though he had for some time a laboratory of his own.   Before long, however, the laboratory was converted into a studio.   His talent insisted on its liberty, and he committed himself to the plastic.   He studied this charming element in Paris, at Düsseldorf ; he began to work in London.   This period of his life was marked by a great calamity, which has left its trace on his career and his work, and which it is needful to mention in order to speak with any fairness of these things. Abruptly, without a warning, his eye-sight partly forsook him, and his activity was cruelly threatened. It is a great pleasure, in alluding to this catastrophe, to be able to speak of it as a signal example of difficulty vanquished. George du Maurier was condemned to many dark days, at the end of which he learned that he should have to carry on his task for the rest of his life with less than half a man's portion of the sense most valuable to the artist. The beautiful work that he has produced in such abundance for so many years has been achieved under restrictions of vision which might well have made any work impossible. It is permitted, accordingly, to imagine that if the artist had had the usual resources, we should not at the present moment have to consider him simply as an accomplished draughts-man in black and white. It is impossible to look at many of his drawings without perceiving that they are full of the art of the painter, and that the form they have taken, charming as it has been, is arbitrary and inadequate.

John Leech died on 27th October 1864, and the first sketches in *Punch* that we recognise as Du Maurier's appeared in that year. The very earliest that we have detected belong, indeed, to 5th December 1863. These beginnings are slight and sketchy head-pieces and vignettes; the first regular "picture" (with a legend beneath it) that we remember is of the date of 11th June 1864. It represents a tipsy waiter (or college servant) on a staircase, where he

has smashed a trayful of crockery. We perceive
nothing else of importance for some time after this,
but suddenly his hand appears again in force, and
from the summer of 1865 its appearances are frequent.
The finish and delicacy, the real elegance of these
early drawings, are extreme : the hand was already
the hand of a brilliant executant. No such manner
as this had hitherto been seen in *Punch*. By the
time one had recognised that it was not a happy
accident, but an accomplished habit, it had become
the great feature, the "attraction," of the comic
journal. *Punch* had never before suspected that it
was so artistic ; had never taken itself, in such
matters, so seriously. Much the larger part of Du
Maurier's work has been done for *Punch*, but he has
designed as well many illustrations for books. The
most charming of these perhaps are the drawings he
executed in 1868 for a new edition of Thackeray's
Esmond, which had been preceded several years
before by a set of designs for Mrs. Gaskell's *Wives
and Daughters*, first ushered into the world as a serial
in the *Cornhill*. To the *Cornhill* for many years Du
Maurier has every month contributed an illustration ;
he has reproduced every possible situation that is
likely to be encountered in the English novel of
manners ; he has interpreted pictorially innumerable flirtations, wooings, philanderings, ruptures.
The interest of the English novel of manners is
frequently the interest of the usual ; the situations
presented to the artist are apt to lack superficial

strangeness. A lady and gentleman sitting in a
drawing-room, a lady and a gentleman going out to
walk, a sad young woman watching at a sick-bed, a
handsome young man lighting a cigarette—this is
the range of incident through which the designer is
called upon to move. But in these drawing-room
and flower-garden episodes the artist is thoroughly
at home; he accepts of course the material that is
given him, but we fancy him much more easily representing quiet, harmonious things than depicting
deeds of violence. It is a noticeable fact that in
Punch, where he has his liberty, he very seldom represents such deeds. His occasional departures from
this habit are of a sportive and fantastic sort, in
which he ceases to pretend to be real: like the
dream of the timorous Jenkins (15th February 1868),
who sees himself hurled to destruction by a colossal
foreshortened cab-horse. Du Maurier's fantastic—
we speak of the extreme manifestations of it—is
always admirable, ingenious, unexpected, pictorial;
so much so, that we have often wondered that he
should not have cultivated this vein more largely.
As a general thing, however, in these excursions into
the impossible it is some *charming* impossibility that
he offers us—a picture of some happy contrivance
which would make life more diverting : such as the
playing of lawn-tennis on skates (on a lawn of ice),
or the faculty on the part of young men on bicycles
of carrying their sweethearts behind them on a
pillion. We recommend the reader to turn to *Punch's*

Almanac for 1865, in which two brilliant full-page illustrations represent the "Probable Results of the Acclimatisation Society." Nothing could be fuller of delicate fancy and of pictorial facility than this prophecy of the domestication in the London streets, and by the Serpentine of innumerable strange beasts —giraffes, ostriches, zebras, kangaroos, hippopotami, elephants, lions, panthers. Speaking of strange beasts, the strangest of all perhaps is the wonderful big dog who has figured of late years in Du Maurier's drawings, and who has probably passed with many persons as a kind of pictorial caprice. He is depicted as of such super-canine proportions, quite overshadowing and dwarfing the amiable family to whom he is represented as belonging, that he might be supposed to be another illustration of the artist's turn for the heroic in the graceful. But, as it happens, he is not an invention, but a portrait—the portrait of a magnificent original, a literally gigantic St. Bernard, the property of the artist—the biggest, the handsomest, the most benignant of all domesticated shaggy things.

We think we are safe in saying that those ruder forms of incongruity which as a general thing constitute the stock-in-trade of the caricaturist fail to commend themselves to this particular satirist. He is too fond of the beautiful—his great passion is for the lovely ; not for what is called ideal beauty, which is usually a matter of not very successful guess-work, but for loveliness observed in the life and manners around him, and reproduced with a generous desire to represent it as usual. The French express a certain difference better than we ; they talk of those who see *en beau* and those who see *en laid.* Du Maurier is as highly developed an example as we could desire of the former tendency—just as Cham and Daumier are examples of the latter ; just, too, if we may venture to select instances from the staff of *Punch,* as Charles Keene and Linley Sambourne are examples of the latter. Du Maurier can see ugliness wonderfully well when he has a strong motive for looking for it, as witness so many of the figures in his crusade against the " æsthetic" movement. Who could be uglier than Maudle and Postlethwaite and all the other apparitions from " passionate Brompton " ? Who could have more bulging foreheads, more protuberant eyes, more retreating jaws, more sloping shoulders, more objectionable hair, more of the signs generally of personal debility ? To say, as we said just now, that Du Maurier carries his specification of types very far is to say mainly that he defines with peculiar completeness his queer people, his failures, his grotesques. But it strikes us that it is just this vivid and affectionate appreciation of beauty that makes him do such justice to the eccentrics. We have heard his ugly creations called malignant—compared (to their disadvantage) with similar figures in Leech. Leech, it was said, is always good-natured and jovial, even in the excesses of caricature ; whereas his successor (with a much greater brilliancy of execution) betrays, in dealing with the oddities of the human family, a taint of "French ferocity." We think the discrimination fallacious ; and it is only because we do not believe Du Maurier's reputation for amiability to be really in danger that we do not hasten to defend him from the charge of ferocity—French or English. The fact is he attempts discriminations that Leech never dreamt of. Leech's characterisations are all simple, whereas Du Maurier's are extremely complicated. He would like every one to be tall and straight and fair, to have a well-cut mouth and chin, a well-poised head, well-shaped legs, an air of nobleness, of happy development. He perceives, however, that nature plays us some dreadful tricks, and he measures her departure from these beautiful conditions with extreme displeasure. He regrets it with all the force of his appreciation of the beautiful, and he feels the strongest desire to indicate the culpability of the aberration. He has an artistic æsthetic need to make ugly people as ugly as they are ; he holds that such serious facts should not be superficially treated. And then, besides that, his fancy finds a real entertainment in the completeness, in the perfection, of certain forms of facial queerness. No one has rendered like Du Maurier the ridiculous little people who crop up in the interstices of that huge and complicated London world. We have no such finished types as these in America. If the English find us all a little odd, oddity, in American society, never ripens and rounds itself off so perfectly as in some of these products of a richer tradition. All those English terms of characterisation which exist in America at the most only as precarious exotics, but which are on every one's lips in England—the snob, the cad, the prig, the duffer—Du Maurier has given us a thousand times the figure they belong to. No one has done the "duffer" so well ; there are a hundred variations of the countenance of Mr. McJoseph, the gentleman commemorated in *Punch* on the 19th August 1876 ; or the even happier physiognomy of the other gentleman who on the 2d November 1872 says to a lady that he "never feels safe from the British snob till he is south of the Danube," and to whom the lady retorts, "And what do the South Danubians say ? " This personage is in profile: his face is fat, complacent, cautious ; his hair and whiskers have as many curves and flourishes as the signature of a writing-master ; he is an incarnation of certain familiar elements of English life—"the great middle class," the Philistinism, the absence of irony, the smugness and literalism. Du Maurier is full of soft irony: he has that infusion of it which is indispensable to an artistic nature, and we may add that in this respect he seems to us more French than English. This quality has helped him immensely to find material in the so-called æsthetic movement of the last few years. None of his duffers have been so good as his æsthetic duffers. But of this episode we must wait a little to speak. The point that, for the moment, we wished to make is, that he has a peculiar perception of the look of breeding, of race; and that, left to himself, as it were, he would ask nothing better than to make it the prerogative of all his characters. Only he is not left to himself. For, looking about into the world he perceives Sir Gorgius Midas and Mr. McJoseph, and the whole multitude of the vulgar who have not been cultivated like orchids and race-horses. But his extreme inclination to give his figures the benefit of the supposition that most people have the feelings of gentlemen makes him, as we began by saying, a very happy interpreter of those frequent works of fiction of which the action goes on for the most part in the drawing-room of the British country house. Every drawing-room, unfortunately, is not a home of the graces; but for the artist, given such an apartment, a group of quiet, well-shaped people is more or less implied. The "fashionable novel," as it flourished about 1830, is no more; and its extinction is not to be regretted. We believe it was rarely accompanied with illustrations; but if it were to be revived Du Maurier would be the man to make the pictures— the pictures of people rather slim and still, with long necks and limbs so straight that they look stiff, who might be treated with the amount of derision justified (if the fashionable novel of 1830 is to be believed) by their passion for talking bad French.

We have been looking over the accumulations of *Punch* for the last twenty years, and Du Maurier's work, which during this long period is remarkably abundant and various, has given us more impressions than we can hope to put into form. The result of sitting for several hours at such a banquet of drollery, of poring over so many caricatures, of catching the point of so many jokes, is a kind of indigestion of the visual sense. This is especially the case if one happens to be liable to confusions and lapses of memory. Every picture, every pleasantry, drives the last out of the mind, and even the figures we recall best get mixed up with another story than their own. The early drawings, as a general thing, are larger than the late ones; we believe that the artist was obliged to make them large in order to make them at all. (They were then photographed, much reduced, upon the block; and it is impossible to form an idea of the delicacy of Du Maurier's work without having seen the designs themselves, which are in pen and ink.) As the years have gone on the artist has apparently been able to use a shorter stroke, there has been less need of reducing it, and the full-page picture has become more rare. The wealth of execution was sometimes out of proportion to the jest beneath the cut; the joke might be as much or as little of a joke as one would, the picture was at any rate before all things a picture. What could be more charming than the drawing (24th October 1868) of the unconscious Oriana and the ingenious Jones? It is a real work of art, a thing to have had the honours of colour, and of the "line" at the Academy; and that the artist should have been able to give it to us for threepence, on the reverse of a printed page, is a striking proof of his affluence. The unconscious Oriana—she is drawn very large—sits in the foreground, in the shadow of some rocks that ornament the sands at a bathing-place. Her beautiful hair falls over her shoulders (she has been taking her bath, and has hung her tresses out to dry), and her charming eyes are bent upon the second volume of a novel. The beach stretches away into the distance —with all the expression of space; and here the ingenious Jones carries out his little scheme of catching a portrait of the object—an object profoundly indifferent—of his adoration. He pretends to sit to an itinerant photographer, and apparently places himself in the line of the instrument, which in reality, thanks to a private understanding with the artist, is focussed upon the figure of his mistress. There is not much landscape in Du Maurier—the background is almost always an interior; but whenever he attempts an out-of-door scene he does it admirably. What could be prettier and at the same time more real than the big view (9th September 1876) of the low tide on Scarborough sands? We forget the joke, but we remember the scene—two or three figures, with their backs to us, leaning over a terrace or balcony in the foreground, and looking down at the great expanse of the uncovered beach, which is crowded with the activities of a populous bathing-place. The bathers, the walkers, the machines, the horses, the dogs, are seen with

distinctness—a multitude of little black points—as
under a magnifying glass; the whole place looks vast
and swarming, and the particular impression the
artist wished to convey is thoroughly caught. The
particular impression—that is the great point with
Du Maurier; his intention is never vague ; he likes
to specify the place, the hour, the circumstances. We
forget the joke, but we remember the scene. This
may easily happen, as one looks over Du Maurier's
work ; we frankly confess that though he often
amuses us, he never strikes us primarily as a joker.
It is not the exuberance of his humour but the
purity of his line that arrests us, and we think of
him much less as a purveyor of fun than as a
charming draughtsman who has been led by circumstances to cultivate a vein of pleasantry. At
every turn we find the fatal gift of beauty, by
which we mean that his people are so charming that
their prettiness throws the legend into the shade.
Beauty comes so easily to him that he lavishes it
with unconscious freedom. If he represents Angelina reprimanding the housemaid, it is ten to one
that Angelina will be a Juno and the housemaid a
Hebe. Whatever be the joke, this element of grace
almost makes the picture serious. The point of
course is not that Angelina should be lovely, but
that the housemaid should be ridiculous ; and you
feel that if you should call the artist's attention to
this he would reply: "I am really very sorry, but
she is the plainest woman I can make—for the

money!" This is what happens throughout—his women (and we may add his children) being monotonously, incorrigibly fair. He is exceedingly fond of children; he has represented them largely at every age and in every attitude; but we can scarcely recall an instance of his making them anything but beautiful. They are always delightful —they are the nicest children in the world. They say droll things, but they never do ugly ones, and their whole child-world is harmonious and happy. We might have referred that critic whom we quoted above, who observed in Du Maurier's manner the element of "ferocity," to the leniency of his treatment of the rising generation. The children of Cham are little monsters; so are Daumier's; and the infants of Gavarni, with a grace of their own, like everything he drew, are simply rather diminutive and rather more sophisticated adults. Du Maurier is fond of large families, of the picturesqueness of the British nursery; he is a votary of the *culte du bébé* and has never a happier touch than when he represents a blooming brood walking out in gradations of size. The pretty points of children are intimately known to him, and he throws them into high relief; he understands, moreover, the infant wardrobe as well as the infant mind. His little boys and girls are "turned out" with a completeness which has made the despair of many an American mother. It may perhaps appear invidious to say that the little girls are even nicer than the little boys, but this is no more than natural, with the artist's delicate appreciation of female loveliness. It begins, to his vision, in the earliest periods and goes on increasing till it is embodied in the stature of those slim Junos of whom we have spoken.

It is easy to see that Du Maurier is of the eminently justifiable opinion that nothing in the world is so fair as the fairness of fair women ; and if so many of his women are fair, it is to be inferred that he has a secret for drawing out their advantages. This secret, indeed, is simply that fineness of perception of which we have already had occasion to speak and to which it is necessary so often to refer. He is evidently of the opinion that almost any woman has beauty if you look at her in the right way—carefully enough, intelligently enough ; and that *a fortiori* the exceptionally handsome women contain treasures of plasticity. Feminine line and surface, curves of shoulder, stretches of arm, turns of head, undulations of step, are matters of attentive study to him ; and his women have for the most part the art of looking as if they excelled in amiability as much as in contour. We know a gentleman who, on being requested to inscribe himself on one of those formidable folios kept in certain houses, in which you indite the name of your favourite flower, favourite virtue, favourite historical character, wrote, in the compartment dedicated to the " three favourite qualities in a woman" the simple words: "Grace. Grace. Grace." Du Maurier might have been this gentleman, for his women are inveterately and imperturbably graceful. We have heard people complain of it ; complain too that they all look alike, that they are always sisters—all products of a single birth. They have indeed a mutual resemblance ; but when once the beautiful type has been found, we see no reason why, from a restless love of change, the artist should depart from it. We should feel as if Du Maurier had been fickle and faithless if he were suddenly to cease to offer us the tall, tranquil persons he understands so well. They have an inestimable look of repose, a kind of Greek serenity. There is a figure in a cut of which we have forgotten both the "point" and the date (we mention it at hazard—it is one in a hundred), which only needed to be modelled in clay to be a truly "important" creation. A couple of children address themselves to a youthful aunt, who leans her hand upon a toilet-table, presenting her back, clothed in a loose gown, not gathered in at the waist, to the spectator. Her charming pose, the way her head slowly turns, the beautiful folds of her robe, make her look more like a statuette in a museum than like a figure in *Punch*. We have forgotten what the children are saying, but we remember her charming attitude, which is a capital example of the love of beauty for beauty's sake. It is the same bias as the characteristic of the poet.

The intention of these remarks has been supposed to be rather a view of Du Maurier in his relation to English society than a technical estimate of his powers—a line of criticism to which we may already appear unduly to have committed ourselves. He is predominantly a painter of social as distinguished from popular life, and when the other day he collected some of his drawings into a volume he found it natural to give them the title of *English Society at Home.* He looks at the luxurious classes more than at the people, though he by no means ignores the humours of humble life. His consideration of the peculiarities of costermongers and "cadgers" is comparatively perfunctory, as he is too fond of civilisation and of the higher refinements of the grotesque. His colleague, the frank and objective Keene, has a more natural familiarity with the British populace. There is a whole side of English life at which Du Maurier scarcely glances — the great sporting element, which supplies half of their gaiety and all their conversation to millions of her Majesty's subjects. He is shy of the turf and of the cricket-field; he only touches here and there upon the river; but he has made "society" completely his own—he has sounded its depths, explored its mysteries, discovered and divulged its secrets. His observation of these things is extraordinarily acute, and his illustrations, taken together, form a complete comedy of manners, in which the same personages constantly reappear, so that we have the sense, indispensable to keenness of interest, of tracing their adventures to a climax. So many of the conditions of English life are spec-

tacular (and to American eyes even romantic) that
Du Maurier has never been at a loss for subjects.
He may have been at a loss for his joke—we
hardly see how he could fail to be, at the rate at
which he has been obliged to produce ; but we repeat
that to ourselves the joke is the least part of the
affair.   We mean that he is never at a loss for
scenes.   English society makes scenes all round
him, and he has only to look to see the most charming combinations, which at the same time have the
merit that you can always take the satirical view of
them.   He sees, for instance, the people in the
Park ; the crowd that gathers under the trees on
June afternoons to watch the spectacle of the Row,
with the slow, solemn jostle of the drive going on
behind it.   Such a spectacle as this may be vain and
unprofitable to a mind bent upon higher business,
but it is full of material for the artist, who finds a
fund of inspiration in the thousand figures, faces,
types, accidents, attitudes.   The way people stand
and sit, the way they stroll and pause, the way they
lean over the rail to talk to one of the riders, the
way they stare and yawn and bore themselves—
these things are charming to Du Maurier, who always
reproduces the *act* with wonderful fidelity.   This we
should bear in mind, having spoken above of his
aversion to the violent.   He has indeed a preference
for quiet and gradual movements.   But it is not in
the least because he is not able to make the movement definite.   No one represents a particular atti-

tude better than he ; and it is not too much to say
that the less flagrant the attitude, the more latent
its intention, the more successfully he represents it.

The postures people take while they are waiting
for dinner, while they are thinking what to say,
while they are pretending to listen to music, while
they are making speeches they don't mean; the
thousand strange and dreary expressions (of face and
figure) which the detached mind may catch at any
moment in wandering over a collection of people
who are supposed to be amusing themselves in a
superior manner—all this is entirely familiar to Du
Maurier ; he renders it with inimitable fidelity.   His
is the detached mind—he takes refuge in the divine
independence of art.   He reproduces to the life the
gentleman who is looking with extraordinary solem-
nity at his boots, the lady who is gazing with sudden
rapture at the ceiling, the grimaces of fifty people
who would be surprised at their reflection if the
mirror were suddenly to be presented to them.   In
such visions as these of course the comical mingles
with the beautiful, and fond as Du Maurier is of the
beautiful, it is sometimes heroically sacrificed.   At
any rate the comic effect is (in the drawing) never
missed.   The legend that accompanies it may sometimes appear to be wanting in the grossest drollery,
but the expression of the figures is always such that
you must say : " How he has hit it ! "   This is the
kind of comedy in which Du Maurier excels—-the
comedy of those social relations in which the incon-

gruities are pressed beneath the surface, so that the picture has need of a certain amount of explanation. The explanation is often rather elaborate—in many cases one may almost fancy that the image came first and the motive afterward. That is, it looks as if the artist, having seen a group of persons in certain positions, had said to himself : " They must—or at least they *may*—be saying so and so ; " and then had represented these positions and affixed the interpretation. He passes over none of those occasions on which society congregates—the garden-party, the picnic, the flower-show, the polo-match (though he has not much cultivated the humours of sport, he has represented polo more than once, and he has done ample justice to lawn-tennis, just as he did it, years ago, to the charming, dawdling, " spooning " tedium of croquet, which he depicted as played only by the most adorable young women, with the most diminutive feet) ; but he introduces us more particularly to indoors entertainments—to the London dinner-party in all those variations which cover such a general sameness ; to the afternoon tea, to the fashionable " squash," to the late and suffocating " small and early," to the scientific *conversazione*, to the evening with a little music. His musical parties are numerous and admirable—he has exposed in perfection the weak points of those entertainments : the infatuated tenor, bawling into the void of the public indifference ; the air of lassitude that pervades the company ; the woe-begone look of certain faces ;

the false and overacted attention of certain others; the young lady who is wishing to sing, and whose mamma is glaring at the young lady who *is* singing; the bristling heads of foreigners of the professional class, which stand out against the sleekness of British respectability.

Du Maurier understands the foreigner as no caricaturist has done hitherto; and we hasten to add that his portraits of continental types are never caricatures. They are serious studies, in which the idiosyncrasies of the race in question are vividly presented. His Germans would be the best if his French folk were not better still; but he has rendered most happily the aspect—and indeed the very temperament—of the German pianist. He has not often attempted the American; and the American reader who turns over the back volumes of *Punch* and encounters the cartoons, born under an evil star, in which, during the long weary years of the War, the obedient pencil of Mr. Tenniel contributed at the expense of the American physiognomy to the gaiety of nations, will not perhaps regret that Du Maurier should have avoided this particular field of portraiture. It is not, however, that he has not occasionally been inspired by the American girl, whom he endows with due prettiness, as in the case of the two transatlantic young ladies who, in the presence of a fine Alpine view, exclaim to a British admirer: " My ! ain't it rustic ? " As for the French, he knows them intimately, as he has a right to do. He thinks better of the English of course; but his

Frenchman is a very different affair from the Frenchman of Leech—the Frenchman who is sea-sick (as if
it were the appanage of his race alone!) on the
Channel steamer. In such a matter as this Du
Maurier is really psychological; he is versed in the
qualities which illustrate the difference of race. He
accentuates first of course the physical variation;
he contrasts—with a subtlety which may not at first
receive all the credit it deserves—the long, fair
English body, inclined to the bony, the lean, the
angular, with the short, plump French personality,
in which the neck is rarely a feature, in which the
stomach is too much of one, in which the calves of
the legs grow fat, in which in the women several of
the joints, the wrists, the shape of the hand, are apt
to be charming. Some of his happiest drawings are
reminiscences of a midsummer sojourn at a French
watering-place. We have long been in the habit of
looking for *Punch* with peculiar impatience at this
season of the year. When the artist goes to France
he takes his big dog with him, and he has more than
once commemorated the effect of this impressive
member of a quiet English family upon the Norman
and Breton populations. There have appeared at
this time certain anecdotic pictures of English travellers in French towns—in shops, markets, tram-
cars—in which some of the deeper disparities of the
two peoples have been (under the guise of its being
all a joke) very sufficiently exposed. Du Maurier
on the whole does justice to the French; his English

figures, in these international tableaux, by no means always come off best. When the English family of many persons troops into the *charcutier*'s or the perfumer's and stands planted there—mute, inexpressive, perpendicular—the demonstrations, the professions, the abundant speech of the neat, plump, insinuating *boutiquière* are a well-intended tribute to the high civilisation of her country. Du Maurier has done the "low" foreigner of the London (or of his native) streets—the foreigner whose unspeakable baseness prompts the Anglo-Saxon observer to breathe the Pharisee's vow of thanks that he is not as these people are; but, as we have seen, he has done the low Englishman quite as well—the 'Arry of the London music-halls, the companion of 'Andsome 'Arriet and Mr. Belville. Du Maurier's rendering of 'Arry's countenance, with its bloated purple bloom, of 'Arry's figure, carriage and costume—of his deportment at the fancy fair, where the professional beauties solicit his custom—is a triumph of exactitude. One of the most poignant of the drawings that illustrate his ravages in our civilisation is the large design which a year or two ago represented the narrow canal beneath the Bridge of Sighs. The hour is evening, and the period is the detested date at which the penny-steamer was launched upon the winding water-ways of the loveliest city in the world. The odious little vessel, belching forth a torrent of black smoke, passes under the covered arch which connects the ducal palace with the ducal

prison. 'Andsome 'Arriet and Mr. Belville (personally conducted) are of course on board, and 'Arriet
remarks that the Bridge of Sighs isn't much of a
size after all. To which her companion rejoins that
it has been immortalised by Byron, any way—" 'im
as wrote ' Our Boys,' you know." This fragment of
dialogue expresses concisely the arguments both for
and against the importation of the cheap and nasty
into Venetian waters.

Returning for a moment to Du Maurier's sketches
of the French, we must recall the really interesting
design in which, at a child's party at the Casino of
a *station balnéaire,* a number of little natives are inviting a group of English children to dance. The French
children have much the better manners ; they make
their little bows with a smile, they click their heels
together and crook their little arms as they offer
them to their partners. The sturdy British infants
are dumb, mistrustful, vaguely bewildered. Presently you perceive that in the very smart attire of
the gracious little Gauls *everything is wrong*—their
high heels, their poor little legs, at once too bare
and too much covered, their superfluous sashes and
scarfs. The small English are invested in plain
Jerseys and knickerbockers. The whole thing is a
pearl of observation, of reflection. Let us recall
also the rebuke administered to M. Dubois, the distinguished young man of science who, just arrived
from Paris and invited to dine by the Duke of Stil-
ton, mentions this latter fact in apology for being

late to a gentleman to whose house he goes on leaving the Duke's. This gentleman, assisted by Mr. Grigsby (both of them specimens of the snob-philistine whom Du Maurier has brought to such perfection), reprehends him in a superior manner for his rashness, reminds him that in England it is "not usual for a professional man" to allude in that promiscuous manner to having dined with a duke—a privilege which Grigsby characterises "the perfection of consummate achievement." The advantage is here with poor M. Dubois, who is a natural and sympathetic figure, a very *gentil* little Frenchman. The advantage is doubtless also with Mlle. Serrurier and her mother, though Mademoiselle is not very pretty, in a scene in which, just after the young lady has been singing at Mrs. Ponsonby de Tomkyns's, the clever Mrs. Ponsonby plays her off on the Duchess (as an inducement to come to another party) and then plays the Duchess off on the little vocalist and her mother, who, in order to secure the patronage of the Duchess, promise to come to the entertainment in question. The clever Mrs. Ponsonby thus gets both the Duchess and the vocalist for nothing. The broad-faced French girl, with small, salient eyes, her countenance treated in the simplest and surest manner, is a capital specimen of Du Maurier's skill in race-portraiture ; and though they may be a knowing couple in their way, we are sure that she and her mamma are incapable of the machinations of Mrs. Ponsonby de Tomkyns.

This lady is a real creation. She is an incident
of one of the later phases of Du Maurier's activity
—a child of the age which has also produced Mrs.
Cimabue Brown and Messrs. Maudle and Postlethwaite. She is not one of the heroines of the æsthetic
movement, though we may be sure she dabbles in
that movement so far as it pays to do so. Mrs.
Ponsonby de Tomkyns is a little of everything, in
so far as anything pays. She is always on the look-
out, she never misses an opportunity. She is not a
specialist, for that cuts off too many opportunities,
and the æsthetic people have the *tort*, as the French
say, to be specialists. No, Mrs. Ponsonby de Tomkyns is—what shall we call her ?—well, she is the
modern social spirit. She is prepared for everything ;
she is ready to take advantage of everything ; she
would invite Mr. Bradlaugh to dinner if she thought
the Duchess would come to meet him. The Duchess
is her great achievement—she never lets go of her
Duchess. She is young, very nice - looking, slim,
graceful, indefatigable. She tires poor Ponsonby
completely out ; she can keep going for hours after
poor Ponsonby is reduced to stupefaction. This
unfortunate husband is indeed almost always stupefied. He is not, like his wife, a person of imagination. She leaves him far behind, though he is so
inconvertible that if she were a less superior person he would have been a sad encumbrance. He
always figures in the corner of the scenes in which
she distinguishes herself, separated from her by

something like the gulf that separated Caliban from Ariel. He has his hands in his pockets, his head poked forward ; what is going on is quite beyond his comprehension. He vaguely wonders what his wife will do next ; her manœuvres quite transcend him. Mrs. Ponsonby de Tomkyns always succeeds. She is never at fault ; she is as quick as the instinct of self-preservation. She is the little London lady who is determined to be a greater one. She pushes, pushes, gently but firmly—always pushes. At last she arrives. It is true that she had only the other day, on 29th June 1882, a considerable failure ; we refer the reader to the little incident of Madame Gaminot, in the *Punch* for that date. But she will recover from it ; she has already recovered from it. She is not even afraid of Sir Gorgius Midas—of the dreadful Midas junior. She pretends to think Lady Midas the most elegant of women ; when it is necessary to flatter, she lays it on as with a trowel. She hesitates at nothing ; she is very modern. If she doesn't take the æsthetic line more than is necessary, she finds it necessary to take it a little ; for if we are to believe Du Maurier, the passion for strange raiment and blue china has during the last few years made ravages in the London world. We may be sure that Mrs. Ponsonby de Tomkyns has an array of fragile disks attached to her walls, and that she can put in a word about Botticelli at the right moment. She is far, however, from being a representative of æstheticism, for her hair is very neatly arranged, and her dress looks French and superficial.

In Mrs. Cimabue Brown we see the priestess of the æsthetic cult, and this lady is on the whole a different sort of person. She knows less about duchesses, but she knows more about dados. Du Maurier's good-natured "chaff" of the eccentricities of the plastic sense so newly and so strangely awakened in England has perhaps been the most brilliant episode of his long connection with *Punch*. He has invented Mrs. Cimabue Brown —he has invented Maudle and Postlethwaite. These remarkable people have had great success in America, and have contributed not a little to the curiosity felt in that country on the subject of the English Renascence. Strange rumours and legends in relation to this great movement had made their way across the Atlantic ; the sayings and doings of a mysterious body of people, devotees of the lovely and the precious, living in goodly houses and walking in gracious garments, were repeated and studied in our simpler civilisation. There has not been as yet an American Renascence, in spite of the taste for " sincere " sideboards and fragments of crockery. American interiors are perhaps to-day as " gracious " as English ; but the movement in the United States has stopped at household furniture, has not yet set its mark upon speech and costume—much less upon the human physiognomy. Du Maurier of course has lent a good deal of his own fame to the vagaries he depicts ; but it is certain that the new æsthetic life has had a good deal of reality. A great many people have discovered themselves to be fitted for it both by nature and by grace; so that noses and chins, facial angles of every sort shaped according to this higher rule have become frequent in London society. This reaction of taste upon nature is really a marvel, and the miracle has not been repeated in America, nor so far as we know upon the continent of Europe. The love of Botticelli has actually remoulded the features of several persons. London, for many seasons, was full of Botticelli women, with wan cheeks and weary eyes, enveloped in mystical, crumpled robes. Their language was apt to correspond with their faces; they talked in strange accents, with melancholy murmurs and cadences. They announced a gospel of joy, but their expression, their manners, were joyless. These peculiarities did not cross the ocean; for somehow the soil of the western world was not as yet prepared for them. American ladies were even heard to declare that there was something in their constitution that would prevent their ever dressing like that. They had another ideal; they were committed to the whalebone. But meanwhile, as I say, there was something irritating, fascinating, mystifying in the light thrown on the subject by *Punch*. It seemed to many persons to be desired that we too should have a gospel of joy; American life was not particularly "gracious," and if only the wind could be made to blow from the æsthetic quarter a great many dry places would

be refreshed.   These desires perhaps have subsided ;
for *Punch* of late has rather neglected the Renascence.
Mrs. Cimabue Brown is advancing in years, and
Messrs. Maudle and Postlethwaite have been through
all their paces.   The new æsthetic life, in short,
shows signs of drawing to a close, after having, as
many people tell us, effected a revolution in English
taste—having at least, if not peopled the land with
beauty, made certain consecrated forms of ugliness
henceforth impossible.

The whole affair has been very curious and, we
think, very characteristic of the English mind.   The
same episode fifty times repeated—a hundred " revo-
lutions of taste," accompanied with an infinite ex-
penditure of money—would fail to convince certain
observant and possibly too sceptical strangers that
the English are an æsthetic people.   They have not
a spontaneous artistic life ; their taste is a matter of
conscience, reflection, duty, and the writer who in
our time has appealed to them most eloquently on
behalf of art has rested his plea on moral standards
—has talked exclusively of right and wrong.   It is
impossible to live much among them, to be a spectator of their habits, their manners, their arrange-
ments, without perceiving that the artistic point of
view is the last that they naturally take.   The sense
of manner is not part of their constitution.   They
arrive at it, as they have arrived at so many things,
because they are ambitious, resolute, enlightened,
fond of difficulties ; but there is always a strange

element either of undue apology or of exaggerated
defiance in their attempts at the cultivation of
beauty. They carry on their huge broad back a
nameless mountain of conventions and prejudices, a
dusky cloud of inaptitudes and fears, which casts a
shadow upon the frank and confident practice of art.
The consequence of all this is that their revivals of
taste are even stranger than the abuses they are
meant to correct. They are violent, voluntary,
mechanical; wanting in grace, in tact, in the sense
of humour and of proportion. A genuine artist like
Du Maurier could not fail to perceive all this, and to
perceive also that it gave him a capital opportunity.
None of his queer people are so queer as some of
these perverted votaries of joy. "Excuse me, it is
not a Botticelli—before a Botticelli I am dumb," one
of them says to a poor plain man who shows him a
picture which has been attributed to that master.
We have said already, and repeated, that Du Maurier
has a great deal of irony—the irony of the thorough-
going artist and of the observer who has a strain of
foreign blood in his veins. There are certain pretensions that such a mind can never take seriously; in
the artist there is of necessity, as it appears to us, a
touch of the democrat—though, perhaps, he is as
unlikely to have more than a certain dose of this
disposition as he is to be wholly without it. Some
of his drawings seem to us to have for the public he
addresses a stinging democratic meaning; like the
adventure of M. Dubois (of whom we have spoken),

who had had the inconvenience of dining with a
duke ; or the reply of the young man to whom Miss
Midas remarks that he is the first commoner she has
ever danced with : " And why is it the commoners
have avoided you so ? "—or the response of the
German *savant* to Mrs. Lyon Hunter, who invites
him to dine, without his wife, though she is on his
arm, to meet various great ladies whom she enumerates : " And pray, do you think they would not
be respectable company for my wife ? " Du Maurier
possesses in perfection the independence of the
genuine artist in the presence of a hundred worldly
superstitions and absurdities. We have said, however, that the morality, so to speak, of his drawings
was a subordinate question : what we wished to insist upon is their completeness, their grace, their
beauty, their rare pictorial character. It is an accident that the author of such things should not have
been a painter—that he has not been an ornament
of the English school. Indeed, with the restrictions
to which he has so well accommodated himself, he is
such an ornament. No English artistic work in
these latter years has, in our opinion, been more
exquisite in quality.

1883.

XI

THE ART OF FICTION

THE ART OF FICTION

I SHOULD not have affixed so comprehensive a title
to these few remarks, necessarily wanting in any
completeness upon a subject the full consideration
of which would carry us far, did I not seem to discover a pretext for my temerity in the interesting
pamphlet lately published under this name by Mr.
Walter Besant. Mr. Besant's lecture at the Royal
Institution — the original form of his pamphlet —
appears to indicate that many persons are interested
in the art of fiction, and are not indifferent to such
remarks, as those who practise it may attempt to
make about it. I am therefore anxious not to lose
the benefit of this favourable association, and to edge
in a few words under cover of the attention which
Mr. Besant is sure to have excited. There is something very encouraging in his having put into form
certain of his ideas on the mystery of story-telling.

It is a proof of life and curiosity—curiosity on
the part of the brotherhood of novelists as well as
on the part of their readers. Only a short time ago
it might have been supposed that the English novel

was not what the French call *discutable.* It had no
air of having a theory, a conviction, a consciousness
of itself behind it—of being the expression of an
artistic faith, the result of choice and comparison.
I do not say it was necessarily the worse for that : it
would take much more courage than I possess to
intimate that the form of the novel as Dickens
and Thackeray (for instance) saw it had any taint of
incompleteness. It was, however, *naïf* (if I may
help myself out with another French word); and
evidently if it be destined to suffer in any way for
having lost its *naïveté* it has now an idea of making
sure of the corresponding advantages. During the
period I have alluded to there was a comfortable,
good-humoured feeling abroad that a novel is a novel,
as a pudding is a pudding, and that our only business with it could be to swallow it. But within a
year or two, for some reason or other, there have
been signs of returning animation—the era of discussion would appear to have been to a certain
extent opened. Art lives upon discussion, upon
experiment, upon curiosity, upon variety of attempt,
upon the exchange of views and the comparison of
standpoints ; and there is a presumption that those
times when no one has anything particular to say
about it, and has no reason to give for practice or
preference, though they may be times of honour, are
not times of development—are times, possibly even,
a little of dulness. The successful application of
any art is a delightful spectacle, but the theory too

is interesting; and though there is a great deal of
the latter without the former I suspect there has
never been a genuine success that has not had a
latent core of conviction. Discussion, suggestion,
formulation, these things are fertilising when they
are frank and sincere. Mr. Besant has set an
excellent example in saying what he thinks, for his
part, about the way in which fiction should be
written, as well as about the way in which it should
be published; for his view of the " art," carried on
into an appendix, covers that too. Other labourers
in the same field will doubtless take up the argument,
they will give it the light of their experience, and
the effect will surely be to make our interest in the
novel a little more what it had for some time threatened to fail to be—a serious, active, inquiring
interest, under protection of which this delightful
study may, in moments of confidence, venture to say
a little more what it thinks of itself.

It must take itself seriously for the public to take
it so. The old superstition about fiction being
" wicked " has doubtless died out in England; but
the spirit of it lingers in a certain oblique regard
directed toward any story which does not more or
less admit that it is only a joke. Even the most
jocular novel feels in some degree the weight of
the proscription that was formerly directed against
literary levity: the jocularity does not always succeed in passing for orthodoxy. It is still expected,
though perhaps people are ashamed to say it, that a

production which is after all only a "make believe"
(for what else is a "story"?) shall be in some
degree apologetic—shall renounce the pretension of
attempting really to represent life. This, of course,
any sensible, wide-awake story declines to do, for it
quickly perceives that the tolerance granted to it on
such a condition is only an attempt to stifle it dis-
guised in the form of generosity. The old evangelical hostility to the novel, which was as explicit as
it was narrow, and which regarded it as little less
favourable to our immortal part than a stage-play,
was in reality far less insulting. The only reason
for the existence of a novel is that it does attempt to
represent life. When it relinquishes this attempt,
the same attempt that we see on the canvas of the
painter, it will have arrived at a very strange pass.
It is not expected of the picture that it will make
itself humble in order to be forgiven; and the analogy
between the art of the painter and the art of the
novelist is, so far as I am able to see, complete.
Their inspiration is the same, their process (allowing
for the different quality of the vehicle), is the same,
their success is the same. They may learn from
each other, they may explain and sustain each
other. Their cause is the same, and the honour of
one is the honour of another. The Mahometans
think a picture an unholy thing, but it is a long
time since any Christian did, and it is therefore the
more odd that in the Christian mind the traces (dis-
simulated though they may be) of a suspicion of the

sister art should linger to this day. The only effec-
tual way to lay it to rest is to emphasise the analogy
to which I just alluded—to insist on the fact that
as the picture is reality, so the novel is history.
That is the only general description (which does it
justice) that we may give of the novel. But history
also is allowed to represent life ; it is not, any more
than painting, expected to apologise. The subject-
matter of fiction is stored up likewise in documents
and records, and if it will not give itself away, as
they say in California, it must speak with assurance,
with the tone of the historian. Certain accomplished
novelists have a habit of giving themselves away
which must often bring tears to the eyes of people
who take their fiction seriously. I was lately struck,
in reading over many pages of Anthony Trollope,
with his want of discretion in this particular. In a
digression, a parenthesis or an aside, he concedes to
the reader that he and this trusting friend are only
"making believe." He admits that the events he
narrates have not really happened, and that he can
give his narrative any turn the reader may like best.
Such a betrayal of a sacred office seems to me, I confess, a terrible crime ; it is what I mean by the
attitude of apology, and it shocks me every whit as
much in Trollope as it would have shocked me in
Gibbon or Macaulay. It implies that the novelist is
less occupied in looking for the truth (the truth, of
course I mean, that he assumes, the premises that we
must grant him, whatever they may be), than the

historian, and in doing so it deprives him at a stroke of all his standing-room. To represent and illustrate the past, the actions of men, is the task of either writer, and the only difference that I can see is, in proportion as he succeeds, to the honour of the novelist, consisting as it does in his having more difficulty in collecting his evidence, which is so far from being purely literary. It seems to me to give him a great character, the fact that he has at once so much in common with the philosopher and the painter; this double analogy is a magnificent heritage.

It is of all this evidently that Mr. Besant is full when he insists upon the fact that fiction is one of the *fine* arts, deserving in its turn of all the honours and emoluments that have hitherto been reserved for the successful profession of music, poetry, painting, architecture. It is impossible to insist too much on so important a truth, and the place that Mr. Besant demands for the work of the novelist may be represented, a trifle less abstractly, by saying that he demands not only that it shall be reputed artistic, but that it shall be reputed very artistic indeed. It is excellent that he should have struck this note, for his doing so indicates that there was need of it, that his proposition may be to many people a novelty. One rubs one's eyes at the thought; but the rest of Mr. Besant's essay confirms the revelation. I suspect in truth that it would be possible to confirm it still further, and that one would not be far wrong in saying that in addition to the people to whom it has never occurred that a novel ought to be artistic, there are a great many others who, if this principle were urged upon them, would be filled with an indefinable mistrust. They would find it difficult to explain their repugnance, but it would operate strongly to put them on their guard. " Art," in our Protestant communities, where so many things have got so strangely twisted about, is supposed in certain circles to have some vaguely injurious effect upon those who make it an important consideration, who let it weigh in the balance. It is assumed to be opposed in some mysterious manner to morality, to amusement, to instruction. When it is embodied in the work of the painter (the sculptor is another affair !) you know what it is : it stands there before you, in the honesty of pink and green and a gilt frame ; you can see the worst of it at a glance, and you can be on your guard. But when it is introduced into literature it becomes more insidious— there is danger of its hurting you before you know it. Literature should be either instructive or amusing, and there is in many minds an impression that these artistic preoccupations, the search for form, contribute to neither end, interfere indeed with both. They are too frivolous to be edifying, and too serious to be diverting ; and they are moreover priggish and paradoxical and superfluous. That, I think, represents the manner in which the latent thought of many people who read novels as an exercise in skipping would explain itself if it were to become articulate. They would argue, of course, that a novel ought to be " good," but they would interpret this term in a fashion of their own, which indeed would vary considerably from one critic to another. One would say that being good means representing virtuous and aspiring characters, placed in prominent positions ; another would say that it depends on a " happy ending," on a distribution at the last of prizes, pensions, husbands, wives, babies, millions, appended paragraphs, and cheerful remarks. Another still would say that it means being full of incident and movement, so that we shall wish to jump ahead, to see who was the mysterious stranger, and if the stolen will was ever found, and shall not be distracted from this pleasure by any tiresome analysis or " description." But they would all agree that the "artistic" idea would spoil some of their fun. One would hold it accountable for all the description, another would see it revealed in the absence of sympathy. Its hostility to a happy ending would be evident, and it might even in some cases render any ending at all impossible. The " ending " of a novel is, for many persons, like that of a good dinner, a course of dessert and ices, and the artist in fiction is regarded as a sort of meddlesome doctor who forbids agreeable aftertastes. It is therefore true that this conception of Mr. Besant's of the novel as a superior form encounters not only a negative but a positive indiffer-ence. It matters little that as a work of art it should really be as little or as much of its essence to supply happy endings, sympathetic characters, and an objective tone, as if it were a work of mechanics : the association of ideas, however incongruous, might easily be too much for it if an eloquent voice were not sometimes raised to call attention to the fact that it is at once as free and as serious a branch of literature as any other.

Certainly this might sometimes be doubted in presence of the enormous number of works of fiction that appeal to the credulity of our generation, for it might easily seem that there could be no great character in a commodity so quickly and easily produced. It must be admitted that good novels are much compromised by bad ones, and that the field at large suffers discredit from overcrowding. I think, however, that this injury is only superficial, and that the superabundance of written fiction proves nothing against the principle itself. It has been vulgarised, like all other kinds of literature, like everything else to-day, and it has proved more than some kinds accessible to vulgarisation. But there is as much difference as there ever was between a good novel and a bad one : the bad is swept with all the daubed canvases and spoiled marble into some unvisited limbo, or infinite rubbish yard beneath the back-windows of the world, and the good subsists and emits its light and stimulates our desire for perfection. As I shall take the liberty of making but a single criticism of Mr. Besant, whose tone is so full of the love of his art, I may as well have done with it at once. He

seems to me to mistake in attempting to say so
definitely beforehand what sort of an affair the good
novel will be.   To indicate the danger of such an
error as that has been the purpose of these few pages;
to suggest that certain traditions on the subject,
applied *a priori*, have already had much to answer
for, and that the good health of an art which undertakes so immediately to reproduce life must demand
that it be perfectly free.   It lives upon exercise, and
the very meaning of exercise is freedom.   The only
obligation to which in advance we may hold a novel,
without incurring the accusation of being arbitrary, is
that it be interesting.   That general responsibility
rests upon it, but it is the only one I can think of.
The ways in which it is at liberty to accomplish this
result (of interesting us) strike me as innumerable,
and such as can only suffer from being marked out
or fenced in by prescription.   They are as various as
the temperament of man, and they are successful in
proportion as they reveal a particular mind, different
from others.   A novel is in its broadest definition a
personal, a direct impression of life : that, to begin
with, constitutes its value, which is greater or less
according to the intensity of the impression.   But
there will be no intensity at all, and therefore no
value, unless there is freedom to feel and say.   The
tracing of a line to be followed, of a tone to be taken,
of a form to be filled out, is a limitation of that
freedom and a suppression of the very thing that we
are most curious about.   The form, it seems to me,

is to be appreciated after the fact : then the author's choice has been made, his standard has been indicated ; then we can follow lines and directions and compare tones and resemblances. Then in a word we can enjoy one of the most charming of pleasures, we can estimate quality, we can apply the test of execution. The execution belongs to the author alone; it is what is most personal to him, and we measure him by that. The advantage, the luxury, as well as the torment and responsibility of the novelist, is that there is no limit to what he may attempt as an executant—no limit to his possible experiments, efforts, discoveries, successes. Here it is especially that he works, step by step, like his brother of the brush, of whom we may always say that he has painted his picture in a manner best known to himself. His manner is his secret, not necessarily a jealous one. He cannot disclose it as a general thing if he would ; he would be at a loss to teach it to others. I say this with a due recollection of having insisted on the community of method of the artist who paints a picture and the artist who writes a novel. The painter *is* able to teach the rudiments of his practice, and it is possible, from the study of good work (granted the aptitude), both to learn how to paint and to learn how to write. Yet it remains true, without injury to the *rapprochement*, that the literary artist would be obliged to say to his pupil much more than the other, " Ah, well, you must do it as you can !" It is a question of degree, a matter

of delicacy.   If there are exact sciences, there are also
exact arts, and the grammar of painting is so much
more definite that it makes the difference.

I ought to add, however, that if Mr. Besant says
at the beginning of his essay that the " laws of fiction
may be laid down and taught with as much precision
and exactness as the laws of harmony, perspective,
and proportion," he mitigates what might appear
to be an extravagance by applying his remark to
" general " laws, and by expressing most of these
rules in a manner with which it would certainly be
unaccommodating to disagree.   That the novelist
must write from his experience, that his " characters
must be real and such as might be met with in actual
life;" that " a young lady brought up in a quiet
country village should avoid descriptions of garrison
life," and " a writer whose friends and personal ex-
periences belong to the lower middle-class should
carefully avoid introducing his characters into
society;" that one should enter one's notes in a
common-place book ; that one's figures should be
clear in outline ; that making them clear by some
trick of speech or of carriage is a bad method, and
" describing them at length " is a worse one ; that
English Fiction should have a " conscious moral purpose;" that " it is almost impossible to estimate too
highly the value of careful workmanship—that is, of
style;" that " the most important point of all is the
story," that " the story is everything " : these are
principles with most of which it is surely impossible

not to sympathise. That remark about the lower
middle-class writer and his knowing his place is perhaps rather chilling ; but for the rest I should find
it difficult to dissent from any one of these recom-
mendations. At the same time, I should find it difficult positively to assent to them, with the exception,
perhaps, of the injunction as to entering one's notes
in a common-place book. They scarcely seem to me
to have the quality that Mr. Besant attributes to the
rules of the novelist—the " precision and exactness "
of " the laws of harmony, perspective, and proportion." They are suggestive, they are even inspiring,
but they are not exact, though they are doubtless as
much so as the case admits of : which is a proof of
that liberty of interpretation for which I just contended. For the value of these different injunctions
—so beautiful and so vague—is wholly in the meaning one attaches to them. The characters, the situation, which strike one as real will be those that touch
and interest one most, but the measure of reality is
very difficult to fix. The reality of Don Quixote or
of Mr. Micawber is a very delicate shade ; it is a
reality so coloured by the author's vision that, vivid
as it may be, one would hesitate to propose it as a
model : one would expose one's self to some very
embarrassing questions on the part of a pupil. It
goes without saying that you will not write a good
novel unless you possess the sense of reality ; but it
will be difficult to give you a recipe for calling that
sense into being. Humanity is immense, and reality

has a myriad forms; the most one can affirm is that
some of the flowers of fiction have the odour of it,
and others have not; as for telling you in advance
how your nosegay should be composed, that is
another affair.   It is equally excellent and incon-
clusive to say that one must write from experience;
to our supposititious aspirant such a declaration
might savour of mockery.   What kind of experience
is intended, and where does it begin and end?   Experience is never limited, and it is never complete;
it is an immense sensibility, a kind of huge spider-
web of the finest silken threads suspended in the
chamber of consciousness, and catching every air-
borne particle in its tissue.   It is the very atmosphere
of the mind; and when the mind is imaginative—
much more when it happens to be that of a man of
genius—it takes to itself the faintest hints of life, it
converts the very pulses of the air into revelations.
The young lady living in a village has only to be a
damsel upon whom nothing is lost, to make it quite
unfair (as it seems to me) to declare to her that she
shall have nothing to say about the military.   Greater
miracles have been seen than that, imagination assist-
ing, she should speak the truth about some of these
gentlemen.   I remember an English novelist, a
woman of genius, telling me that she was much com-
mended for the impression she had managed to give
in one of her tales of the nature and way of life of
the French Protestant youth.   She had been asked
where she learned so much about this recondite being,

she had been congratulated on her peculiar opportunities. These opportunities consisted in her having once, in Paris, as she ascended a staircase, passed an open door where, in the household of a *pasteur*, some of the young Protestants were seated at table round a finished meal. The glimpse made a picture; it lasted only a moment, but that moment was experience. She had got her direct personal impression, and she turned out her type. She knew what youth was, and what Protestantism; she also had the advantage of having seen what it was to be French, so that she converted these ideas into a concrete image and produced a reality. Above all, however, she was blessed with the faculty which when you give it an inch takes an ell, and which for the artist is a much greater source of strength than any accident of residence or of place in the social scale. The power to guess the unseen from the seen, to trace the implication of things, to judge the whole piece by the pattern, the condition of feeling life in general so completely that you are well on your way to knowing any particular corner of it—this cluster of gifts may almost be said to constitute experience, and they occur in country and in town, and in the most differing stages of education. If experience consists of impressions, it may be said that impressions *are* experience, just as (have we not seen it?) they are the very air we breathe. Therefore, if I should certainly say to a novice, " Write from experience and experience only," I should feel that this was rather a tantalising monition if I were not careful immediately to add, "Try to be one of the people on whom nothing is lost!"

I am far from intending by this to minimise the importance of exactness — of truth of detail. One can speak best from one's own taste, and I may therefore venture to say that the air of reality (solidity of specification) seems to me to be the supreme virtue of a novel—the merit on which all its other merits (including that conscious moral purpose of which Mr. Besant speaks) helplessly and submissively depend. If it be not there they are all as nothing, and if these be there, they owe their effect to the success with which the author has produced the illusion of life. The cultivation of this success. the study of this exquisite process, form, to my taste, the beginning and the end of the art of the novelist. They are his inspiration, his despair, his reward, his torment, his delight. It is here in very truth that he competes with life ; it is here that he competes with his brother the painter in *his* attempt to render the look of things, the look that conveys their meaning, to catch the colour, the relief, the expression, the surface, the substance of the human spectacle. It is in regard to this that Mr. Besant is well inspired when he bids him take notes. He cannot possibly take too many, he cannot possibly take enough. All life solicits him, and to "render" the simplest surface, to produce the most momentary illusion, is a very complicated business His case would be easier, and the rule

would be more exact, if Mr. Besant had been able
to tell him what notes to take. But this, I fear, he
can never learn in any manual; it is the business of
his life. He has to take a great many in order to
select a few, he has to work them up as he can, and
even the guides and philosophers who might have
most to say to him must leave him alone when it
comes to the application of precepts, as we leave the
painter in communion with his palette. That his
characters "must be clear in outline," as Mr. Besant
says—he feels that down to his boots; but how he
shall make them so is a secret between his good
angel and himself. It would be absurdly simple if
he could be taught that a great deal of "description"
would make them so, or that on the contrary the
absence of description and the cultivation of dialogue,
or the absence of dialogue and the multiplication of
"incident," would rescue him from his difficulties.
Nothing, for instance, is more possible than that he
be of a turn of mind for which this odd, literal opposition of description and dialogue, incident and description, has little meaning and light. People often
talk of these things as if they had a kind of inter-
necine distinctness, instead of melting into each other
at every breath, and being intimately associated parts
of one general effort of expression. I cannot imagine
composition existing in a series of blocks, nor conceive, in any novel worth discussing at all, of a
passage of description that is not in its intention
narrative, a passage of dialogue that is not in its

intention descriptive, a touch of truth of any sort
that does not partake of the nature of incident, or
an incident that derives its interest from any other
source than the general and only source of the success of a work of art—that of being illustrative. A
novel is a living thing, all one and continuous, like
any other organism, and in proportion as it lives
will it be found, I think, that in each of the parts
there is something of each of the other parts. The
critic who over the close texture of a finished work
shall pretend to trace a geography of items will mark
some frontiers as artificial, I fear, as any that have
been known to history. There is an old-fashioned
distinction between the novel of character and the
novel of incident which must have cost many a
smile to the intending fabulist who was keen about
his work. It appears to me as little to the point as
the equally celebrated distinction between the novel
and the romance—to answer as little to any reality.
There are bad novels and good novels, as there are
bad pictures and good pictures ; but that is the only
distinction in which I see any meaning, and I can as
little imagine speaking of a novel of character as I
can imagine speaking of a picture of character.
When one says picture one says of character, when
one says novel one says of incident, and the terms
may be transposed at will. What is character but
the determination of incident ? What is incident
but the illustration of character ? What is either a
picture or a novel that is *not* of character ? What

else do we seek in it and find in it ? It is an incident for a woman to stand up with her hand resting on a table and look out at you in a certain way; or if it be not an incident I think it will be hard to say what it is. At the same time it is an expression of character. If you say you don't see it (character in *that—allons donc !*), this is exactly what the artist who has reasons of his own for thinking he *does* see it undertakes to show you. When a young man makes up his mind that he has not faith enough after all to enter the church as he intended, that is an incident, though you may not hurry to the end of the chapter to see whether perhaps he doesn't change once more. I do not say that these are extraordinary or startling incidents. I do not pretend to estimate the degree of interest proceeding from them, for this will depend upon the skill of the painter. It sounds almost puerile to say that some incidents are intrinsically much more important than others, and I need not take this precaution after having professed my sympathy for the major ones in remarking that the only classification of the novel that I can understand is into that which has life and that which has it not.

The novel and the romance, the novel of incident and that of character—these clumsy separations appear to me to have been made by critics and readers for their own convenience, and to help them out of some of their occasional queer predicaments, but to have little reality or interest for the producer, from whose point of view it is of course that we are attempting

to consider the art of fiction. The case is the same
with another shadowy category which Mr. Besant apparently is disposed to set up—that of the "modern
English novel"; unless indeed it be that in this matter
he has fallen into an accidental confusion of standpoints. It is not quite clear whether he intends the
remarks in which he alludes to it to be didactic or
historical. It is as difficult to suppose a person intending to write a modern English as to suppose
him writing an ancient English novel : that is a label
which begs the question. One writes the novel, one
paints the picture, of one's language and of one's time,
and calling it modern English will not, alas ! make the
difficult task any easier. No more, unfortunately, will
calling this or that work of one's fellow-artist a romance
—unless it be, of course, simply for the pleasantness
of the thing, as for instance when Hawthorne gave
this heading to his story of *Blithedale*. The French,
who have brought the theory of fiction to remarkable completeness, have but one name for the novel,
and have not attempted smaller things in it, that I
can see, for that. I can think of no obligation to
which the "romancer" would not be held equally
with the novelist; the standard of execution is
equally high for each. Of course it is of execution
that we are talking—that being the only point of a
novel that is open to contention. This is perhaps
too often lost sight of, only to produce interminable
confusions and cross-purposes. We must grant the
artist his subject, his idea, his *donnée :* our criticism is

applied only to what he makes of it. Naturally I
do not mean that we are bound to like it or find it
interesting: in case we do not our course is perfectly simple—to let it alone. We may believe that
of a certain idea even the most sincere novelist can
make nothing at all, and the event may perfectly
justify our belief; but the failure will have been a
failure to execute, and it is in the execution that the
fatal weakness is recorded. If we pretend to respect
the artist at all, we must allow him his freedom of
choice, in the face, in particular cases, of innumerable
presumptions that the choice will not fructify. Art
derives a considerable part of its beneficial exercise
from flying in the face of presumptions, and some of the
most interesting experiments of which it is capable are
hidden in the bosom of common things. Gustave Flaubert has written a story about the devotion of a servant-
girl to a parrot, and the production, highly finished as
it is, cannot on the whole be called a success. We are
perfectly free to find it flat, but I think it might have
been interesting; and I, for my part, am extremely
glad he should have written it; it is a contribution to
our knowledge of what can be done—or what cannot.
Ivan Turgénieff has written a tale about a deaf and
dumb serf and a lap-dog, and the thing is touching,
loving, a little masterpiece. He struck the note of
life where Gustave Flaubert missed it—he flew in
the face of a presumption and achieved a victory.

Nothing, of course, will ever take the place of the
good old fashion of "liking" a work of art or not

liking it : the most improved criticism will not abolish
that primitive, that ultimate test. I mention this to
guard myself from the accusation of intimating that
the idea, the subject, of a novel or a picture, does
not matter. It matters, to my sense, in the highest
degree, and if I might put up a prayer it would be
that artists should select none but the richest. Some,
as I have already hastened to admit, are much more
remunerative than others, and it would be a world
happily arranged in which persons intending to treat
them should be exempt from confusions and mis-
takes. This fortunate condition will arrive only, I
fear, on the same day that critics become purged
from error. Meanwhile, I repeat, we do not judge
the artist with fairness unless we say to him, " Oh, I
grant you your starting-point, because if I did not I
should seem to prescribe to you, and heaven forbid I
should take that responsibility. If I pretend to tell
you what you must not take, you will call upon me
to tell you then what you must take ; in which case
I shall be prettily caught. Moreover, it isn't till I
have accepted your data that I can begin to measure
you. I have the standard, the pitch ; I have no
right to tamper with your flute and then criticise
your music. Of course I may not care for your idea
at all ; I may think it silly, or stale, or unclean ; in
which case I wash my hands of you altogether. I
may content myself with believing that you will not
have succeeded in being interesting, but I shall, of
course, not attempt to demonstrate it, and you will

be as indifferent to me as I am to you. I needn't remind you that there are all sorts of tastes : who can know it better? Some people, for excellent reasons, don't like to read about carpenters ; others, for reasons even better, don't like to read about courtesans. Many object to Americans. Others (I believe they are mainly editors and publishers) won't look at Italians. Some readers don't like quiet subjects ; others don't like bustling ones. Some enjoy a complete illusion, others the consciousness of large concessions. They choose their novels accordingly, and if they don't care about your idea they won't, *a fortiori*, care about your treatment."

So that it comes back very quickly, as I have said, to the liking : in spite of M. Zola, who reasons less powerfully than he represents, and who will not reconcile himself to this absoluteness of taste, thinking that there are certain things that people ought to like, and that they can be made to like. I am quite at a loss to imagine anything (at any rate in this matter of fiction) that people *ought* to like or to dislike. Selection will be sure to take care of itself, for it has a constant motive behind it. That motive is simply experience. As people feel life, so they will feel the art that is most closely related to it. This closeness of relation is what we should never forget in talking of the effort of the novel. Many people speak of it as a factitious, artificial form, a product of ingenuity, the business of which is to alter and arrange the things that surround us, to translate them into conventional, traditional moulds. This, however, is a view of the matter which carries us but a very short way, condemns the art to an eternal repetition of a few familiar *clichés*, cuts short its development, and leads us straight up to a dead wall. Catching the very note and trick, the strange irregular rhythm of life, that is the attempt whose strenuous force keeps Fiction upon her feet. In proportion as in what she offers us we see life *without* rearrangement do we feel that we are touching the truth ; in proportion as we see it *with* rearrangement do we feel that we are being put off with a substitute, a compromise and convention. It is not uncommon to hear an extraordinary assurance of remark in regard to this matter of rearranging, which is often spoken of as if it were the last word of art. Mr. Besant seems to me in danger of falling into the great error with his rather unguarded talk about "selection." Art is essentially selection, but it is a selection whose main care is to be typical, to be inclusive. For many people art means rose-coloured window-panes, and selection means picking a bouquet for Mrs. Grundy. They will tell you glibly that artistic considerations have nothing to do with the disagreeable, with the ugly ; they will rattle off shallow commonplaces about the province of art and the limits of art till you are moved to some wonder in return as to the province and the limits of ignorance. It appears to me that no one can ever have made a seriously artistic attempt without becoming conscious of an immense increase

—a kind of revelation—of freedom. One perceives
in that case—by the light of a heavenly ray—that
the province of art is all life, all feeling, all observation, all vision. As Mr. Besant so justly intimates,
it is all experience. That is a sufficient answer to
those who maintain that it must not touch the sad
things of life, who stick into its divine unconscious
bosom little prohibitory inscriptions on the end of
sticks, such as we see in public gardens—" It is forbidden to walk on the grass ; it is forbidden to touch
the flowers ; it is not allowed to introduce dogs or
to remain after dark ; it is requested to keep to the
right." The young aspirant in the line of fiction
whom we continue to imagine will do nothing without taste, for in that case his freedom would be of little
use to him ; but the first advantage of his taste will
be to reveal to him the absurdity of the little sticks
and tickets. If he have taste, I must add, of course
he will have ingenuity, and my disrespectful reference
to that quality just now was not meant to imply that
it is useless in fiction. But it is only a secondary
aid ; the first is a capacity for receiving straight
impressions.

Mr. Besant has some remarks on the question of
" the story " which I shall not attempt to criticise,
though they seem to me to contain a singular ambiguity, because I do not think I understand them.
I cannot see what is meant by talking as if there
were a part of a novel which is the story and part of
it which for mystical reasons is not—unless indeed

the distinction be made in a sense in which it is
difficult to suppose that any one should attempt to
convey anything. "The story," if it represents anything, represents the subject, the idea, the *donnée*
of the novel; and there is surely no "school"—Mr.
Besant speaks of a school—which urges that a novel
should be all treatment and no subject. There must
assuredly be something to treat; every school is
intimately conscious of that. This sense of the
story being the idea, the starting-point, of the novel,
is the only one that I see in which it can be spoken
of as something different from its organic whole;
and since in proportion as the work is successful the
idea permeates and penetrates it, informs and animates it, so that every word and every punctuation-
point contribute directly to the expression, in that
proportion do we lose our sense of the story being
a blade which may be drawn more or less out of its
sheath. The story and the novel, the idea and the
form, are the needle and thread, and I never heard
of a guild of tailors who recommended the use of
the thread without the needle, or the needle without
the thread. Mr. Besant is not the only critic who
may be observed to have spoken as if there were
certain things in life which constitute stories, and
certain others which do not. I find the same odd
implication in an entertaining article in the *Pall Mall
Gazette*, devoted, as it happens, to Mr. Besant's
lecture. "The story is the thing!" says this graceful
writer, as if with a tone of opposition to some other

idea. I should think it was, as every painter who, as the time for "sending in" his picture looms in the distance, finds himself still in quest of a subject—as every belated artist not fixed about his theme will heartily agree. There are some subjects which speak to us and others which do not, but he would be a clever man who should undertake to give a rule—an index expurgatorius—by which the story and the no-story should be known apart. It is impossible (to me at least) to imagine any such rule which shall not be altogether arbitrary. The writer in the *Pall Mall* opposes the delightful (as I suppose) novel of *Margot la Balafrée* to certain tales in which "Bostonian nymphs" appear to have "rejected English dukes for psychological reasons." I am not acquainted with the romance just designated, and can scarcely forgive the *Pall Mall* critic for not mentioning the name of the author, but the title appears to refer to a lady who may have received a scar in some heroic adventure. I am inconsolable at not being acquainted with this episode, but am utterly at a loss to see why it is a story when the rejection (or acceptance) of a duke is not, and why a reason, psychological or other, is not a subject when a cicatrix is. They are all particles of the multitudinous life with which the novel deals, and surely no dogma which pretends to make it lawful to touch the one and unlawful to touch the other will stand for a moment on its feet. It is the special picture that must stand or fall, according as it seem to possess truth or to lack it.

Mr. Besant does not, to my sense, light up the subject by intimating that a story must, under penalty of not being a story, consist of "adventures." Why of adventures more than of green spectacles? He mentions a category of impossible things, and among them he places "fiction without adventure." Why without adventure, more than without matrimony, or celibacy, or parturition, or cholera, or hydropathy, or Jansenism? This seems to me to bring the novel back to the hapless little *rôle* of being an artificial, ingenious thing—bring it down from its large, free character of an immense and exquisite correspondence with life. And what *is* adventure, when it comes to that, and by what sign is the listening pupil to recognise it? It is an adventure—an immense one—for me to write this little article; and for a Bostonian nymph to reject an English duke is an adventure only less stirring, I should say, than for an English duke to be rejected by a Bostonian nymph. I see dramas within dramas in that, and innumerable points of view. A psychological reason is, to my imagination, an object adorably pictorial; to catch the tint of its complexion—I feel as if that idea might inspire one to Titianesque efforts. There are few things more exciting to me, in short, than a psychological reason, and yet, I protest, the novel seems to me the most magnificent form of art. I have just been reading, at the same time, the delightful story of *Treasure Island*, by Mr. Robert Louis Stevenson and, in a manner less consecutive, the

last tale from M. Edmond de Goncourt, which is
entitled *Chérie*. One of these works treats of murders,
mysteries, islands of dreadful renown, hairbreadth
escapes, miraculous coincidences and buried doubloons.
The other treats of a little French girl who lived in
a fine house in Paris, and died of wounded sensibility
because no one would marry her. I call *Treasure
Island* delightful, because it appears to me to have
succeeded wonderfully in what it attempts ; and I
venture to bestow no epithet upon *Chérie*, which
strikes me as having failed deplorably in what it
attempts—that is in tracing the development of the
moral consciousness of a child. But one of these
productions strikes me as exactly as much of a novel
as the other, and as having a " story" quite as much.
The moral consciousness of a child is as much a part
of life as the islands of the Spanish Main, and the
one sort of geography seems to me to have those
" surprises" of which Mr. Besant speaks quite as
much as the other. For myself (since it comes back
in the last resort, as I say, to the preference of the
individual), the picture of the child's experience has
the advantage that I can at successive steps (an
immense luxury, near to the " sensual pleasure" of
which Mr. Besant's critic in the *Pall Mall* speaks) say
Yes or No, as it may be, to what the artist puts
before me. I have been a child in fact, but I have
been on a quest for a buried treasure only in supposition, and it is a simple accident that with M. de
Goncourt I should have for the most part to say No.

With George Eliot, when she painted that country with a far other intelligence, I always said Yes.

The most interesting part of Mr. Besant's lecture is unfortunately the briefest passage—his very cursory allusion to the " conscious moral purpose " of the novel.   Here again it is not very clear whether he be recording a fact or laying down a principle ; it is a great pity that in the latter case he should not have developed his idea.   This branch of the subject is of immense importance, and Mr. Besant's few words point to considerations of the widest reach, not to be lightly disposed of.   He will have treated the art of fiction but superficially who is not prepared to go every inch of the way that these considerations will carry him.   It is for this reason that at the beginning of these remarks I was careful to notify the reader that my reflections on so large a theme have no pretension to be exhaustive.   Like Mr. Besant, I have left the question of the morality of the novel till the last, and at the last I find I have used up my space. It is a question surrounded with difficulties, as witness the very first that meets us, in the form of a definite question, on the threshold.   Vagueness, in such a discussion, is fatal, and what is the meaning of your morality and your conscious moral purpose ? Will you not define your terms and explain how (a novel being a picture) a picture can be either moral or immoral ?   You wish to paint a moral picture or carve a moral statue : will you not tell us how you would set about it ?   We are discussing the Art of

Fiction ; questions of art are questions (in the widest sense) of execution ; questions of morality are quite another affair, and will you not let us see how it is that you find it so easy to mix them up ? These things are so clear to Mr. Besant that he has deduced from them a law which he sees embodied in English Fiction, and which is " a truly admirable thing and a great cause for congratulation." It is a great cause for congratulation indeed when such thorny problems become as smooth as silk. I may add that in so far as Mr. Besant perceives that in point of fact English Fiction has addressed itself preponderantly to these delicate questions he will appear to many people to have made a vain discovery. They will have been positively struck, on the contrary, with the moral timidity of the usual English novelist ; with his (or with her) aversion to face the difficulties with which on every side the treatment of reality bristles. He is apt to be extremely shy (whereas the picture that Mr. Besant draws is a picture of boldness), and the sign of his work, for the most part, is a cautious silence on certain subjects. In the English novel (by which of course I mean the American as well), more than in any other, there is a traditional difference between that which people know and that which they agree to admit that they know, that which they see and that which they speak of, that which they feel to be a part of life and that which they allow to enter into literature. There is the great difference, in short, between what they

talk of in conversation and what they talk of in
print.   The essence of moral energy is to survey the
whole field, and I should directly reverse Mr. Besant's
remark and say not that the English novel has a
purpose, but that it has a diffidence.   To what degree
a purpose in a work of art is a source of corruption I
shall not attempt to inquire ; the one that seems to
me least dangerous is the purpose of making a perfect
work.   As for our novel, I may say lastly on this
score that as we find it in England to-day it strikes
me as addressed in a large degree to "young people,"
and that this in itself constitutes a presumption that
it will be rather shy.   There are certain things which
it is generally agreed not to discuss, not even to mention, before young people.   That is very well, but the
absence of discussion is not a symptom of the moral
passion.   The purpose of the English novel—"a
truly admirable thing, and a great cause for congratulation"—strikes me therefore as rather negative.

There is one point at which the moral sense and
the artistic sense lie very near together ; that is in
the light of the very obvious truth that the deepest
quality of a work of art will always be the quality of
the mind of the producer.   In proportion as that
intelligence is fine will the novel, the picture, the
statue partake of the substance of beauty and truth.
To be constituted of such elements is, to my vision,
to have purpose enough.   No good novel will ever
proceed from a superficial mind ; that seems to me an
axiom which, for the artist in fiction, will cover all

needful moral ground : if the youthful aspirant take
it to heart it will illuminate for him many of the
mysteries of "purpose." There are many other useful things that might be said to him, but I have
come to the end of my article, and can only touch
them as I pass. The critic in the *Pall Mall Gazette*,
whom I have already quoted, draws attention to the
danger, in speaking of the art of fiction, of general-
ising. The danger that he has in mind is rather, I
imagine, that of particularising, for there are some
comprehensive remarks which, in addition to those
embodied in Mr Besant's suggestive lecture, might
without fear of misleading him be addressed to the
ingenuous student. I should remind him first of
the magnificence of the form that is open to him,
which offers to sight so few restrictions and such innumerable opportunities. The other arts, in comparison, appear confined and hampered ; the various
conditions under which they are exercised are so
rigid and definite. But the only condition that I can
think of attaching to the composition of the novel is,
as I have already said, that it be sincere. This freedom is a splendid privilege, and the first lesson of
the young novelist is to learn to be worthy of it.
" Enjoy it as it deserves," I should say to him ; " take
possession of it, explore it to its utmost extent, publish
it, rejoice in it. All life belongs to you, and do not
listen either to those who would shut you up into
corners of it and tell you that it is only here and
there that art inhabits, or to those who would per-

suade you that this heavenly messenger wings her way outside of life altogether, breathing a superfine air, and turning away her head from the truth of things. There is no impression of life, no manner of seeing it and feeling it, to which the plan of the novelist may not offer a place ; you have only to remember that talents so dissimilar as those of Alexandre Dumas and Jane Austen, Charles Dickens and Gustave Flaubert have worked in this field with equal glory. Do not think too much about optimism and pessimism ; try and catch the colour of life itself. In France to-day we see a prodigious effort (that of Emile Zola, to whose solid and serious work no explorer of the capacity of the novel can allude without respect), we see an extraordinary effort vitiated by a spirit of pessimism on a narrow basis. M. Zola is magnificent, but he strikes an English reader as ignorant ; he has an air of working in the dark ; if he had as much light as energy, his results would be of the highest value. As for the aberrations of a shallow optimism, the ground (of English fiction especially) is strewn with their brittle particles as with broken glass. If you must indulge in conclusions, let them have the taste of a wide knowledge. Remember that your first duty is to be as complete as possible—to make as perfect a work. Be generous and delicate and pursue the prize."

1884.

BIBLIOGRAPHICAL AND OTHER NOTES

Partial Portraits was first published 8 May 1888; 2000 copies were printed and bound copies were exported to the United States. Later that year there appeared the first American edition.

RALPH WALDO EMERSON (1803–82). James's review of J. E. Cabot's memoir of Emerson first appeared in *Macmillan's Magazine* in December 1887.

P. 30. James's allusion to his going to the Louvre with Emerson refers to their meeting in Paris during the autumn of 1872. Later that winter they met in Rome and James escorted Emerson to the Vatican to look at the classical sculptures.

GEORGE ELIOT (1819–80). "The Life of George Eliot" by her husband J. W. Cross was reviewed by James in the *Atlantic Monthly* in the May 1885 issue.

James had reviewed her at various times during the 1860's and had written a long article on her, his first full-length critical portrait, in 1866. He met her for the first time in 1869, and saw her on a number of occasions thereafter.

P. 60. The quotations from Daudet are a record of James's 1884 talk with the French novelist. See notes on Daudet below.

"Daniel Deronda: A Conversation" appeared in the *Atlantic Monthly* in December 1876.

ANTHONY TROLLOPE (1815–82). This essay was first published in the *Century Magazine* in July 1883.

P. 98–99. James here alludes to his crossing the Atlantic late in 1875 to take up residence in Paris. A fellow passenger was Trollope. James later had some observation of him in London drawing rooms, but never got to know him well.

ROBERT LOUIS STEVENSON (1850–94). James's essay first appeared in the *Century Magazine* in April 1888, a month before publication of *Partial Portraits.*

James had met Stevenson briefly in London some years before. In 1885 at Bournemouth, he came to know him better and the friendship they then formed endured to the end of Stevenson's life. Some of James's finest letters were written to Stevenson after the latter had settled in Samoa. For an account of their friendship see Leon Edel, *The Life of Henry James*—the sections entitled *The Middle Years* (1962) and *The Treacherous Years* (1969).

P. 138. James here describes his conception of the "literary portrait."

CONSTANCE FENIMORE WOOLSON (1840–94). The essay on Miss Woolson was first published in *Harper's Weekly* 12 February 1887. For an account of James's friendship with the authoress see the chapters devoted to her in Edel's *The Middle Years* (1962).

ALPHONSE DAUDET (1840–97). This essay first appeared in the *Century Magazine* in August 1883. At the time of its writing James remembered Daudet from their early meetings at Flaubert's in 1875. In 1884 the friendship was renewed in Paris. For an account of this see James's letter to T. B. Aldrich, 13 February 1884 (in Leon Edel, *Selected Letters of Henry James* (1955). In 1889 James translated Daudet's *Port-Tarascon.* For an account of their later meetings see Edel's *The Treacherous Years* (1969).

GUY DE MAUPASSANT (1850–93). The essay first appeared in the *Fortnightly Review,* March 1888. James had met Maupassant when he was still young and unpublished at Flaubert's. They subsequently met in London. See *The Middle Years* (1962).

IVAN TURGÉNIEFF (1818–83). This memorial tribute was first published in the *Atlantic Monthly* in January 1884, a few weeks after the death of the Russian novelist. For a detailed account of the friendship see L. Edel, *The Conquest of London.*

GEORGE DU MAURIER (1834–96). This essay was originally published under the title "Du Maurier and London Society" in the *Century Magazine,* May 1883. The friendship is documented in *The Treacherous Years* (1969).

THE ART OF FICTION. This essay was first published by James in *Longman's Magazine* in September 1884.

P. 375. Walter Besant (1836–1901), Victorian novelist and historian, delivered the lecture at the Royal Institution on 25 April 1884. It was entitled "Fiction as a Fine Art."

P. 388. "A woman of genius." James is here alluding to Anne Thackeray Ritchie, daughter of the novelist, whose first novel *The Story of Elizabeth* he here describes.

P. 395. The allusion to Flaubert's story about a girl and a parrot, "Un Coeur Simple." Turgenev's story about a serf and a lapdog is entitled "Mumu."

P. 401. The author, fairly obviously, is Henry James himself and the story to which he alludes is "An International Episode" (1879).

P. 401. *Margot la Balafrée* by Fortuné du Boisgobey (1884).

INDEX

Selected Ann Arbor Paperbacks
Works of enduring merit

For a complete list of Ann Arbor Paperback titles write:
THE UNIVERSITY OF MICHIGAN PRESS ANN ARBOR